MARINE REPORTING AND TERRITORIAL MARITIME CONTROLS

J MARK ROWBOTHAM

www.seamanshiptutor.com

First published in 2011 by SeamanshipTutor Ltd,
57 Melbrack Road,
Liverpool, L18 9SF
Email: info@seamanshiptutor.com
Copyright © 2011, J Mark Rowbotham

All rights reserved. No part of this publication may be reproduced, stored in a retrieval system, or transmitted in any form or by any means, electronic, mechanical, photocopying, recording or otherwise, without the written permission of the copyright holder. Applications for the copyright holder's written permission to reproduce any part of this publication should be addressed to the publisher.

Although great care has been taken with the writing and production of this publication, neither SeamanshipTutor Ltd nor the author can accept any responsibility for any errors, omissions or their consequences.

This publication has been prepared to deal with the subject of marine reporting and territorial controls. This should not however, be taken to mean that this publication deals with comprehensively with all the issues of the subject.

The opinions expressed are those of the author only and are not necessarily to be taken as policies or views of any organisation with which he has any connection.

ISBN 978-0-9563971-2-6

www.SeamanshipTutor.Com

CONTENTS

Acknowledgements vii

INTRODUCTION 1

CHAPTER 1 – THE LEGAL PERSPECTIVE 3

The Basic Principle behind Vessel Reporting and Territorial Controls
The Principle of the Territorial Sea and its Convention
Overview and History of the UN Convention of the Law of the Sea (UNCLOS)
Definition of Areas covered by UNCLOS

CHAPTER 2 – DEFINITION OF AREAS COVERED BY THE UNCLOS 12

Baselines
Internal Waters
Territorial Sea
Straits
Contiguous Zone
Continental Shelf
High Seas
Innocent Passage
The Coastal State

CHAPTER 3 – THE PRACTICAL PERSPECTIVE 33

Types and Nature of Vessels
Hazardous or Dangerous Cargoes and the IMDG Code
The Marine Environment – Pollution of the Seas
The Duty of Disclosure

CHAPTER 4 – REPORTING REGIMES 49

Port Information
The Maritime and Coastguard Agency (MCGA)
EC Directive 2002/59/EC
Policing the Territorial Waters
Customs Maritime Cargo Reporting & Controls
Marine Accident Reporting
Ship Routeing and Traffic Separation Schemes (TSS)
CNIS Reporting
Marine Reporting – 24 Hours in Advance
A European Maritime Reporting System
The Consolidated European Reporting System (CERS)
The EU Entry Summary Declaration (ENS)

CHAPTER 5 – CONVENTIONS, CODES AND CONTROLS 87

The International Maritime Organisation (IMO)
The IMO FAL Convention
ISPS
VTS
Automatic Identification System (AIS)
LRIT
Small & Leisure Craft

CHAPTER 6 – ROLES AND RESPONSIBILITIES 133

Multimodal Information and the International Supply Chain
The Vessel Perspective
The Shore Perspective
The Role of the Agency
Perceived Anomalies

CHAPTER 7 – MARINE ACCIDENTS AND THEIR AFTERMATH 156

Tankers – Erika, Prestige & Amoco Cadiz
Container Vessels – Hyundai Fortune & MSC Napoli

CHAPTER 8 – PRACTICAL SOLUTIONS 173

Summary and Appraisal
Towards an Integrated Reporting System

CHAPTER 9 – CASE STUDIES 196

Case Study 1 – The 1936 Montreux Convention Regarding The Regime Of The Turkish Straits
Case Study 2 – Scandinavian Waters: The Storebaelt and Öresund
Case Study 3 – UK Waters: The North Channel and the Pentland Firth
Case Study 4 – Canada - A Blueprint for a more Secure Maritime Future?

References 229

ACKNOWLEDGEMENTS

UKHO
CNIS Dover
Maritime & Coastguard Agency
HM Revenue & Customs
Royal Navy (HMNB Faslane)
Scottish Executive (Scottish Fisheries Protection)
International Maritime Organisation (IMO)
Royal Danish Administration of Navigation and Hydrography
Swedish Customs (Tullverket), Malmö
Swedish Maritime Administration (Sjöfartsverket), Malmö
Canadian Coast Guard Authority
Lloyd's Register Fairplay
Clydeport (Greenock & Hunterston Operations)
Port of Tyne
Port of Heysham
Port of Barrow
Port of Aberdeen
Royal Institute of Navigation
Chartered Institute of Logistics & Transport UK
Institute of Chartered Shipbrokers
South Tyneside College, Maritime Training Unit

Special thanks to

ABP (Associated British Ports) Southampton for the cover image,
Mr. Amir Hameed for the cover design.

INTRODUCTION – ATTENTION ALL SHIPPING...

The words "Attention all Shipping" may remind us of those dark winter nights, when we have the radio tuned to Radio 4, and the gentle tones of Ronald Binge's Melody "Sailing By" soothe our innermost thoughts, prior to our sympathies being roused for those unfortunate mariners caught in some squall or Force 8 gale in areas as evocative as Viking, Forties, North Utsire, Rockall, Bailey or Biscay.

But behind the seemingly endless stream of lists of weather conditions around the British Coastline delivered from the Meteorological Office, there lurks another major issue – that of the reporting of shipping to the various national authorities whose coastlines are located within the areas illustrated above. The issue of Marine Reporting covers a variety of circumstances, from vessels sailing through the Strait of Dover, through the reporting of hazardous or dangerous cargoes to the Port of Destination, to the reporting of marine incidents or accidents. Several Reporting regimes presently exist, but are by no means standardised, harmonised or integrated. Furthermore, it would appear that no one single Marine Reporting regime covers the ability of a national authority to control or monitor not only the shipping movements close to its coasts, other than the regime operating in the Channel between Dover and Cap Gris Nez, but also the intentions of the ships concerned and the nature of their cargoes, crews or passengers. Indeed, it would also appear that the powers held by certain national authorities to control maritime movements both within and outwith the scope of national maritime territorial controls are extremely limited, despite the basic need for a nation to exercise complete control and sovereignty over its defined territory.

A hornet's nest was stirred on the ship and conference venue *HQS Wellington*, permanently moored alongside the Victoria Embankment on the River Thames in London, in June 2005, when I addressed a gathering of a variety of delegates at a CILT seminar on the subject of Marine Reporting. As a result of my address, many questions were raised as to the effectiveness of national maritime controls around EU waters, and what was being done to address such issues. The UK Maritime & Coastguard Agency (MCA) stated that progress was being made towards a common EU policy on such issues, but that this would take some time to resolve. The overall conclusion of the seminar was that there was no fully co-ordinated policy to take into account all the diverse marine reporting regimes which existed at the time, i.e. no appearance of "joined-up thinking" with reference to the issues at stake. This was borne out by certain organisations I consulted for the purpose of my research, and led me to believe that much work was required, not only to create an integrated international regime for marine reporting, but also to ensure that such a regime also fulfilled the relevant articles of the UN Convention of the Law of the Sea (UNCLOS).

This text seeks to define and explain certain elements of the UNCLOS pertaining to national maritime territory and national maritime controls, as well as to address the issues relating to present-day marine reporting mechanisms and systems, and to recommend proposals for the review, overhaul and restructuring of such marine reporting mechanisms and regimes to account for all the above anomalies, using case studies as examples of present-day reporting mechanisms.

It also seeks to review marine reporting mechanisms in the light of the threats posed by terrorism and the maritime risks associated therewith, as well as the need for greater degrees of control over shipping movements and the risks posed by ever-increasing tonnage of vessels on the high seas with relation to how they may affect both other ships in the vicinity, the ports they visit, and the risks they may pose to the national interest and well-being of any coastal State. Such controls must inevitably also cover the identification of such vessels, their intentions while sailing, and their cargoes, as increasing tonnage of vessels also means increasing volumes of cargo carried, and how such carriage encroaches upon the national interest and the issue of security, including customs and fiscal controls as defined within the scope of the UNCLOS as well as for the purposes of national interests.

CHAPTER ONE

THE LEGAL PERSPECTIVE

THE BASIC PRINCIPLE BEHIND VESSEL REPORTING AND TERRITORIAL CONTROLS

The oceans of the world comprise over 70% of the earth's surface, and they are a major and critical part of the world's existence. As well as being a major source of resources, both in terms of marine life and minerals, they are also a major means of transport, given that the vast majority of trade throughout the world is carried by some form of marine transport. This transport is shared out amongst a large number of nations, and plies regularly around many parts of the world. Marine vessels are flagged according to the nations where their owners are based, or have offices for the purpose of convenience, often for tax purposes. They operate in international waters, and visit many different ports worldwide. Because of their different nationalities, they are visiting different countries, and require free access to the ports of these countries, although upon entry into the waters of those countries, they become subject to the jurisdiction of the country concerned for fiscal, customs, immigration and sanitary purposes, and therefore they must obey and be subject to the laws of that country, seen as a coastal State, although they are also subject to the laws of the country where they are flagged or owned. For the purposes of this exercise, a coastal state is a country which has a coastline bordering on an international sea or ocean.

The principle of the free use of the oceans and high seas has existed for more than three centuries, although its basis effectively prevailed from biblical times, when the vessels of the Mediterranean plied waters around the coasts of Europe and North Africa, especially in the times of the Roma Empire. Beyond the limits of a coastal State's zone of jurisdiction, i.e. its territorial sea (only fully defined in the 20th century), lay the high seas – *mare liberum* – upon which there was freedom of navigation. A basic concept of the closed sea – *mare clausum* – existed, for a brief period during the 18th century whereby certain maritime powers, namely Britain, Portugal and Spain, proposed a seaward extension of the territorial sea, beyond the customary international law, as it stood at the time, of a three-nautical mile limit (traditionally accepted as the distance a cannon shot could be fired out to sea from the country's shoreline), and varying to as much as one hundred or more nautical miles from their coastline.

During the second half of the 20th century, merchant shipping underwent rapid and significant changes and development, especially with the introduction of larger, faster and more specialised vessels, in particular bulk carriers and container vessels. Substantial changes in vessel design have occurred in the bulk carrier sector, with the introduction of the OBO (Ore-Bulk-Oil) vessel, capable of carrying both ore and oil commodities. The rapid increase in the number and size of container vessels, ro-ro vessels and vehicle ferries has demonstrated just how much shipping has become part of a more closely-integrated and globalised transport system. The increase in the size of vessels has come to pose significant navigational problems in restricted waters, related to the available depth of water and passage through confined space such as the Strait of Dover, the Öresund (The Sound), the Storebaelt (Great Belt) and the Malacca Straits and Straits of

Singapore, as well as canals such as the Suez Canal and the Panama Canal, each of which have their own designation for the size of vessels capable of navigating them, as in the case of the Suezmax bulk carriers and the more universally-known "Panamax" standard and size of vessel, i.e. the largest vessel which can negotiate the locks of the Panama Canal, generally in the region of some 37000grt for container vessels. Increasing demands for petroleum-based products and commodities has led to an increase in the size of crude oil carriers and to the development of new types of tankers carrying liquefied petroleum gas (LPG) and liquefied natural gas (LNG). To maintain maritime transport operating costs at a minimum, large tankers (and even dry bulk carriers in the iron ore trade) with a tonnage of 100,000 to 350,000 deadweight range have been developed, the largest dry bulk carrier to date being the Bergesen-owned *Berge Stahl* of 364,000 tonnes. However, some of the larger vessels, such as the tankers *Torrey Canyon* (wrecked 1967), *Erica*, *Prestige*, *Amoco Cadiz* and *Exxon Valdez* (grounded off Alaska in April 1989), have been responsible for maritime disasters of unimaginable magnitude, leading to the need for greater controls over maritime movements and maritime environmental controls, as well as the need for stringent regulatory controls over the transportation of oil on the high seas on a global scale. Even non-environmental marine disasters involving vessels such as the dry bulk carriers *Berge Istra*, *Berge Vanga* and *Derbyshire*, and the container vessels *Hyundai Fortune* and *MSC Napoli* demonstrate the need for a more cohesive and integrated international maritime reporting and monitoring regime concerning commercial vessels in general. Hence there is an urgent need for comprehensive global policies on a national and international scale on the subjects of coastal zone management, the protection of natural marine resources and the marine environment, and the international control over worldwide shipping movements and the extent to which such vessels can be monitored and controlled, especially within the framework of national and international maritime control mechanisms and regimes.

According to international law and the principle of international relations, every country has the right to govern itself. In order for a country to have full statehood, the following criteria must be satisfied by any nation-state:

- A people;
- A territory;
- A government;
- National sovereignty.

A nation therefore has the right to govern its territory, and to apply the full rule of law over that territory at all times. It also has the right to defend that territory, and to apply such forces as necessary to uphold and exercise that defence. According to the United Nations Convention of the Law of the Sea (UNCLOS), it also has the right to defend the waters off its shore up to an internationally-designated limit, defined as being its territorial waters. It therefore has overall control over all issues pertaining to these waters, including shipping and maritime activity.

All vessels approaching or entering these waters must therefore make themselves known to the country concerned, and its national authorities dealing with maritime and territorial matters. Once a vessel enters national waters, it comes under the jurisdiction and control of the country governing these territorial waters, and therefore must declare its intention to enter port, as well as submitting details of its identity and its complement, including passengers and cargoes. If it is passing close to the coastline of a coastal State while en route to the port of another State, it may pass through the territorial waters of that State, and therefore must report its identity and intentions to that State, despite its international rights of passage through the waters concerned under the principle of the right of innocent passage. Similarly, if that vessel is passing through a limited section of international waters which are not considered part of a country's territorial sea, from one area of the high seas to another, such as a strait, then it must still declare its intentions to pass through the strait to the national authority closest to its intended course, in spite of the international principles of the right of innocent passage as defined by the UNCLOS. This text seeks to examine such principles and apply the scope of the UNCLOS to such vessel movements.

THE PRINCIPLE OF THE TERRITORIAL SEA AND ITS CONVENTION

Territorial waters, or a territorial sea, as defined by the 1982 UN Convention on the Law of the Sea, is a belt of coastal waters extending at most twelve nautical miles from the baseline (usually the mean low-water mark) of a coastal State. The territorial sea is regarded as the sovereign territory of the state, although foreign ships (both military and civilian) are allowed innocent passage through it; this sovereignty also extends to the airspace over and seabed below, including all activity relating to exploitation of the area beneath the seabed, as in the case of offshore oil and gas exploration.

The term "territorial waters" is also used informally to describe any area of water over which a state has jurisdiction, including also internal waters, the contiguous zone, the exclusive economic zone and potentially the continental shelf, all of which are described later in this text. All these areas form part of a coastal State's territory, and are subject to that State's jurisdiction and controls. A state's territorial sea extends up to 12 nautical miles (22 km) from its baseline. If this were to overlap with the territorial sea of another state, the border is then taken as the median point between the baselines of both states, unless the states in question agree otherwise. A state can also choose to claim a smaller territorial sea if it so desires, especially in cases where the breadth of the territorial sea may be limited owing to its proximity to a strait.

From the 18th century until halfway through the 20th century, the territorial waters of the former British Empire, the United States, France and many other nations measured three nautical miles (5 km). Originally, this was traditionally the length of a cannon shot, hence it became the portion of an ocean that a sovereign state could defend from the shore. However, Iceland claimed two nautical miles (3.7 km), Norway claimed four nautical miles (7.4 km), and Spain claimed six nautical miles (11.1 km) during this period. During incidents such as nuclear weapons testing and fisheries disputes some nations arbitrarily extended their maritime claims to as much as fifty or even two hundred nautical miles (370 km), including the Icelandic authorities, which claimed these limits during the so-called "cod wars". Since the late 20th century the 12-mile limit has become almost universally accepted. The UK extended its territorial waters from three to twelve nautical miles (22 km) in 1987.

Historically, the definition of the territorial sea has been open to interpretation, and the need arose to define its existence and how coastal States should claim it and govern over it. For this reason, the Territorial Sea Convention (TSC) was agreed internationally in 1958, and came into force in September 1964. However, its articles were, in certain cases vague, and it only sought to define the territorial sea for each signatory coastal State, and how such territory should be controlled. As well as generally defining the territorial sea, the 1958 Convention on the Territorial Sea and Contiguous Zone made the provision that coastal States cannot suspend the innocent passage of foreign ships through straits which are used for international navigation between one part of the high seas and another part of the high seas, or the territorial sea of a foreign coastal State.

In time, the need arose to review the Convention, and it was duly effectively replaced by the UN Convention of the Law of the Sea in 1982. In 1987, the UK passed the Territorial Sea Act, defining the extent of its national territorial sea limits. A further Statutory Order of the same year further extended this jurisdiction by defining the UK's continental shelf, beyond the UK' territorial sea boundaries, in the form of the **Continental Shelf (Designated Areas)(Extended Territorial Sea) Order 1987**. This also defined the activities which could be carried out under UK control, such as offshore oil and gas exploration, within these limits.

OVERVIEW AND HISTORY OF THE UN CONVENTION OF THE LAW OF THE SEA (UNCLOS)

The UN Convention of the Law of the Sea (UNCLOS) was agreed in 1982 and was signed by 159 Countries. It did not enter into force until a year after it had been ratified by 60 States. The 60th instrument of ratification was deposited on 16 November 1993, and the Convention entered into force on 16 November 1994. The UK, along with Germany and the United States, was not originally party to the Convention because of disagreements concerning the deep sea bed mining regime, but an agreement to resolve these difficulties was adopted by the UN General Assembly in July 1994. The Territorial Sea Act of 1987 extended UK territorial waters from 3 Miles offshore to 12 nautical miles offshore. However, although the United States and Germany subsequently ratified the Convention, the UK delayed acceding to the Convention because of concern about the legality of the Rockall fisheries zone (The UK Exclusive Economic Zone encompassed by the 200-mile limit), but eventually did accede to the Convention on 25 July 1997 with effect from 24 August 1997.

The UNCLOS concerns all aspects of the management and regulation of worldwide maritime activities, including national and international jurisdiction over the high seas, and refers, *inter alia*, to the following issues:

- National Territorial Limits;

- Exclusive Economic Zones;

- The Continental Shelf;
- Contiguous Zones;
- Rights of Innocent Passage;
- Movement of Vessels;
- The Marine Environment;
- Marine Pollution.

It is administered by the International Maritime Organisation (IMO), which is based in London, and covers not only the High Seas themselves but also Shipping Movements upon the High Seas.

The Convention on the Law of the Sea (UNCLOS) covers the following areas and definitions:

- Baselines;
- Internal waters;
- The territorial sea;
- Straits;
- Archipelagos;
- The contiguous zone;
- The continental shelf;
- The exclusive economic zone
- Delimitation of maritime boundaries;
- High seas;
- The international sea bed area;
- Navigation;
- Fishing;
- The prevention of marine pollution and the protection of the marine environment;

- Marine scientific research and the transfer of technology;
- Military uses of the sea;
- Landlocked and geographically-disadvantaged States;
- Settlement of disputes.

The purpose of this text is to use the above definitions to define the need for maritime reporting of vessels within the framework of the UNCLOS and the assess the effectiveness of the present reporting systems within this framework, especially concerning recent EU vessel monitoring initiatives and the issues surrounding national and international maritime security. Certain areas, such as fishing, marine research, military uses of the sea and landlocked states, are not deemed part of this text, as they are separate areas and are not covered by systems pertaining to marine reporting.

There were four early attempts to codify the peacetime rules of the international law of the sea. The first was initiated by the League of Nations, which appointed a committee of experts in 1924 to draw up a list of maritime subjects suitable for codification, among which were considered territorial waters, piracy, exploitation of marine resources and the legal status of State-owned merchant ships. The committee circulated "questionnaires" to governments on the first three of these. Subsequently, a Preparatory Commission was established to prepare three topics, namely nationality, State responsibility and territorial waters, for codification. These preparations involved the circulation of a "Schedule of Points" to governments and, following the receipt of responses from these governments, the drafting of "Bases of Discussion" on which the Codification Conference could base its work. Reports were also drawn up for the Committee and Preparatory Commission. However, the Conference, which convened at The Hague in 1930, did not succeed in adopting a convention on territorial waters. A further committee was established to study the subject, and a report was produced setting out such agreements as had been reached by the conference. This report included draft articles on matters such as the nature and extent of the right of coastal states over the territorial sea, and the right of innocent passage by vessels through limited straits and international waterways. However, it was not possible to reach agreement on the vital question of the breadth of territorial waters. As a result, the conference could do no more than refer the draft articles to governments, in the hope that agreement could be reached at a later date to be determined.

These draft articles were to influence later discussions, and when the League of Nations was replaced by the United Nations after the Second World War, it was deemed desirable to provide for the establishment of a body charged with the "progressive codification" of international law. The organisation established was called the International Law Commission (ILC), a body of 34 eminent international lawyers, serving in individual capacities but nominated and elected by national governments, whose first members were appointed in 1948. During the first years of its existence, the ILC embarked on the preparation of draft articles on the high seas and the territorial sea, and their work drew significantly on the articles produced as a result of the 1930 conference. By 1956, the ILC had produced a report covering most aspects of the law of the sea of contemporary importance, and this report formed the basis of the work of the first post-war conference of the law of the sea.

The first United Nations Conference on the Law of the Sea (UNCLOS I) was held at Geneva in 1958, and was attended by eighty-six states, almost double the number of countries which had attended the conference at The Hague in 1930. From this conference, four Conventions were adopted, namely the following:

- The Convention on the Territorial Sea and the Contiguous Zone;
- The Convention on the High Seas;
- The Convention on the Continental Shelf;
- The Convention on Fishing and the Conservation of Living Resources of the High Seas.

The first three Conventions were ratified by substantial numbers of States, and were also largely based on customary international law, as presented in the reports of the ILC. As a result, these first three conventions comprised the core of the generally-accepted rules of the law of the sea with regard to maritime zones. The fourth Geneva Convention, and an optional Protocol on dispute settlement, proved less popular, partly because they went further than the existing obligations which customary law imposed on national States. However, the one major issue which was still not solved by the 1958 Geneva conference was that concerning the breadth of the territorial sea. As a result, a second conference, UNCLOS II, was convened in 1960 to discuss this issue, as well as the associated question of fishery limits. It failed, by only one vote, to adopt a compromise formula providing for a six-mile territorial sea plus a six-mile fishery zone. It was necessary for an agreement on the breadth of the territorial sea to await the preparation of the Convention drawn up by the third UN Conference on the Law of the Sea (UNCLOS III), in the 1980s.

The origins of UNCLOS III lay in the Sea Bed Commission established in 1967 by the UN General Assembly to examine the question of the deep sea bed lying beyond the limits of national jurisdiction. Any internationalism of the sea bed beyond national jurisdiction required a definition of the limits of national jurisdiction over the sea bed and a revision of parts of the 1958 Convention on the Continental Shelf and of the 1958 Convention on the High Seas. However, many States were reluctant to review the law of the sea, which had already been significantly codified in the 1950s. By this time, many newly-independent States had emerged, which had had no say in the formation of the original 1958 Conventions, and they provided a substantial majority in favour of reviewing the earlier law. Furthermore, there was increasing concern by many States over the problems of over-fishing and marine pollution off their coasts, neither of which could be satisfactorily controlled within the narrow scope of jurisdictional limits upon which the 1958 regime of Conventions was based. The prevalence of these factors, along with the recognition that the various parts of the law of the sea were inter-related, led to widespread support for an extensive review of the whole of the law of the sea. As a result, it was agreed in 1970 in UN General Assembly Resolution 2570, that a new comprehensive UN Conference on the Law of the Sea be agreed.

This Conference, the third UN Conference on the Law of the Sea (UNCLOS III), held its first session in 1973, and worked for several months each year until it finally adopted a new Convention in 1982, over fifty years since the original conference held at The Hague in 1930. The conference was divided into three main committees. Committee One dealt with the problem of the legal regime of the deep sea bed. Committee Two dealt with the regimes of the territorial sea and the contiguous zone, the continental shelf, exclusive economic zone, the high seas, and fishing and conservation of the living resources of the high seas, as well as with specific aspects of these topics, such as the questions of straits, such as the Öresund between Denmark and Sweden, the Strait of Dover and the Malacca Strait, and archipelagic States such as Indonesia and the Philippines. Committee Three dealt with the questions of the preservation of the marine environment and scientific research.

The UNCLOS III, unlike its predecessors and the Hague Conference of 1930, had no "Bases of Discussion" or ILC Report to guide its work. It was seen as a political, rather than a legal, enterprise, and to this extent it was assigned to the UN General Assembly's First Committee (Political and Security) rather than its sixth Committee (Legal). In time, a number of loose groupings emerged, namely a group of 120 countries (known as the 'Group of 77' developing States), and the groups of Western and East European States, several of which were at the time part of the East European Socialist bloc, as well as smaller, special interest groups, such as the archipelagic States, the straits States, the coastal and 'maritime' States, all of which played important roles during the negotiations on various parts of the Convention. Agreement amongst member States was reached by consensus, rather than by outright formal voting. The subsequent negotiating texts showed greater levels of agreement on issues such as the extent of the territorial sea, the legal regimes of the territorial sea, contiguous zones, continental shelf, exclusive economic zone and high seas, and the regulation of scientific research and marine pollution. The result of these agreements was that the provisions of the texts resulting from the UNCLOS agreements began to be incorporated into national legislation, thus exerting a strong influence on customary international law. The 1982 Convention gave rise to the establishment of rights to 200-mile Exclusive Economic Zones (EEZs), some years before the actual Convention itself entered into force.

The text of the Convention was finally adopted on 30 April 1982, and on 10 December that same year, the formal UN Convention on the Law of the Sea (UNCLOS) was opened for signature at Montego Bay in Jamaica by States and by international organisations such as the European Communities (EC), now the European Union (EU), to which its member States have delegated competence in matters pertaining to the UN Convention (UNCLOS, Articles 305-7). By the end of the Convention's period for signature, it had been signed by 159 States and other supranational entities, namely the EC, although certain members of the EC, namely West Germany (still separated from its eastern neighbour) and the UK, as well as the United States refused to sign it at the time owing to their opposition to parts of the Convention's regime for the deep sea bed. Over the next ten years, the Convention was embodied in national legislation as well as customary international law. Many States extended their national territorial seas to twelve miles (the 12-mile limit), and their fisheries jurisdiction to 200 miles (the EEZ). The sixtieth ratification of the Convention was made by Guyana on 16 November 1993, and the Convention duly entered force one year later, on 16 November 1994, as provided for in Article 308 of the Convention. A further Implementation Agreement was also concluded in 1994 which was designed to meet the concerns of the industrialised nations which remained outside the UNCLOS regime, especially concerning guarantees and priorities being given to the deep-sea mining companies of the industrialised nations. This Agreement entered force on 28 July 1996.

CHAPTER TWO

DEFINITION OF AREAS COVERED BY THE UN CONVENTION ON THE LAW OF THE SEA (UNCLOS)

BASELINES AND TERRITORIAL MARITIME LIMITS

In order to determine the extent of a coastal State's territorial sea and other maritime zones, it is first of all necessary to establish from what points on the country's coast the outer limits of such zones are to be measured. The definition of the normal baseline is covered in **Part II, Article 5** of the UNCLOS and **Article 3** of the Territorial Sea Convention, and states that the normal baseline for measuring the breadth of the territorial sea is the low-water line along the coast as marked on large-scale charts officially recognised by the coastal State. The effect of this definition is to push the outer limit of the territorial sea and other zones seawards, particularly on coasts where there is an extensive tidal range. Hence, the baseline is the line from which the outer limits of the territorial sea and other coastal State zones, i.e. the contiguous zone, the exclusive fishing zone and the exclusive economic zone (EEZ) are measured. The waters on the landward side of the baseline are known as internal waters. Thus, the baseline also forms the boundary between internal waters and the territorial sea, i.e. the demarcation between that maritime area (internal waters) where other States enjoy no general rights, as stated in **Article 8** of the UNCLOS, and those maritime areas (territorial sea and other zones) where other States do enjoy certain general rights. Since coasts are generally not straight, but vary according to promontories, headlands, bays and coves, as well as sandbanks and harbour installations, the baselines have to be defined to account for these discrepancies. Cases where offshore islands exist which are part of national territory also affect baseline definition. The Outer Hebrides containing the islands of Barra, North and South Uist, Benbecula, Harris and Lewis, are part of Scotland and hence UK national territory. The Minch, the stretch of water separating them from the Scottish mainland, is therefore included in internal waters, as the baseline pertaining to international maritime territory is located on their western side. The same applies to the Pentland Firth, the stretch of water separating the Orkney Islands from the Scottish mainland, and the North Channel, separating the province of Ulster, on the Irish landmass, from the landmass of Scotland. In this respect, these areas are classed as internal waters, yet international shipping has right of access, i.e. innocent passage, through these waterways, thus provided for by Section 2 of Article 8 of the UNCLOS.

BAYS

Originally, customary international law had recognised that the baseline could, in principle, be drawn across the mouth of bays, as well as estuaries, and, in the case of Scotland, firths, enclosing them as internal waters. But customary international law failed to provide clear rules on two essential points, namely the criteria by which an indentation of the coast would be recognised as a bay, and the maximum length of the closing line across a bay. Factors to be taken into account in deciding whether an indentation was a bay included the penetration of the bay inland, and the security and economic interests of the coastal State therein. For example, Lyme Bay is a wide curved indentation covering the eastern area of the English county of Devon, but it only extends a few miles out to sea into the Channel. The Bay of Bengal, however, is a huge expanse of water dividing the Indian sub-continent from South-East Asia. And yet, both expanses of water are described on the world map as bays. Article 7 of the Territorial Sea Convention established clear and precise rules for the determination of both these uncertain points, and Article 10 of the UNCLOS repeats these rules, stating that as long as the distance between the low-water marks of the natural entrance points of the bay does not exceed 24 nautical miles, a closing line may be drawn between these two low-water marks, and the waters enclosed thereby can be considered as internal waters. Lyme Bay falls within this category, whereas the Bay of Bengal does not. It is worth noting that Lyme Bay was the location where the stricken container vessel *MSC Napoli* was beached in January 2007, as a result of a hull fracture sustained during a savage storm in the Channel.

Historic Bays, such as the Bay of Bengal, which borders on several countries, and Lough Foyle, which separates the UK province of Ulster from the Irish Republic, do not fall within the category set out above, and are referred to in **Article 7** of the Territorial Sea Convention of 1958. They comprise international waters, and are thus not solely contained in the national territory of one country alone. In such cases, the baseline is constituted by the low-water baseline around the shores of the bay, rather than across the mouth of the bay. Indeed, the Bay of Bengal may be classified more as a Gulf, than a Bay, as it is an arm of the Indian Ocean in the same way that the Bay of Biscay (Fr. *Golfe de Gascogne*) is an indentation of the Atlantic Ocean.

River mouths and estuaries, as well as inlets such as Scottish Firths, are covered by **Article 9** of the UNCLOS and **Article 13** of the Territorial Sea Convention. In this case, the baseline may be a straight line across the mouth of the river between points on the low-water line of its banks. **Article 8** of the Territorial Sea Convention and Article 11 of the UNCLOS state that, in the case of ports and harbours, the outermost harbour works which form an integral part of the harbour system, such as jetties and breakwaters, are to be regarded as forming part of the coast and thus can serve as the baseline. However, Article 11 of the UNCLOS also adds that offshore installations and artificial islands are not to be considered as permanent harbour works. Only those harbour works attached to the coast, or at least very close to the coast, can be used as baselines.

INTERNAL WATERS

Internal, national or interior waters are those which lie landward of the baseline from which the breadth of the territorial sea and other maritime zones are measured, as defined by **Article 8** of the UNCLOS. Internal waters of a maritime character mostly comprise bays, estuaries and ports, and waters enclosed by straight baselines. The coastal State enjoys full territorial sovereignty over its internal waters, and thus may deal freely with such waters as it pleases, as these waters lie within national territory. For this reason, such waters have not been made the subject of detailed regulation in any of the Conventions on the Law of the Sea.

The existence of national sovereignty over internal waters and the absence of any general right of passage through them logically implies the absence of any right under customary international law for foreign ships to enter a State's ports or other internal waters. While it holds that the international ports of a State are assumed to be open to international merchant traffic, thus excluding foreign warships unless otherwise stated, this assumption has not acquired the status of a *right* under customary international law, as a State's international port could be closed to foreign vessels under specific issues pertaining to national security. Under this principle, the master of an incoming vessel, especially that of a foreign nationality, must report to the port authority prior to arrival at the port. It is clear that States have the right to nominate those ports which are to be open to international trade, i.e. to those vessels which the State chooses or binds itself by treaty to admit to its ports, although certain restrictions may be made concerning the right to entry, as exemplified by US requirements concerning the entry of foreign vessels into US territorial waters as defined by the 2002 US Trade Act and detailed in the CT-PAT (Customs and Trade Partnership against Terrorism) initiative. Under these provisions, the United States reserves the right to prevent the entry into US of any vessel it deems unsuitable, or where it has not received advance details of the vessel's complement of crew, passengers or cargo. The rule concerning the nomination by a State of its ports deemed open to international trade is often found in legislation designating approved ports of entry for customs, immigration and international trade purposes, as the relevant national authorities must approve such ports accordingly. This is also reinforced by the provision of the 3-mile territorial limit, which dictates that any vessel entering this maritime limit must report to a port of destination in order to satisfy the national authorities of its intentions, as the 3-mile limit is imposed by Customs as a point at which the vessel becomes subject to national Customs controls. Within this area, a national State enjoys absolute sovereignty, except insofar as it may have undertaken Treaty obligations to admit foreign vessels, whether Commercial or Naval, into its Ports. Under such obligations, such a vessel will be required to report into the Port in question at least 24 hours in advance.

States may also prescribe conditions for access to their ports. There are provisions in multilateral treaties which envisage the refusal of entry to ports to vessels which do not comply with measures adopted under such treaties, exemplified by the SOLAS (Safety of Lives at Sea) and MARPOL (Marine Pollution) Conventions. Even where vessels do arrive in port, they may still be subject to rigorous checks made by officials of the national maritime administration under the scope of Port State Control, which reserves the right of any such official to detail a vessel if it does not meet the national requirements for safety and seaworthiness, which are in general seen as elements of the international regulations imposed by the International Maritime Organisation (IMO). Indeed, the 1982 UNCLOS clearly implies the provision that States may set their own conditions for entry into their ports. However, there is one clear customary law which gives the automatic right of entry for ships in distress. If a vessel needs to enter a port or internal waters to shelter in order to preserve human life or at least render its comparative safety, international law gives it a right of entry. This right was exercised in early 2007, when the container vessel *MSC Napoli* foundered in heavy seas in the Channel while en route for the South Atlantic and Asia. Owing to the pronounced fractures in her hull, she was beached on a shallow reef in Lyme Bay off the coast of Devon, in South-West England. Although Lyme Bay was not a port facility in any way, it was considered sheltered enough water to facilitate the comparative safety of the vessel in order to easily rescue its crew. However, in cases where severe pollution may arise as a result of the adverse condition of the vessel, it is deemed better that coastal States may forbid such vessels to enter their internal waters if measures have been taken to save the lives of persons on board. The decision should be taken by weighing the gravity of the vessel's situation against the probability, degree and kind of harm to the environment of the coastal State that would arise if the vessel were allowed to enter internal waters.

Concerning the general right of entry into foreign ports, there are many bilateral treaties concerning commerce and navigation which allow such rights, although under any such treaty and the obligations imposed by it, the vessel will be required to report to the port of destination at least 24 hours before its arrival. The provisions of the EC Treaty of Rome in 1957 allowed for non-discrimination and the free movement of goods between all member States of the Community. The treaty thus gave a similar reciprocal right of access for all vessels belonging to each Member States into the ports of the other Member States, thus implying that, under the treaty of free market, a Dutch vessel had an automatic right of entry into a UK port, and so on. This is qualified by the system of Authorised Regular Operators, which allow the free access of vessels under such conditions on the basis that their operator has been approved by the EU authorities for regular sailings between the predetermined Member States covered by the authorisation, such as daily Ro-Ro ferry operations across the North Sea between the UK and the Netherlands.

It should, however, be stated that although rights of access imply a right to leave ports as well as enter them, that right of exit is subject to important limitations. Thus States are entitled to arrest vessels in port, in accordance with their normal legal processes, such as for safety or seaworthiness violations, or for customs offences such as illicit trade in the form of contraband or smuggling. Similarly, vessels in port are liable to arrest or seizure as security in civil actions or actions against the vessel itself, such as the arrest of the cruise vessel *Van Gogh* at the port of Funchal in April 2008 as a result of a legal dispute concerning the liquidation of the company formerly responsible under a charter party agreement for her operation. However, under the 1952 Brussels Convention on the Arrest of Sea-Going Ships, vessels of party States are subject to civil arrest only in the case of "maritime claims" as defined in Article 1 of that Convention. Furthermore, States may detain vessels which are in an unseaworthy condition, or otherwise unfit to proceed to sea, especially where defined by the national maritime administration such as the UK Maritime and Coastguard Agency (MCA). States may also require the masters or agents of foreign ships to obtain clearance documentation from the port authorities, certifying compliance with customs and health formalities, before they leave port.

By entering foreign ports and other internal waters, vessels subject themselves to the territorial jurisdiction of the coastal state, and are therefore required by law to declare their presence and their intentions. Accordingly, that State is entitled to enforce its laws and regulations against the ship, its crew, passengers and cargo, subject to the normal rules concerning sovereign and diplomatic immunities, which arise mainly in the case of visiting warships. But given that vessels are essentially self-contained units, with the laws of their flag State or the country of registry of their owners applying to them, but also a system for the enforcement of those flag State laws through the powers of the vessel's master and the authority of the local Consul, coastal States will generally enforce their laws only in cases where their interests are engaged, other than the application of international rules concerning reporting requirements, which apply to all vessels entering the internal waters of any coastal State, regardless of their nationality. Matters relating solely to the internal economy and administration of the vessel, i.e. issues concerning the vessel itself, are in practice left to the authorities of the flag State, i.e. the State where the vessel is owned or registered. It should be noted that the ownership of the vessel may apply to one country, whereas the flag of registry may be located elsewhere. For example, the cruise liner *Black Prince* is owned by the Norwegian-based company Fred Olsen, but she has been registered for some years in Nassau, Bahamas.

The main reason for the application of local law to ships visiting a specific port is their temporary presence within the territorial jurisdiction of the coastal State concerned. There are occasions where the coastal State seeks to impose obligations on foreign vessels which, if they are to be complied with in the State's ports, must be complied with throughout the voyage or at very least part of it. A case in point concerns the consumption and sale of alcoholic beverages on board vessels plying the North Sea, particularly Ro-Ro vehicle ferries. When the vessel is outbound from a UK port, UK Excise rates on such products apply, whereas if the product is purchased on a vessel leaving a continental port, the Excise rates of that country apply. However, to avoid confusion concerning the rate applicable to the direction of sailing, compromises are often reached to maintain stability in prices. The principal rule is that, if a vessel is sailing within EU waters, EU Excise rules apply. In cases where the vessel leaves EU waters for a non-EU destination, then alcohol and other excisable products may be sold at duty-free prices.

THE TERRITORIAL SEA

Territorial Maritime Limits can, in many cases, be defined at 3 specific levels:

- 200 Mile Exclusive Economic Zone (The Continental Shelf);
- The 12-Mile Limit;
- The 3-Mile Limit.

The UK and its waters

The sovereignty of a national State also extends to its **Territorial Sea** (UNCLOS, Article 2), also known as Territorial Waters", but this differs from Internal Waters in that it is subject to a right of "Innocent Passage" by foreign vessels (UNCLOS, Article 17). The right of Innocent Passage does not exempt the vessel from being required under certain Rules, such as the requirement to report to either UK or French Coastguards when passing through the Strait of Dover, and also stipulates requirements for such vessels to identify themselves by their national flag or flag of convenience. Certain other restrictions are placed on the passage of vessels, such as the requirement for all Submarines of any nationality to remain surfaced while passing through the defined Strait. In general, Territorial Sea limits are defined as being at a 12-Mile Limit from the national shore, although this may vary due to tidal fluctuations and the existence of islands or archipelagos controlled by that National State.

The final text submitted to the Hague Conference of 1930 by its Territorial Waters Committee accordingly included a provision stating that the territory of a State includes a belt of sea described in the Convention as the territorial sea. Sovereignty over this belt is exercised subject to the conditions prescribed by the Convention and the other rules of international law. The text was not adopted as a convention, mainly because of a failure to agree on the vital question of the breadth of the territorial sea. However, there has never been a serious challenge to the principle of coastal sovereignty over the territorial sea since the Hague Conference, other than wartime violations of British sovereign waters by German U-boats, most notably the sinking of the Royal Navy battleship *HMS Royal Oak* in Scapa Flow by the German U-boat *U-47* in 1939. The 1930 Conference may justly be regarded as the occasion when the doubts over that sea's juridical status, which had prevailed up to the preceding decade, were finally dispelled. Eventually, all States adopted the sovereignty doctrine concerning the Territorial Sea, including the States which gained their independence in the years following the Second World War. However, it does not follow that the municipal law of every State treats the sea in the same way that it does the land, so that municipal laws apply there. UK territorial waters remain as a matter of domestic law outside the realm, the UK laws apply therein only to the extent specifically provided. For example, Oil and Gas installations located in UK territorial waters are governed by UK jurisdiction, but they are located outside UK Customs jurisdiction, in that they are deemed to lie in offshore waters outside such domestic Customs control, and as such fall into the category of continental shelf activities and controls.

In order to emphasise that the right of innocent passage by vessels through territorial waters rendered the rights of coastal States over the territorial sea less extensive than those over their land territory, the Hague formula was amended to provide for two specific points:

1) The sovereignty of a State extends, beyond its land territory and its internal waters, to a belt of sea adjacent to its coast, described as the territorial sea;

2) This sovereignty is exercised subject to the provisions of these articles and to other rules of international law.

(Territorial Sea Convention, Article 1)

A similar provision, in which a reference to archipelagic waters was inserted after that referring to internal waters, appears in the Law of the Sea Convention (**UNCLOS, Arts. 2[1], 2[3]**).

The breadth of the territorial sea has always been a controversial issue. The original rule concerning the breadth of this expanse of water was defined by the premise that the rights of coastal States over marginal waters extended up to the point at which those waters could be controlled by shore-based cannon fire, i.e. the point at which a cannon ball landed in the water after being fired seawards by a shore-based cannon. This "cannon-shot" doctrine was probably not intended to support the establishment of a continuous belt of maritime territory along the whole coast, but rather to acknowledge the possibility of "pockets" of control by actual cannon present at various places on shore, especially as practised by Dutch and Mediterranean States. Conversely, Scandinavian countries did not apply this cannon-shot rule, but claimed maritime dominion over fixed distances from the shore along the whole coastline, regardless of the actual presence or absence of shore batteries. Over the years, these distances were progressively reduced from those claimed around the 16th century, and by the mid-18th century had generally settled at the four-mile Scandinavian 'league'. Eventually, the cannon-shot and fixed-distance approaches converged at the end of the 18th century, and the three-mile limit was chosen by most countries, mainly as a matter of reasonableness and convenience, and became the standard measurement adopted by the major powers throughout the 19th century, although it was never unanimously accepted. The Scandinavian countries consistently maintained a 4-mile limit, and several other countries, such as Spain, claimed zones of more than three miles for specific purposes.

The 1930 Hague Conference attempted to reach agreement upon the width of the territorial sea, and failed. At the final meeting of its Territorial waters Committee, 20 States sought territorial seas of three miles, 12 countries sought six miles, and the 4 Scandinavian States sought recognition of their own historic four-mile claim. Furthermore, several countries wanted the right to claim contiguous zones beyond their territorial seas. As a result, no general agreement was reached. In the event, the generally-applied 3-mile limit was assumed to apply, more by a negative approach in that the validity of claims of up to three miles could no be denied. Only after the third UN Conference on the Law of the Sea in 1982 was a definitive limit agreed. A consensus was reached by the finish of the UNCLOS III in favour of a 12-mile limit to the territorial sea. Article 3 of the Convention of the Law of the Sea thus sets the limit to the territorial sea for all coastal States which are party to the Convention at 12 miles.

The right of "innocent passage" through a territorial sea includes not only actual passage through the territorial sea but also stopping and anchoring insofar as this is part of normal navigation or is made necessary by *force majeure* or distress, a stated in the Territorial Sea Convention, Article 14(3), and the Law of the Sea Convention, Article 18(2). Other than these stipulations, and a further exception where one vessel may assist another ship or person in distress, vessels are not allowed to cruise around or loiter in the territorial sea unnecessarily, because, regardless of whether they are "innocent", they would not be engaged in passage. This implies that passage must be "continuous and expeditious", as stated in the Law of the Sea Convention, Article 18(2), meaning that all vessels engaged in innocent passage must be transiting through the territorial sea on their way to another destination, either a port in the country exercising control over the territorial sea in question, or to a port in another country which lies beyond the territorial sea. According to Article 14(6) of the Territorial Sea Convention, and Article 20 of the Law of the Sea Convention, all submarines and underwater vehicles must navigate on the surface.

A problem with regard to the right of innocent passage has arisen in the past concerning vessels carrying hazardous cargoes (HAZMAT). Some States regard these vessels as a threat to their peace and good order, especially those vessels carrying nuclear materials, namely the vessels belonging to Pacific Nuclear transport ltd (PNTL), which make regular voyages between Japan and the European Union. Influences such as Greenpeace and forces within certain governments of various countries have made the journeys of these vessels more inconvenient, despite the need to transport such materials by sea for reprocessing elsewhere. The IMO has set out specific guidelines for the transportation of nuclear materials, and these rules, published in the IMDG (International Movement of Dangerous Goods) Code as a separate INF Code, are accepted worldwide. Article 23 of the Law of the Sea Convention requires all vessels carrying nuclear or other inherently dangerous or noxious substances, to carry specific documentation and observe internationally agreed precautionary measures, such as those included in the 1974 SOLAS Convention, when exercising their right to innocent passage. Article 22 of the Law of the Sea Convention specifically authorises Coastal States to require such vessels to confine their passage to and sea lanes which have been designated in their territorial seas. However certain countries, including Chile, have excluded such vessels from their waters on many occasions and have thus denied the right of innocent passage to them. Under existing legislation, vessels carrying hazardous or dangerous materials must submit reports in advance of entering the territorial waters of most States under the HAZMAT rules and national reporting system regimes implemented by many nations worldwide.

STRAITS

The term "Strait" describes a narrow natural passage or arm of water between two land masses connecting two larger bodies of water, such as seas or oceans. It is the legal status of the waters constituting the strait and their use by international shipping, rather than the definition of the word 'strait', that determines the rights of coastal and flag States. **Article 16(4)** of the Territorial Sea Convention provides that there shall be no suspension of the innocent passage of foreign vessels through straits which are used for international navigation between one part of the high seas and another part of the high seas, or the territorial sea of a foreign State.

According to Article 37 of the Law of the Sea Convention, the regime of transit passage of vessels applies to straits which are used for international navigation between one part of the high seas or an exclusive economic zone and another part of the high seas or an exclusive economic zone. Three categories of strait are excluded from this definition. The first, defined by Article 36 of the UNCLOS, is the category of straits through which there is a high-seas route, or a route through an exclusive economic zone, of a similar manner with respect to its navigational and hydrographical characteristics, exemplified by the Florida Strait between the United States and

Cuba. The second category, defined in Article 38(1) of the UNCLOS, is that of straits formed by an island bordering the strait and its mainland, where a route of similar navigational and hydrographical convenience exists through the exclusive economic zone or high seas seaward of the island, such as the Straits of Messina between the island of Sicily and the Italian mainland. The third category, defined by Article 45 of the UNCLOS, is that of straits connecting an area of the high seas or an exclusive economic zone with the territorial sea of a third State, exemplified by the Straits of Tiran, between the Sinai and Arabian peninsulas at the northern end of the Red Sea. In all three cases, the right of innocent passage exists, although this may be regulated in the same way that innocent passage can be regulated through other parts of their territorial seas.

In all cases of passage through straits by international maritime traffic, such as through the Malacca Straits, the Strait of Gibraltar, the Öresund or the Strait of Dover, transit passage is the exercise of freedom of navigation for the continuous and expeditious transit of the strait between one area of high seas or economic zone and another, or in order to enter or leave a State bordering the strait, as stated in **Article 38(2)** of the UNCLOS. This implies that the vessel cannot stop while in transit through the strait, and this provision for constant and consistent movement of vessels is further reinforced by the Traffic Separation Scheme (TSS) in force in the Strait of Dover. While in transit, vessels must comply with generally accepted international regulations, procedures and practices for safety at sea, and for the prevention of pollution from ships, as stated by **Article 39(2)** of the UNCLOS, including the SOLAS conventions and the IMO pollution conventions. Where required, they must also report their identification, position and destination, in accordance with any national or supranational reporting requirements as determined by the coastal States they are passing at the time.

To this extent, the IMO has allowed for the implementation of Traffic Separation Schemes (TSS), ensuring that vessels passing through the Strait must maintain course along a designated shipping lane assigned to them by the national authority on whose side of the Strait they are navigating at the time. They must also ensure that their identification is known to the national authority in question, should the need arise for interception of the vessel or for communication to be made by the national authority with the vessel while it is passing through the Strait.

CONTIGUOUS ZONES

The Contiguous Zone is a zone of sea contiguous to and seaward of the territorial sea in which States have limited powers for the enforcement of customs, fiscal, sanitary and immigration laws. Different countries historically applied different criteria for the definition of the contiguous zone, mainly to deter acts such as smuggling, and for policing for customs and security purposes, as well as fishery protection in other cases. General State practice with regard to such jurisdiction differed between many coastal States until the Geneva Conference of 1958, which eventually agreed upon the establishment of a contiguous zone within which the coastal State could enjoy limited jurisdiction. That provision, set out in Article 24 of the Territorial Sea Convention, ultimately became Article 33(1) of the 1982 UNCLOS. This article states that in the contiguous zone, the coastal State may exercise the control necessary to:

a) Prevent infringement of its customs, fiscal, immigration or sanitary laws and regulations within its territory or territorial sea;

b) Punish infringement of the above laws and regulations committed within its territory or territorial sea.

Unlike the definition of the territorial sea and its breadth, States are not obliged to maintain contiguous zones, as they are to maintain territorial seas, and to this extent, the UNCLOS contains no provision for the delimitation of the contiguous zone between opposite and adjacent States, mainly because such a delimitation would, in cases where coastal States also claim an Exclusive Economic Zone (EEZ), amount to a delimitation of part of the EEZ, and should therefore be considered as part of the EEZ. Unlike the continental shelf, the contiguous zone is not automatically given to the coastal State. Under both the 1958 and 1982 Conventions, a State must choose whether to claim a contiguous zone, and in reality over one-third of the world's coastal States have chosen to do so, with 50 States claiming a contiguous zone by 1997. Owing to differing claims by several countries with regard to the breadth of the contiguous zone, UNCLOS III of 1982 decided to move the contiguous zone seaward, setting the outer limit at 24 miles from the national baseline, as stated by Article 33 of the UNCLOS, thus allowing a 12-mile contiguous zone beyond the 12-mile territorial sea limit.

National Sovereign States are given the option of claiming a contiguous zone adjacent to their territorial sea, in which they may exercise the control necessary to prevent and punish infringement of their customs, fiscal, immigration and sanitary laws within their territory or territorial sea (UNCLOS, Article 33). Under the Territorial Sea Convention, the contiguous zone could not exceed 12 (Twelve) miles from the baselines of the territorial sea, but this distance has been extended to 24 miles by the Law of the Sea Convention. However, this extension cannot apply to Straits such as the Strait of Dover and the Öresund, where the maximum distance across the Strait from one shoreline to the other does not exceed 20 miles (The Strait of Dover) and 10 miles (The Öresund).

Thus, Contiguous Zones are those areas of water subject to national territorial controls which extend beyond territorial waters up to a distance of not greater than 24 nautical miles from the national coastline or baseline. A country which imposes a contiguous zone may operate its own maritime protection forces within that zone for the purposes of defence of its sovereignty with relation to Customs, fiscal immigration or sanitary laws and regulations. In Straits of a limited width such as the Strait of Dover, the Öresund, the Strait of Gibraltar or the Malacca Straits, then contiguous zones do not apply, as there is insufficient width of waterway to allow for both a territorial sea and a contiguous zone owing to the fact that under such limited conditions, the territorial sea limits of each coastal State overlooking the Strait would overlap in mid-Channel.

A lesser degree of national territorial control is permissible in Straits used for international navigation between parts of the high seas or exclusive economic zones, such as the Straits of Dover and Gibraltar. In these, a new right of "transit passage" has been introduced by the

Convention of the Law of the Sea, conferring freedom of navigation and overflight on foreign ships and aircraft for the purpose of continuous and expeditious transit (UNCLOS, Article 38). However, the vessel concerned must identify itself and show that it is bound for a port outside these areas, and its movement is still monitored by the national authorities concerned in order to comply with the applying rules. There is no requirement that the passage should be innocent, as defined in the rules pertaining to Territorial Seas, but ships must refrain from activities not incidental to normal transit (e.g. warfare, terrorism or aggression), and must comply with international regulations, procedures and practices for the safety at sea (SOLAS – Safety of Lives at Sea) and control of marine pollution (UNCLOS, Article 39). However, the scope of national legislation and regulation is limited, and at present the only available measures of control are as follows (UNCLOS, Article 42):

- Prevention of Fishing;
- International Standards on Maritime Safety;
- International Standards on Pollution;
- Customs & Fiscal Enforcement;
- Immigration Controls;
- Sanitary and Health Controls.

It should be noted that with initiatives towards electronic Cargo Reporting and Declaration, combined with a downsizing in personnel employed by many national Customs Authorities, even Customs controls over such activities have become less evident, and in most cases, especially within parts of the European Union such as the UK, such maritime fiscal controls can no longer be exercised owing to the lack of human resources for such a task. In this case, the application and enforcement of Article 42 of the UNCLOS would appear to be less defined and practical.

THE CONTINENTAL SHELF

The Continental Shelf was defined in the 1958 Continental Shelf Convention as the seabed and subsoil of the submarine areas adjacent to the national coastline but outside the Territorial Sea to a depth of 200 meters or, beyond that limit, to where the depth of the superjacent waters admits and permits the exploration and exploitation of their natural resources, be they mineral or otherwise. This definition has been replaced by the UN Convention of the Law of the Sea, which refers instead to the natural prolongation of the land territory to the outer edge of the continental margin or a minimum distance of 200 nautical miles from the territorial sea baselines (usually 12 Miles), subject to a maximum of 350 miles from the baselines or 100 miles from the 2,500 metre isobath (UNCLOS, Article 76). These areas must also be specifically defined and must be charted and mapped for official purposes. However, for the purposes of most practical exercises, the Continental Shelf is generally still deemed to refer to the geographic maritime area generally bounded by the 200-Mile Limit, where the seabed closer to national shores is at a much shallower level than out in the main body of the Ocean. On the landward side, the continental shelf boundary is deemed to start where the limitation of the territorial sea ends, i.e. at 12 miles from the shore. It is this area which is used primarily for the exploration of Oil & Gas reserves. In the case of the UK, specific areas used for Oil & Gas exploration are the area to the West of the Shetland Islands, and the North Sea from the German Bight to the waters of the Norwegian Basin between the Shetland Islands and the Norwegian Coast.

The inner or landward limit of the continental shelf has always been regarded as being the outer limit of the territorial sea. Article 1 of the 1958 Continental Shelf Convention defined the continental shelf as being the sea bed and subsoil of the submarine areas adjacent to the coast but outside the area of the territorial sea, to a depth of 200 metres or, beyond that limit, to where the depth of the surrounding waters admits the exploitation of the natural resources of the stated areas. However, it was recognised at the 1958 conference on the continental shelf that the addition of the exploitability test rendered the seaward limit of the continental shelf dangerously imprecise. It became clear that new technology, especially in the offshore mineral resource sector, namely oil and gas exploration, would push the limit further and further from the shore, and "exploitability", which ranged from trawling for sedentary fish to the establishment of a full-scale profit-making offshore oil production complex, was itself an elusive criterion. Between 1958 and the UNCLOS III conference, increasing attention was paid to the sea bed and to what extent it could be exploited, and by the time of the UNCLOS III conference, there was significant difficulty in reaching agreement on the outer limit of the continental shelf. The consolidation of the emergent rules on the EEZ automatically included the acceptance of an outer limit of at least 200 miles from the baselines of coastal States. This brought about approximately 36% of the total sea bed within national jurisdiction, including in some areas parts of the sea bed lying beyond the physical continental margin.

Article 76(1) of the UNCLOS thus provides that the continental shelf of a coastal State comprises the sea-bed and subsoil of the submarine areas which extend beyond its territorial sea throughout the natural prolongation of its land territory to the outer edge of the continental margin, or to a distance of 200 nautical miles from the baselines from which the breadth of the territorial sea is measured where the outer edge of the continental margin does not extend up to that distance. In this way, the legal definition of the continental shelf is quite distinct and different from the geological definition of the shelf. Areas of the sea bed which lie beyond the physical continental margin, i.e. in deeper water, are included in the legal scope of the continental shelf, as long as they are located within 200 miles of the coast. In broad terms, therefore, a coastal State is entitles to a continental shelf comprising:

a) The sea bed reaching 200 miles from the baselines, i.e. the coastline; and

b) Any area of physical continental margin (often known as the "outer" continental shelf) beyond it.

Therefore, the limits established by the 1982 UNCLOS allow the inclusion within national jurisdiction of substantially the whole of the physical continental margin.

A coastal state has sovereign rights over the continental shelf for the purpose of exploring it and exploiting its natural resources, but these are confined to mineral and other non-living resources (i.e. fish and crustaceans) together with sedentary species of living organisms (**UNCLOS, Article 77**).

The exploration for Oil and Gas has meant a huge amount invested in the construction and installation of Offshore Production Platforms, and these are protected by the UNCLOS in the form of an exclusion zone comprising a 500-metre radius around each platform. However, there is no reporting mechanism governing the safe passage of vessels within the areas containing such platforms, namely the various Oil and Gas fields in the North Sea and to the West of the Shetland Islands. The Supply Vessels serving these platforms must report to the relevant Harbour Authority of Departure, such as the Port of Tyne or Aberdeen, concerning their general destination (a designated oilfield), prior to sailing from the Port in question. They must also be in possession of correct cargo manifests pertaining to all consignments loaded aboard vessel prior to departure for the satisfaction of both Port Authority and Customs Control requirements. However, once the vessel has sailed, there is no specific means of the vessel reporting its intentions, other than the AIS System (detailed later in this text) or the VTS system (also detailed later in the text) pertaining to the vessel's course and position.

The offshore Oil and Gas sector is an area which is vulnerable to maritime threats or incidents. Oil and Gas production platforms are located well outside the 12-mile limit of UK territorial waters, and have little or no protection around them. To this extent, the provisions of the UN Convention of the Law of the Sea (UNCLOS) have afforded them an automatic 500-metre exclusion zone, prohibiting the incursion of any vessel other than those authorised to unload materials and supplies onto them.

We live in an era of political uncertainty, with the constant risk of threats and acts of international terrorism. Because of the lack of a major security initiative controlling these maritime areas, as well as the lack of a more secure marine reporting regime, there is always the great risk of sabotage or at worst a major disaster in one of the oilfields cause by acts of terrorism or collision in adverse weather conditions. A fictional scenario, far-fetched as it may have seemed at the time, depicted in the 1980s film "North Sea Hijack", illustrated such risks in graphic and chilling detail. Indeed, tragic events such as the 1980s Piper Alpha disaster show how easy it is for a simple error or cost-cutting exercise to become a major international disaster, as well as a menace to shipping in the vicinity. A huge area of the North Sea, and indeed much of the Northern European Continental Shelf, is now covered by Oil or Gas Platforms. Some are operational and some are non-operational, but each poses its own hazard to shipping in the area. In fine weather, these platforms are clearly visible to ships in the area, whereas in less-clement weather conditions, they are only identifiable on the radar screens until approached at close quarters. Given that each platform is surrounded by a 500-metre radius exclusion zone bestowed upon it by the UN Convention of the Law of the Sea, there is a great need for vigilance on the part of ships' masters to ensure that they will only approach the platform for legitimate supply purposes, and will otherwise avoid the area. This said, there is an increasing need for all vessels in the area of the North Sea Oil and Gas fields to make their positions known to the platforms located in these fields, in order to ensure complete maritime security and to equally ensure that their presence is monitored and accounted for.

The Continental Shelf is also an area protected by international interests because of its environmental considerations and its fishing grounds. In the European Continental Shelf, the waters are fished by several nations, each requiring large catches to satisfy national demand and to ensure a commercial living. But in recent years, the levels of fish in these areas have been severely depleted, many as a result of over-fishing by the fleets of several nations, and as a result, strict quotas have been imposed by the European Commission on yearly catches by each of the maritime nations. This does not stop illegal incursion into the fishing grounds by many vessels in direct violation of these quotas, and the net result has been for several nations, including the UK, to impose controls on these areas by using Fishery Protection Vessels. These vessels do not use conventional identification systems such as active AIS systems, in order to remain undetectable by fishing vessels, but by using passive AIS and other monitoring systems, can detect other vessels conducting illegal activities and if required detain or arrest them. There are, however, only limited resources available concerning the operations of these vessels, and they can only be in one location at once.

THE EXCLUSIVE ECONOMIC ZONE (EEZ)

The Exclusive Economic Zone (EEZ) is a zone extending up to 200 miles from the baseline, within which the coastal State enjoys extensive rights in relation to natural resources and related jurisdictional rights, and third States enjoy freedoms of navigation, and the laying of cables and pipelines. The EEZ is a reflection of the aspiration of the developing countries for economic development and their desire to gain greater control over the economic resources off their coasts, particularly fish stocks, which in many cases have been largely exploited by the distant-water fleets of developed States. However, the developed States also can impose an EEZ to protect their own fishing and mineral resources, as exemplified by the European Union, which imposes an EEZ over the area of the North Atlantic off its western coastline. Under the UNCLOS, there is no obligation on a State to claim an EEZ. However, most coastal States have exercised their rights to make such a claim, with the exceptions of the States bordering the Mediterranean and some States bordering other semi-enclosed seas, where it is impossible for geographical reasons to establish an EEZ of a full 200 miles breadth. States such as the UK have preferred to claim a 200-mile EFZ (Exclusive Fishing Zone) rather than a 200-mile EEZ because the former entity, together with the exclusive rights they already have over sea-bed resources under the continental shelf regime, gives such States all that they require at present from an EEZ.

According to Article 55 of the UNCLOS, the inner limit of an EEZ is the outer limit of the territorial sea. Article 57 states that the zone's outer limit shall not extend beyond 200 nautical miles from the baselines from which the breadth of the territorial sea is measured. In many regions, however, States are unable to claim a full 200-mile zone because of the presence of neighbouring States, and it is therefore necessary to delimit the EEZs of opposite and adjacent States to a breadth deemed appropriate to allow an area of high seas in the form of international waters, thus ensuring that the EEZ of one country does not impinge upon the EEZ of the country lying opposite it.

An interesting consideration of the extent of the EEZs of the European Union and Iceland is that concerning the width of the Atlantic Ocean to the north of the UK. Because of the relatively shore distance between the Shetland Isles, the Faeroe Islands (belonging to Denmark, Iceland and Greenland, the continental shelf extends right across the ocean, and thus eliminates the status of high seas at that point. The status of the Shetland Isles and the Faeroe Islands as archipelagic states (albeit owned by member States of the European Union) extends the EEZ regime of the Atlantic up to the Icelandic EEZ, which itself extends to the EEZ around Greenland (which is also owned by Denmark). Given the proximity of Greenland to the North American continent, the EEZ therefore extends to the EEZ of Canada. This therefore removes high sea status from that part of the Atlantic Ocean, and effectively the EEZ domain right across the Atlantic.

In brief, the maritime limits defined by international law are as follows:

The **200-Mile** Exclusive Economic Zone (EEZ) is patrolled by Fishery Protection Vessels, especially those of the Royal Navy, and serves to protect fishing rights within these waters and restrict them to EU vessels.

The **12-Mile Limit** refers to the absolute offshore limit pertaining to national territorial controls, and thus defines the territorial sea. Within this limit, waters are deemed as being under national territorial control, and are not deemed to be international waters.

The **3-Mile Limit** refers (in the case of the UK) to the rights of Admiralty and HM Customs & Excise to control all shipping and maritime movements within these waters. All vessels operating within the 3-Mile Limit are subject to Admiralty and Customs controls, and may be subject to boarding by Officers belonging to such authorities where required.

HIGH SEAS

The regime of the high seas has traditionally been characterised by the prevalence of the principles of free use and the exclusivity of flag State jurisdiction, in direct contrast to the powers of States over their coastal waters. In other words, once a vessel is out of waters subject to national controls, it becomes subject to the rules imposed by its owners, or the flag State to which it belongs. The 1958 High Seas Convention, which claimed to codify customary international law, gave four examples of the freedom of the high seas, namely:

- Freedom of Navigation;
- Freedom of Fishing;
- Freedom of laying of Submarine Cables and Pipelines; and
- Freedom of Overflight.

The high seas were defined in the 1958 High Seas Convention as "all parts of the sea not included in the territorial sea or in the internal waters of a state" (Article 1, High Seas

Convention). With the introduction of Exclusive Economic Zones and the concept of archipelagic waters, i.e. waters surrounding islands and archipelagos such as the Philippines and Galapagos islands, this definition required modification. Article 86 of the UNCLOS, while not as such offering a definition of the high seas, states that the high-seas rules as incorporated in the Convention apply to all parts of the sea which are not included in the exclusive economic zone, in the territorial sea or in the internal waters of a State, or in the archipelagic waters of an archipelagic State.

The high seas are open to all States, and hence access to vessels belonging to such States, and no State may validly claim to render any part of them subject to its own national sovereignty (Article 2, High Seas Convention; Articles 87 & 89, UNCLOS), and this rule of customary law is a cornerstone and very basis of modern international law. From the rule that no State can subject areas of the high seas to its own national sovereignty, or indeed to its jurisdiction, it follows that no State has the right to prevent ships of other States from using the high seas for any "lawful purpose". A corollary of the status of the high seas is that apart from a few special cases, generally created by treaty, no State has jurisdiction over foreign ships on the high seas. Thus, users of the high seas remain at liberty to do as they please apart from a few restrictive rules as defined by the UNCLOS. Further to stating the freedoms of the high seas, Article 2 of the 1958 High Seas Convention continued by stating that these freedoms, and others which are recognised by the general principles of international law, should be exercised by all States with reasonable regard to the interests of other States in their exercise of the freedom of the high seas. Therefore, all States, whether coastal or not, have the right to exercise high-seas freedoms. In general, the flag State, i.e. the State which has granted to a ship the right to sail under its national flag, has the exclusive right to exercise legislative and enforcement jurisdiction over its ships on the high seas, as stated by Article 6 of the High Seas Convention and Article 92 of the UNCLOS. This means that all vessels must exercise due care and attention to all the rules imposed over passage through the high seas, and must ensure that they do not unduly interfere with other vessels engaged in the same activity, unless called upon to do so for legitimate purposes, such as coming to the rescue of ships in distress. It also means that acts of piracy, where vessels are intercepted for whatever unlawful reason, are by nature illegal, and thus every State has the long-established right to act against such actions, even where one of its vessels is sailing in waters far removed from its own national territory, for example off Somali waters or through the Malacca Straits.

Piracy remains a serious, and increasing, problem, mainly off parts of South-East Asia and East Africa. It is consistently being monitored by the International Maritime Organisation (IMO) and the international shipping industry. Piracy involves any illegal act of violence, detention or depredation committed for private purposes by the crew or passengers of a private ship against another ship or persons or property on board that vessel, on the high seas. If a ship is intended to be or has been used for such purposes by the persons in dominant control of it, it is deemed to be a pirate ship, as stated by Article 17 of the High Seas Convention and Article 103 of the UNCLOS. The IMO has become concerned at the increasing numbers of piracy incidents, and also of terrorist acts threatening the safety of navigation, and duly prepared the Convention for the Suppression of Unlawful Acts against the Safety of Maritime Navigation (known as the "SUA" Convention) in 1988, which entered into force in 1992. Article 3 of this Convention specifies certain acts against shipping as offences, including the seizure of ships and the endangering of safe navigation by the use of violence against persons on board or by damage to the ship, its cargo or equipment, and attempts to commit these acts. Article 6(1) declares that countries which have adopted this Convention must establish jurisdiction over offences committed on or against their ships, or in their territory, or by their nationals. This Article is more difficult to enforce, given that certain countries, such as Somalia, wilfully and clearly allow their citizens to commit such offences, and take no action in seeking to deter such offences. In other cases, acts of piracy are known about but little action is taken as a deterrent or as a means of eradication. Indeed, countries where piracy occurs are also some of the most politically unstable. A protocol to the SUA Convention, adopted in 1989, also extends these principles to acts committed against fixed oil and gas platforms located on the continental shelf.

Provision is also made for States to act against unauthorised vessels encroaching on areas governed by the rules pertaining to EEX or continental shelf activity, such as fisheries. Given that under the provisions of the UNCLOS, fisheries are to be protected by national authorities, unauthorised fishing by vessels not belonging to the State in question may be intercepted by warships of that country and boarded and seized where necessary. Similarly, vessels engaged in acts of illicit trade, smuggling or contraband may also be challenged by vessels belonging to the national authority, such as warships or Customs vessels, as long as the vessels concerned are operating within territorial waters and, perhaps the EEZ, and this is embodied in the principle of hot pursuit.

INNOCENT PASSAGE

The existence of the right of innocent passage through the territorial sea, or in areas of limited international water, such as straits between two national territories, has evolved over many years. The right was never well-defined, but remained at the discretion of national States seeking to exercise their national sovereignty over areas of territorial sea and the contiguous zones beyond those defined territories. The definition of "passage" includes not only the actual passage through or close to the territorial sea, but also stopping and anchoring in such territorial areas inasmuch as this action is incidental to ordinary navigation or becomes necessary in the event of *force majeure*, such as major storms, distress or accident, as covered by the Territorial Sea Convention (TSC), Article 14(3) and the UNCLOS, Article 18(2). The UNCLOS extends the exception of distress to cases where one vessel goes to assist another vessel or person in danger or distress (UNCLOS, Article 18(2)). Other than this exception, vessels are not allowed to "loiter" or cruise around in or close to the territorial sea because, regardless of whether they are deemed to be "innocent", they would not be engaged in passage. Therefore, passage must be "continuous and expeditious" (UNCLOS, Article 18(2)). All underwater or submersible vehicles, especially submarines, must navigate on the surface (TSC, Article 14(6); UNCLOS Article 20).

The articles of the 1930 Hague Conference introduced a new element into the definition of passage, which had not been previously adopted in international State practice, by including vessels passing through the territorial sea to or from internal national waters within the scope of the right of innocent passage. On this basis, coastal States retained the right to make, impose and enforce conditions for the admission of foreign vessels to internal national waters, and these provisions were included in the TSC (Article 16(2)) and subsequently the UNCLOS (Article 25(2)). However, this element was primarily introduced for the convenience of bringing such vessels within the legal regime and scope of vessels in innocent passage, for the general purposes of coastal State control and jurisdiction. Article 14(2) of the Territorial Sea Convention adopted the same position, and this article was carried through into the UNCLOS, although it was slightly modified to include within the overall scope of "passage" the voyages of vessels navigating the territorial sea in order to call at port facilities or terminals outside internal waters (UNCLOS, Article 18(1)).

The concept of "innocence" was effectively defined by the 1930 Hague Conference, which adopted a text which stated that passage is not innocent when a vessel makes use of the territorial sea of a coastal State for the purpose of doing any act prejudicial to the security, to the public policy or to the fiscal interests of that State (**League of Nations Document C. 351(b). M. 145(b). 1930. v, p.213**). During the preparation of the Territorial Sea Convention, the 1930 Hague draft was used, with specific reference to acts prejudicing the interests of coastal States rather than the manner of passage. The final text drafted by the International Law Commission stated that passage was innocent as long as the vessel did not commit any acts prejudicial to the security of the coastal State or contrary to existing rules ("present rules"), or to any other rules of international law, as stated in the ILC Yearbook 1956, Volume II. The term "present rules" was understood to refer to the duty which was imposed by another of the draft articles to comply with coastal State legislation on issues such as public health, immigration, customs and fiscal matters, navigation, fishing, and the protection of the products of the territorial sea, these being the interests which the coastal State was entitled to protect in its territorial sea, including offshore facilities for subsea exploration such as oil and gas energy resources. However, this draft was not accepted by the 1958 conference. After various proposed amendments, a compromise text was adopted as Article 14(4) of the Territorial Sea Convention, which stated that passage is innocent as long as it is not prejudicial to the peace, good order or security of the coastal State concerned. Such passage was to take place in conformity with the articles in question and with other rules of international law. Unlike the 1930 Hague draft, article 14(4) detailed the circumstances in which passage was deemed to be innocent. To this extent, the 1958 provision does not require the committing of a particular act or violation of any specific law before innocence is lost. There is, however, a case where innocence may be lost in the case of violation prejudicing coastal interests, and this is contained in Article 14(5), which refers to the passage of foreign fishing vessels, which may not be considered innocent if they do not observe the laws and regulations made and published by a coastal State in order to prevent these vessels from fishing within the definitions and boundaries of a territorial sea. Subsequently, the definition of innocent passage was significantly amended in the UN Convention of the Law of the Sea. Article 19 of the 1982 Convention retains the text of Article 14(4) of the 1958 Convention. However, it continues by stating in Paragraph 2 that passage of a foreign vessel shall be considered to be prejudicial to the peace, good order or security of the coastal State if, while in the territorial sea, it engages in any of the following activities, including:

- Weapons practice;

- Spying;

- Propaganda;

- Taking on board military devices;

- Embarking or disembarking persons or goods contrary to customs, fiscal, immigration or sanitary regulations;

- Wilful and serious pollution;

- Fishing;

- Research or survey activities;

- Interference with coastal communication or other facilities.

The list was then completed by two rather broader categories of activity:

- Any threat or use of force against the sovereignty, territorial integrity or political independence of the coastal State, or in any other manner in violation of the principles of international law embodied in the charter of the United Nations;

- Any other activity not having a direct bearing on passage (UNCLOS, Article 19(2)(a)).

Thus, the simple definition of innocence as stated in the 1958 Convention was replaced by the more detailed provisions of the 1982 Convention so as to produce a more objective definition, allowing less scope for interpretation on the part of coastal States, and hence less opportunity for abuse of their right to prevent non-innocent passage. However, a coastal State may exercise such measures as to reasonably protect its national territory, and this includes the defence of its territorial sea, including the interception of vessels deemed to be abusing their right of innocent passage according to the criteria explained in this section. What is paramount in the whole of the law referring to the right of innocent passage by foreign vessels is that coastal States may not under any circumstances suspend, even temporarily, the innocent passage of vessels through straits which are open to shipping between two areas of high seas.

THE COASTAL STATE

The rights of a coastal State to exercise jurisdiction over the territorial sea have historically varied according to what degree the coastal State considered its overall control over its sector of territorial sea. The most commonly accepted issues have generally included navigation, customs, fishing, sanitation (pollution) and security, although the general criminal and civil laws of a State were not seen as extending to foreign vessels. To this end, any activity of a coastal State interfering with a foreign vessel was very limited. As with many other issues, the 1930 Hague Convention failed to resolve the matter at an overall level, although the Hague Draft included an article, namely Article 6, obliging foreign vessels to comply with the laws and regulations enacted by any coastal State, especially those relating to navigation, pollution and resources of the territorial sea. This position was further pursued by the International Law Commission, although it also included the requirement for foreign vessels to conform with national laws and regulations pertaining to transport and navigation, and this revised definition was eventually adopted as Article 17 of the Territorial Sea Convention. The UNCLOS modified this article to allow the coastal State to adopt laws concerning navigation, protection of cables and pipelines, fisheries, pollution, scientific research and customs, fiscal and sanitary regulations, which must be appropriately publicised. These provisions are contained in Article 21(3) of the UNCLOS. Under Articles 21(4) and 22 of the UN Convention, foreign vessels are obliged to comply with laws enacted by the coastal State within the UNCLOS, as long as they are within sea lanes designated by the coastal State, and these regulations include the prevention of collisions at sea. Although coastal State legislative jurisdiction over the territorial sea may be limited in many cases, enforcement of jurisdiction may still be carried out under many circumstances, especially in cases of fishery protection and illicit trade such as smuggling or violations of national immigration policy. It is also the right of a coastal State to engage in measures to ascertain the identity of vessels approaching its territory, especially where its jurisdiction over the territorial sea is concerned, and this infers the adoption of a maritime reporting regime to undertake such controls.

However, the enforcement of jurisdiction can only effectively be undertaken if a violation has been carried out within the confines of the country's national territorial sea limits. Under Article 19(5) of the 1958 Territorial Sea Convention, if a violation occurred outside such boundaries, and the vessel subsequently simply passed through the territorial sea on its way to another location elsewhere, then enforcement of the country's jurisdiction could not be undertaken as there is no legal basis to do so. To this extent, the 1982 UN Convention of the Law of the Sea adopted exactly the same principles, applying them to Articles 27 and 28 of the UNCLOS. If, however, a violation occurs within the confines of a coastal State's territorial sea, then appropriate action may be taken against that vessel, especially concerning fishery, customs, fiscal or immigration violations. However, it is also the express duty of the coastal State to give appropriate notice of its national laws and regulations to all countries involved in the UN Convention with regard to its controls over its territorial sea, as well as notice of all known navigational hazards, including undersea pipelines and known wrecks, as stipulated by Article 15(1) of the TSC and Article 24(1) of the UNCLOS. This information also includes the provision of basic navigational services such as lighthouses and rescue facilities. According to Article 15(1) of the TSC and Article 24(1) of the UNCLOS, coastal States must not interfere with or impede the right of innocent passage for any vessel, and this has been seen as a limitation upon the jurisdiction of any coastal State, but it is applied in a general sense and is designed to prevent any unreasonable interference with innocent passage by the establishment of installations in the territorial sea, including offshore oil and gas platforms, despite, in many cases, their proximate location to well-established shipping routes.

CHAPTER 3

THE PRACTICAL PERSPECTIVE

TYPES AND NATURES OF VESSELS

CRUISE VESSELS

The concept of the passenger liner has changed over the latter part of the 20th century and into the 21st century, with the demise of the conventional and traditional passenger liner and the emergence of the more specialised and purpose-built cruise liner. Cruising as a means of maritime passenger transport commenced between the two world wars, as the passenger liners normally associated with the regular sailings on routes such as the North Atlantic, became less attractive or economical for such purposes, and were transferred to cruising to accommodate the demands for more leisure-based commercial sailing activities. In the years following the Second World War, cruising, especially to warmer climates such as the Mediterranean and Caribbean, became more popular, and some of the passenger liners of the post-war period which were, like their prewar counterparts, normally used for regular sailings across the North Atlantic, were adapted for cruising activities over the winter months, when passenger levels on their regular routes dwindled.

The 1960s were a turbulent time in the passenger liner market, as airline fares became cheaper, and the intercontinental jets decimated the business originally held by the passenger liners. The great Cunard liners *Queen Mary* and *Queen Elizabeth*, built at a time when transatlantic passenger liner travel was at its zenith, were abruptly retired, as their passenger numbers fell drastically. An intended successor for the 1960s, the '*Q3*' liner project, envisaged as a three-class North Atlantic liner to rival the French Line's flagship *France*, was hurriedly abandoned when it became clear that her construction would have bankrupted Cunard Line. Instead, a hybrid design for a smaller ship was approved by Cunard, which allowed for a dual-role passenger liner capable of plying the North Atlantic in the summer months, and transferring to pure cruising activities in the winter months. This vessel was duly constructed and launched as the vessel Queen Elizabeth 2, and entered service with Cunard Line in 1969. Five years later, the French Line announced its intention to sell its flagship *France*, owing to her decrease in viability on the regular transatlantic route. She was purchased by the Kloster Group of Norway for its Norwegian Caribbean cruise operations, and became the *Norway*. She was extensively rebuilt for cruise operations, and survived until the early part of the 21st century.

By the mid-1970s, the traditional passenger liner had disappeared. Gone were the multiple-class arrangements of the North Atlantic services, replaced by one-class accommodation, although in recent years several price categories exist for the more luxurious hybrid liners, especially those of Cunard Line, which still ply the North Atlantic route as part of their varied itineraries. The old traditional styles of liners were replaced by purpose-built cruise vessels, capable of accommodating more than 2000 passengers on any single cruise. Many of the traditional shipping lines also disappeared, such as Swedish-America Line, Nord-Deutscher Lloyd and Shaw Savill

Line. Others, such as Holland-America Line, Cunard Line and P&O, were swallowed up by other major cruise companies such as Carnival Cruise Corporation, based in Miami, Florida. However, new companies, such as the Norwegian-owned Royal Caribbean International Line, emerged, with huge vessels such as *Freedom of the Seas* (completed 2006) and her sister vessel *Liberty of the Seas* (completed 2007), two of the most recent cruise liners built and the largest pure cruise liners at the time of writing, each displacing some 158,000 grt. Each vessel can accommodate over 4300 passengers and has a complement of 1300 crew on fifteen passenger decks. Today, there are a large number of specialist cruise lines, each offering a wide variety of itineraries and prices designed for an equally-wide variety of clientele. The vessels vary in size from as small as 3000 grt up to the largest at 158,000 grt, and offer a wide variety of facilities on board. To this extent, such vessels have become floating hotels, shopping malls and entertainment centres rolled into one, a far cry from the days of the traditional North Atlantic passenger liners of the first part of the 20th century.

RO-RO VESSELS

The Ro-Ro vessel, namely the passenger and vehicle ferry, has become increasingly important to maritime traffic, capable of handling all kinds of road transport such as trailers, coaches and cars. Some Ro-Ro vessels are designed solely for the carriage of commercial traffic such as trailers or chassis-mounted containers (with or without the tractor) and the drivers of these vehicles, where the vehicle is accompanied. Such vessels operate on freight-only routes, chiefly across the North Sea and also in the Mediterranean Sea. They can accommodate several hundred trailers on any voyage, and operate on voyages classed as frequent regular sailings.

Other Ro-Ro vessels are designed for the carriage of not only road trailers but also cars and coaches. From small beginnings after the Second World War, when a car ferry displaced some 2000 tonnes, these huge ferries of the present day are also designed as semi-cruise vessels, with a displacement of up to 70,000 grt in some cases. There are two vessels of 59,000 tonnes each plying the route between Hull and Europoort/Rotterdam, owned by P&O North Sea Ferries, namely the *Pride of Hull* and the *Pride of Rotterdam*, but the biggest vessels of such a category are the two new vessels in the Norwegian-owned Color Line fleet, the *Color Fantasy* and the *Color Magic* are both 70,000 tonnes, and ply the route between Oslo (Norway) and Kiel (Germany).

The purpose of these vessels is to carry both passengers and vehicles on overnight or daytime sailings between the major ferry ports on a mixture of commercial and leisure activities, and their operation has given rise to a certain extent to the phrase "Booze Cruise", where passengers use these vessels to make day or weekend trips to Continental ports in order to take advantage of the duty-reduced or duty-free prices on such commodities as alcoholic or tobacco goods. This activity is particularly prevalent on the Cross-Channel services between Dover and Calais, where French prices of such items are vastly lower than their UK counterparts. The ferries operating these routes have also increased over the last several decades, from some 2000 tonnes to 35,000 tonnes at present. There are smaller ferries operating in other parts of the UK, especially between the Scottish mainland and the Scottish islands; these vessels range from approximately 2500 tonnes to the largest vessel at 6700 tonnes.

GENERAL CARGO VESSELS

Maritime cargo vessels vary in their nature according to the kind of cargoes they carry, as well as the volume of cargo transported. Before the era of containerisation, most cargo was carried by general cargo vessels, equipped with their own cranes ands derricks capable of loading and unloading cargoes at most docksides and wharves without the need for specialist cranes mounted on the quayside itself. This form of cargo carriage remained standard practice until the 1960s, when sea freight containers became a more efficient form of cargo transportation.

The function of the general cargo vessel was that it could transport, load and unload cargoes of a variety of shapes, sizes and volumes and sail to any part of the world, either on regular "liner" sailings, or as a "tramp" vessel, transporting cargoes when and where required. All cargoes were packed and stowed in the vessel's holds, and inevitably the process of loading and unloading was time-consuming and laborious once the vessel was berthed alongside the quay.

General cargo vessels still exist, and have an important part to play in the international maritime carriage of goods, but their role is somewhat more limited in the present day, partly because of their size and function, and partly because of the heavy demands placed on the carriage of goods because of the container system. However, their onboard cranes and derricks enable them to serve international seaports which other vessels, such as the huge container vessel cannot, and this enables them to serve more niche maritime markets. They are also capable of carrying more specialist maritime loads, especially cargoes which may be considered too voluminous for other carriers, and which require specific forms of transportation. A present example of such vessels is the MV *Apollogracht*, seen above, which is equipped with heavy-purpose cranes and capable of transporting heavy items such as oilfield equipment around the world.

CONTAINER VESSELS

Although the issue of containerisation is covered later in this text, it is worthwhile considering the container vessel as a means of maritime transport in its own right. The container vessel has evolved over the past fifty years, with the first commercial vessel to carry containers being a converted oil tanker, the *Ideal X*. She sailed in 1956 with her first cargo of some 30 containers mounted on her deck from Port Newark, New Jersey, around the US Coast to Port Houston, Texas. The container age was born, and soon other vessels were being equipped to carry this revolutionary form of cargo transport. The first dedicated container vessel were constructed in the early 1960s, primarily for the newly-formed US container line, Sea-Land, owned and founded by the person responsible for introducing the container, Malcom McLean.

As the concept of containers became more prevalent by the early 1970s, the second generation of container vessels were constructed in the 1970s, and were capable of carrying larger numbers of containers, up to 2500 TEUs (Twenty-Foot Equivalent Units), and could transport such loads round the world. By this time, several container shipping lines existed, including Sea-Land, ScanDutch (a consortium of several European Shipping Lines including Nedlloyd of the Netherlands and Wilhelm Wilhelmsen of Norway), OCL (Overseas Container Lines, a subsidiary of the P&O Group).

The third generation of container vessels, constructed in the 1980s, increased both the size of the vessel and the number of containers carried, up to 4000 TEUs, namely the Panamax vessels, so called because they belonged to the 1985 Panamax standard, being the largest vessels capable of negotiating the lock systems on the Panama Canal. The fourth generation of container vessels increased capacity yet further to 5000 TEUs, and were known as the Post-Panamax vessels given that they exceeded the size allowable to negotiate the Panama Canal. The Post-Panamax standard was introduced in 1988, and referred to container vessels of capacity up to 5000 TEUs. These vessels were constructed in the period between 1988 and 2000, and became the main vessels to sail the seas, weighing in at some 100,000 grt and carrying huge numbers of containers, largely across the Pacific Ocean and from the Far East to Europe.

The present range of vessels, the fifth generation, has taken the carrying capacity through 8000 TEUs to 12000+ TEUs, with a displacement of 150,000 gross tonnes. These vessels are somewhat limited in the number of container ports they can serve, and it is already established that they will only serve a limited number of European Ports because of their size and berthing requirements, as well as trans-shipment requirements for containers to be transferred to smaller feeder vessels for more regional voyages. The new Maersk Line vessels, introduced in 2006 and capable of handling up to 14,000 TEUs, are in this category, as are several new vessels belonging to the Chinese Shipping Lines. However, where the largest vessels are more limited in the number of ports which they can serve, the smaller container vessels are able to serve more ports and are thus more versatile in the markets which they can serve. This said, the larger vessels are more convenient for the specific high-density markets, where the requirement exists to serve a limited number of ports, thus reducing laytime (the length of time a vessel spends berthed at port) and maximising the time the vessel spends at sea between ports. All other traffic can be maintained on a hub-and-spoke basis, with smaller feeder vessels serving the larger deep-sea vessels at a system of limited trans-shipment ports.

A variation on the design of the container vessel is that of the Ro-Ro Container vessel. Several shipping lines have used these vessels over the past decades, with a notable present user being Atlantic Container Line (ACL), sailing out of Liverpool across the North Atlantic ocean. These vessels not only handle containers, but also can accommodate road trailers by way of an angled ramp located at the stern of the vessel.

BULK CARRIERS

The bulk carrier is of itself a vital form of maritime cargo transport. Whereas container vessels and general cargo vessels carry all kinds of general cargoes, the bulk carrier is specialist in the carriage of bulk cargoes, such as minerals, grain, liquefied gas or crude petroleum. Although owned by specific shipping companies, they are often chartered out to other companies for the purpose of the carriage of specific cargoes from one port to another, on either a voyage charter (single voyage) or time charter (multiple voyage) basis. In some cases, even the vessel may be transferred from one owner to another in the middle of the voyage, an activity particularly prevalent with petroleum-carrying VLCCs (Very large Crude Carriers). This practice is less common at present, but it still occurs from time to time depending upon the needs of the customer. In general, however, the petroleum carriers are owned by the large oil companies, and spend their time on the high seas carrying petroleum on behalf of those companies.

Some bulk carriers are equipped to carry different types of bulk cargo with little modification, whereas others are equipped solely for the carriage of a specific type of cargo. Those carriers which can be modified for the carriage of both mineral and petroleum loads are known as "OBO" (Ore/Bulk/Oil) carriers, whereas other carriers, such as the 364,768 tonne Norwegian-owned *Berge Stahl* are equipped solely for the carriage of iron ore. The MV Berge Stahl operates between just three ports in the world – Europoort/Rotterdam (Europe), Terminal Maritimo de Ponta da Madeira (Brazil) and Saldanha Bay (South Africa). This vessel makes some 10 journeys per year, mainly between the ports of Ponta da Madeira and Europoort, carrying huge quantities of iron ore from Brazil to Europe.

As with the large container vessels, the large bulk carriers are only able to service certain ports worldwide owing to their immense size; the draft of the *Berge Stahl* at 15m means that she can only just negotiate the mouth of the Maas/Rhine estuary at Europoort which is not much deeper. This means that she can only enter the port safely at high tide, and even then the clearance between her keel and the seabed is extremely limited.

Another distinction between the various types of bulk carrier is that some are "geared" and others are not. A geared carrier is one which has its own cargo lifting gear mounted on board vessel, enabling it to load and discharge at ports which may not have the correct lifting gear mounted on the quay. A non-geared vessel relies entirely on the lifting gear installed at the dedicated terminal at the port to load it and discharge its cargo. Vessels such as the *Berge Stahl* fall into this category, hence the limitations imposed upon her scope of activity.

The VLCC vessels require even more dedicated terminal facilities. Because they carry only petroleum commodities, which are classed as hazardous or dangerous hydrocarbons, they require a specific terminal for the purpose of loading and discharging their cargoes. There is a specific procedure for handling these vessels at each port, as well as a specific form of both documentation and controls. Every tanker is subject to a different set of rules and regulations from its more general commercial counterparts, and the carriage of such commodities is strictly controlled by the maritime authorities. This is not only because of the nature of the cargo itself, but also because of the inference of the impact of such commodities upon the environment, given the number of marine accidents and disasters involving tankers, especially where the tanker grounded on a coastline, or even where an oil spillage occurred at sea, thus damaging the marine environment to a significant degree.

Other examples of bulk carrier include the car carriers dedicated to the bulk carriage of cars on the high seas. These were particularly designed to serve the Far East markets, in order to transport cars from the Far East to Europe, but they are also used to transport cars from the European plants, especially those of Toyota and Nissan to overseas destinations. It is commonplace to witness such a vessel at the Port of Tyne loading with cars destined for overseas markets, and also at the Port of Liverpool, bringing in vehicles from the Far East for sale in the UK.

SHORT SEA VESSELS

The short sea business, although different from its deep sea counterpart in the sense that the voyages are generally much shorter than a long-distance deep sea voyage, is nevertheless as important to the commercial maritime sector as the deep sea business. The short sea sector involves maritime traffic within regions such as the North Sea, the Baltic Sea, the Mediterranean and the Far East, where distances between regional ports are limited and traffic is of lower quantities but made on a frequent basis. Short Sea vessels are divided into much the same categories as the deep sea business, namely general cargo vessels, container vessels, this time of the feeder variety in that they only accommodate in general up to 1000-1500 TEUs, and short sea bulk carriers such as petroleum or petrochemical carriers.

OILFIELD SUPPLY VESSELS

The other category of vessel now increasingly common as far as the nature of maritime cargo carriage is concerned is the Oilfield Supply Vessel. This type of vessel is designed for the supply of offshore oil and gas field equipment to the Offshore Oil and gas platforms, located in areas of the globe such as the North Sea, the South Atlantic Ocean off the coasts of Brazil and Angola, and the seas off the coast of Australia. These vessels can carry a variety of equipment, and are equipped with their own handling gear such as cranes and derricks for the loading and offloading of such equipment on to other vessels or on to the platforms themselves. Most of these vessels are also equipped with a helicopter landing pad, where personnel may also be offloaded and loaded for deployment in such operations and areas. They are designed for deep sea operations as well as Continental Shelf maritime operations close to the European coastline, and can withstand the severe forces of mid-ocean conditions without problem.

Examples of such a vessel are the *Toisa Perseus* and *Toisa Polaris*, operated by the company Subsea 7, which undertakes to supply oilfield equipment from Europe to several offshore oilfields worldwide. They are often seen in the ports of Aberdeen and Tyne loading equipment to such locations, and can be away from her home ports for as much as six months at a time. This time is spent calling at overseas ports to load and unload cargo as well as directly serving the overseas offshore oil and gas fields, transferring equipment to the offshore platforms as well as laying sub-sea flowlines for the purpose of facilitating the undersea flow of oil or gas from the wellhead to a shore-based installation. At tonnages of some 6000 grt, they are capable of operating in relatively-sheltered waters such as the North Sea, as well as in the deep sea conditions of the North Atlantic and South Atlantic Oceans.

HAZARDOUS OR DANGEROUS CARGOES AND THE IMDG CODE

Other than passenger ships such as cruise liners, every vessel which carries cargo, be it by container, trailer or bulk, has the capacity to carry hazardous or dangerous goods of some description. It is the express duty of the shipper to notify the carrier and their agent of the nature of such goods, as the need then arises to impose specific conditions upon the carriage of such goods, as covered by the Carriage of Goods by Sea Acts, Special provision must be mad eon board vessel for the carriage of such goods, and prior permission for the loading of such cargoes must be obtained from the master of the vessel, as well as specific documentation being raised for such carriage. Furthermore, the vessel carrying such cargoes must notify the port of arrival at least 24 hours in advance prior to arrival at the port for specific arrangements to be made for the handling and unloading of such consignments, especially where they are of a specific nature which could compromise the safety of the port and the vessel if they were not handled in a particular way.

The Safety of Lives at Sea (SOLAS) Regulations concern the requirements by Ship's Masters and Shipowners to ensure that all necessary Health and Safety Regulations pertaining to the Crews of Ships are maintained and obeyed. On ships carrying general commercial cargoes or passengers, these Regulations refer to general practice under normal commercial activities, but on ships whose cargoes are primarily of a hazardous or dangerous nature, then the regulations become more stringent. Furthermore, the Regulations pertaining to the reporting of such vessels to shore-based authorities are equally more stringent. Ships carrying such cargoes are not only obliged by Regulation to report to the British and French Authorities under the Channel Navigation Information System (CNIS), but they are also required by law to report to the Port Authority of their destination prior to arrival at the port, so that appropriate measure can be taken to ensure their safe berthing and unloading, as well as their safe passage into national waters.

Cargoes subject to such requirements are:

- Hydrocarbons (i.e. Petroleum);
- Liquefied Natural or Petroleum Gas;
- Other Liquefied Gas;
- Chemicals;
- Explosives.

In the case of bulk cargoes carried at sea, this requirement is clearly evident, since the quantities of such cargoes carried in any vessel could result in catastrophic disasters should an accident occur either at sea or in port. The disasters pertaining to the ships "Erika" and "Prestige" proved such a scenario – the oilspills resulting from the "Erika" disaster on the French Coast proved extremely damaging to the coastline, as did previous disasters resulting from the grounding of the tankers *"Torrey Canyon"*, *"Amoco Cadiz"* and *"Erika"*. Other international disasters include the grounding of the tanker *"Exxon Valdez"* off the Alaskan Coast some years ago, with the resulting destruction of the local marine environment.

In the case of hazardous or dangerous cargoes carried in containers alongside more general containerised cargoes on deep sea or feeder vessels, the same risks exist although in reduced form. However, given the documentary regimes requiring the issuing of Dangerous Goods Notes for the carriage of such cargoes coupled with the interests of the insured parties concerning such marine ventures under the insurance principle of *"Uberrimae Fidei"* (Utmost Good Faith), the Master of the Ship and the Shipowners should be well aware of the risks of carrying such cargoes on board vessel. Indeed, there are strict rules within the framework of the Law of Carriage of Goods at Sea (**Carriage of Goods by Sea Act (1971)**) and the Hague/Visby Rules (**Art IV, Rule 6**) concerning where and how on board ship such consignments must be stowed, and the liability of the carrier for such cargoes. For the purposes of Ro-Ro carriage of hazardous or dangerous consignments, there are equally strict rules set out in the CMR Convention of 1956 (**Articles 6(f) and 7**), concerning the exact details to be included in the CMR Consignment Note and the duties and responsibilities of the shipper when both notifying the carrier of the nature and description of the consignment, especially its classification under the IMDG Code, and the liabilities incurred should the cargo be damaged or cause damage to the vessel while in carriage. In this respect, it is the express duty of the shipper to inform the carrier of the nature of the consignment so that adequate provisions may be made for the safe stowage of the consignment in either a container or a trailer aboard vessel in a position which is likely to minimise the risk of damage to the container, trailer or the vessel itself, as well as minimising the risk of compromise or prejudice to the ultimate safety of the vessel and its crew.

Under the rules of Marine Reporting, all ships carrying any kind or quantity of Dangerous or Hazardous Goods must report to the Port of Destination prior to arrival at the Port, usually 24 hours in advance of the vessel's arrival at port, in order to allow for special provisions for the berthing and unloading of the vessel upon its arrival at port where hazardous or dangerous cargoes are concerned. However, certain cargoes are declared to Customs, the Carriers and the Insurers in such a fashion as to disguise their true nature, either because of the risk of the liability of higher Insurance Premiums or because of the desire of their owners to hide their true nature from national authorities. The Buyer or the Seller of such consignments has a Duty of Disclosure to inform the Carrier of the full and true nature of the cargo being carried, although there are occasions when this duty is not exercised. It is also stated in the Hague/Visby Rules, **Art IV Rule 6**, that if cargoes of a hazardous or dangerous nature are carried without the prior knowledge of the Carrier, if the Carrier discovers their true nature they may destroy or land the cargo at any place and hold the owner of the cargo liable for damages or expenses incurred in such action. However, if the Carrier is unaware of the nature of the nature of such cargoes and fails to report the vessel's movement to the Port of Destination in advance under the Hazardous Goods rules, then the Carrier may be held liable for not informing the Port Authority accordingly and running the risk of endangering the Port, its personnel and other vessels in the vicinity.

The transport of Dangerous and Hazardous Goods is covered by the IMDG (International Maritime Dangerous Goods) Code, which has been adopted by the IMO. The IMDG Code was developed as a uniform international code for the transport of dangerous or hazardous cargoes by sea, and was designed to cover such matters as packing, container traffic and stowage, with particular reference to the segregation and isolation of incompatible substances, where the potential contact of such substances could lead to severe accidents or could prejudice or compromise the safety and security of the vessel and her crew.

The development of the IMDG Code dates from the 1960 Conference of the Safety of Life at Sea, which recommended as its outcome that Governments should adopt a uniform international code for the transport of dangerous and hazardous cargoes by sea to supplement the regulations contained in the 1960 International Convention for the Safety of Life at Sea (SOLAS), which eventually became a full set of international regulations in 1974. A resolution adopted by the 1960 Conference stated that the proposed Code should cover such matters as packing, stowage aboard vessel and container traffic in general, although in 1960, container traffic was still in its infancy, the first containers having been carried by maritime means in 1956 along the East Coast of the USA. The full IMDG Code, resulting from a working group of the IMO Maritime Safety Committee which began to prepare the Code in 1961, was adopted by the fourth IMO Assembly in 1965, although since its adoption it has undergone many changes, both in appearance and content, to maintain pace with the ever-changing needs of industry as well as the overall maritime transport of goods, especially with the ever-increasing use of sea containers to transport cargoes worldwide.

Amendments to the Code originate from two sources. These are:

- Proposals submitted directly to the IMO by member states;
- Amendments which are required to take account of and provide for changes to the United Nations Recommendations on the Transport of Dangerous Goods, which set the basic requirements for all transport modes.

Amendments to the provisions of the UN Recommendations are made on a two-yearly cycle, and approximately two years after their adoption by the UN, they are adopted by the authorities responsible for regulating the various transport modes, which in the case of the UK is the Department for Transport (DfT). In this way, a basic set of requirements applicable to all modes of transport is established and implemented, thus ensuring that difficulties are not encountered at intermodal interfaces, such as the transport of containers by both sea and road, and equally the transport of cargoes by trailer using both road and sea means, especially where Ro-Ro maritime transport is involved.

For classification and definition purposes, the IMDG Code is divided into 7 Parts contained in Volume 1:

- General Provisions, Definitions and Training;
- Classification;
- Consignment Procedures;
- Construction and Testing of Packagings, International Bulk Containers, Large Packagings, Portable Tanks and Road Tank Vehicles;
- Transport Operations.

Volume 2 of the Code contains Sections on:

- Dangerous Goods List;
- Limited Quantities Exceptions;
- Proper Shipping Names;
- Glossary of Terms;
- Index.

The application of the IMDG Code (now Amended Version 2006), is mandatory, but it also contains provisions of a recommendatory nature which are stated in Chapter 1.1 of the Code. The classification of a cargo into its applicable category according to the provisions of the IMDG Code is the direct responsibility of the shipper or consignor, regardless of who is arranging the shipment according to the International Terms of Delivery (INCOTERMS), or by the appropriate designated competent authority where specified in the Code. This Code can include a Freight Agent, where that agent has been specifically empowered as the competent authority by the shipper or consignor/consignee.

Although the IMDG Code applies in general to ships carrying bulk cargoes of a hazardous or dangerous nature, it also applies to vessels carrying more general and varied containerised cargoes, amongst which may be cargoes of a dangerous or hazardous nature. The Code also refers to the responsibilities of agents and traders in ensuring that cargoes are correctly described and declared to the Shipping Line prior to loading aboard vessel. The need exists, therefore, for agents and traders trading in hazardous or dangerous goods to be equipped with an up-to-date copy of the IMDG Code at all times, to allow for changes in the Code as well as for the overall purpose of compliance with the regulations pertaining to the carriage of dangerous goods by sea.

The ship owner or operator will only accept and handle dangerous goods by prior written arrangement, and then only on the express condition that the shipper provides a full and adequate description of the cargo to be shipped. If this arrangement is accepted, a special stowage order, often referred to as a dangerous goods form, will be issued which indicates to the master of the vessel that the cargo conforms to the prescribed code of acceptance laid down by the ship owner or operator. The shipment will not take place until a special stowage order, which is the authority for shipment, has been issued by the ship owner or operator, given that the dangerous or hazardous cargo must be stowed in a specific location as far from the vessel's accommodation quarters as possible. Furthermore, the shipper must fully describe and classify the cargo, and ensure that it is correctly packed, marked and labelled. This can be achieved through the services of a freight forwarder.

Before dangerous goods can be authorised for shipment, the following information is required:

- Name of sender/consignor;

- Correct technical name of the dangerous/hazardous goods to be carried;

- Class of dangerous/hazardous goods, as given in the IMDG Code;

- Flashpoint (if applicable);

- UN Number to identify the substance;

- Details of outer packing;

- Details of inner packing;

- Quantity to be shipped in individual packages and in total;

- Additional information for radioactive materials, explosives and consignments in bulk (e.g. tank containers, road tankers etc.).

The Dangerous Goods authority form will have a reference number and will also show the sailing details, including the ports of departure and destination for which the consignment is authorised, plus the following details:

- The hazard class;
- UN Number;
- Labels;
- Key number (in case of emergency);
- Any special instructions.

On the arrival of the goods at the port of loading, the consignment and the authority to ship are submitted to the master of the vessel for ultimate approval prior to customs clearance and loading, although in reality, the customs export declaration will have been submitted in advance of the consignment being despatched to the port of loading. The Dangerous Goods Note (DG Note) issued for the consignment must also be completed, along with a Container Vehicle Packing Certificate, and these documents must accompany the goods.

THE MARINE ENVIRONMENT – POLLUTION OF THE SEAS

The UN Convention of the Law of the Seas (UNCLOS) covers Marine Pollution and the Marine Environment as much as it covers the High Seas themselves, and such controls are contained in Section XII of the UNCLOS. The issue of pollution covers a wide variety of activities, from the deliberate spillage or dumping of pollutants and debris to tank cleaning as part of a ship's operational activities. Either form of activity renders significant harm to the Marine environment, and can lead to a variety of forms of short-term or long-term contamination of the sea, the seabed and the shoreline.

There are four main sources of marine pollution, namely shipping, dumping, sea-bed activities and land activities. For the purposes of this text, only shipping and dumping are addressed, as these pertain to vessel activities and require a monitoring regime on the part of the national authorities to ensure that the Law of the Sea is obeyed at all times.

As far as shipping is concerned, some pollution results from the operation of ships, given that most vessels are powered by marine diesel engines which consume large quantities of fuel oil. Some oil is discharged with the bilge (waste) water, and the fumes discharged as exhaust through the vessel's funnel into the atmosphere will eventually return to the surface of the sea. Some vessels use their fuel tanks (bunkers) for ballast water, and subsequently may discharge this oily ballast water into the sea. All vessels will pollute the sea if they discharge rubbish overboard or discharge their sewage directly into the sea. By far, however, the greatest amount of pollution from ships comes from their cargoes, especially hydrocarbons and petroleum. The tanks of crude tankers are cleaned at sea, and the seawater which is pumped into the tanks for such purposes is pumped out again into the sea once the tanks have been cleaned out. This residue caused by the cleaning process appears as an oil slick on the surface of the water, and often drifts to shore causing adverse effects on the marine environment in the process. Accidents, such as collisions or leaking, can also cause marine pollution, and the risks caused by such incidents increases with the growing number of vessels on the high seas.

In the case of dumping, especially the dumping of waste from ships, international conventions, including the UNCLOS, treat dumping as a source of pollution separate from shipping. This is usually because dumping, unlike other pollution from ships, is always seen as being deliberate, and partly because dumping is an extension of pollution from land, although it is still considered to be separate from land-based sources because the areas where marine dumping takes place are legally different from land territory.

There is also a growing risk of collisions of vessels with submerged containers, caused by such containers breaking loose from their securing fasteners on board vessel and falling overboard, especially in heavy seas and inclement weather. Such containers do not always sink to the sea bed, but often remain close to the surface of the water, and thus pose a significant risk to other vessels in the vicinity. There have been occasions when submerged containers have caused significant damage to vessels, such as the reefer vessel *Horncliff*, which encountered such a problem when it was holed by one of its own containers which had fallen off its deck in heavy seas west of the UK in early 2008. The UK and French authorities prevented the container vessel *NYK Antares* from proceeding through the Channel in late 2007 when it was discovered that she had already lost several stacks of empty containers off her deck, and that several more were in danger of being lost overboard. The risk of such large numbers of containers falling into Channel waters in some of the world's busiest shipping lanes was too great for the authorities to allow the vessel to proceed any further under such circumstances.

The problem with such hazards is that they cannot be defined clearly under the Law of the Sea, as they are not considered to be deliberate dumping, as well as the fact that they often occur outside territorial maritime limits. The main issue is that any incidents, where containers fall off the deck of a vessel, must be reported immediately to the nearest national authority by the master of the vessel, and their location defined, so as to avoid the risk of damage to other vessels as much as possible. Where such incidents occur within contiguous zones, territorial waters or internal waters, it is the responsibility of the coastguard to ensure that all action is taken to retrieve such obstacles as quickly as possible, and to bring them ashore. Within territorial waters, the contents of containers which have fallen off a ship are considered as wrecks, and thus come under the scope of the Receiver of Wrecks. The contents must be immediately reported to the authorities, including coastguards and Customs. Such was the scenario when the container vessel *MSC Napoli* foundered in the Channel in early 2007, and many of her containers were washed up on the beach of South Devon, much to the delight of local residents. Similarly, the cargo vessel *Ice Prince* foundered in the Channel in early 2008, and her entire cargo of timber was subsequently washed up on the beaches of the South Coast of England. Outside territorial limits, the situation is less clear, as the nature of the high seas implies that no one single State can be made responsible for the retrieval and removal of floating obstructions such as containers, and that there is no clear means for the reduction of such risks, unless they occur within defined shipping lanes and could be seen as being a significant risk to the safety of vessels in the area. In this case, all the coastal States involved may seek to employ suitable measures, such as coastguard vessels or specialist removal vessels, to remove the obstacles before they cause major problems to shipping.

The control of pollution from ships is the responsibility of the Department for Transport and its Maritime and Coastguard Agency (MCA), based in Southampton. The statutory basis of their functions was clarified by the 1995 Merchant Shipping Act, Section 293. Under Sections 137–141 of the Act, the Secretary of State for Transport is empowered to intervene where a shipping accident, such as a collision, is likely to cause significant pollution in the United Kingdom or its waters, and this jurisdiction has been enlarged to include the Continental Shelf by the 1997 Merchant Shipping and Maritime Security Act, Section 2. It should be noted, however, that although this provision exists in law and that other provisions exists for the prevention of Marine Pollution under the Collision Regulations (COLREGS), Oil & Gas Offshore Installations on the UK and Norwegian areas of the Continental Shelf are also protected under the UNCLOS by the provision of a 500-Metre Exclusion Zone around each installation, thus theoretically preventing any vessel from entering into such a zone unless specifically authorised, such as Supply Vessels used to convey equipment to the various installations for use in the sector.

Section 1 of the 1997 Merchant Shipping and Maritime Security Act of the UK allows the Secretary of State for Transport to designate temporary exclusion zones around ships or structures to prevent interference with counter-pollution or safety measures. It also enables the Secretary of State to order the removal of ships in UK waters (s.10) and to impose charges on vessels to recover the costs of exercising his maritime functions (Schedule 2). In addition, it gives him new powers to regulate the provision and use of waste reception facilities in Ports (s.5). In addition, the 2003 Marine Safety Act gives the Secretary of State the powers to issue safety directions to personnel in charge of coastal land, requiring them to allow their facilities to be used after a marine accident in order to safeguard a ship or to prevent pollution.

Powers to control pollution, particularly that as a result of oil spills, from ships on the seaward side of the baseline of territorial waters are provided by the Merchant Shipping (Prevention of Oil Pollution) Order 1983, SI 1983/1106 (amended by SI 1985/2002, SI 1991/2885 and SI 1993/1580), and the Merchant Shipping (Prevention of Pollution) (Law of the Sea Convention) Order 1996, SI 1996/282. The geographical scope of these powers was extended from 12 Miles (The Limit of the Territorial Sea) out to the Continental Shelf in accordance with the Law of the Sea Convention on 5 September 1996 by the Merchant Shipping (Prevention of Pollution) (Limits) Regulations 1996.

Any ship in UK-controlled waters, or any UK ship anywhere in the world, must not discharge oil or oily substances or mixtures into the sea, *unless* they are on a voyage, are outside "special areas" (Baltic, Mediterranean, Black Sea, North-West European waters and Antarctic), the oil content is less than 15 parts per million, and the ship has oil filtering and oil discharge monitoring and control systems in operation. No discharge may contain chemicals or other substances in concentrations likely to harm the marine environment. The same rules apply to tankers and other commercial ships alike.

This stated, the ability by shore-based agencies such as the MCA to identify and monitor such discharges is limited. The MCA states that its primary role is that of Search and Rescue (SAR) with relation to marine accidents, and in any case, the number of MCA Centres located around the UK is at very least sparse. The ability by the MCA to police the UK coastlines in the event of an oil or chemical spill, or even to prevent a catastrophe from occurring as a result of such a spill is at best limited, if not impossible. Assuming that a ship involved in such activities is beyond the horizon, even the horizon of a clear day, then it would be impossible for any MCA station to identify the ship involved and to monitor or control the situation. Only in limited areas such as the Strait of Dover are such policing activities possible, although the physical ability on the part of the MCA to prevent such spillage activities from occurring, even within UK maritime territorial controls, is somewhat limited.

However, the Department for Transport (DfT) has established a series of Marine Environmental High Risk Areas (MEHRAs) around the UK coast, adjacent to internal UK waters, i.e. they are within the UNCLOS baseline defining the inner limit of the UK's territorial sea, within the 12-mile limit. There is no domestic UK legislation allowing permanent restrictions to apply to shipping movements in the internal waters within the UK baseline. The other locations of the MEHRAs face onto the UK's territorial sea, and lie outside the 12-mile limit.

Other measures include a number of recommendations by the IMO concerning navigation around the UK coastline, including the use of Admiralty Chart 5500 Mariner's Routeing Guide, for ships navigating in the English Channel and the Dover Strait. In accordance with the provisions of the International Law of the Sea (UNCLOS), the right of innocent passage is recognised throughout UK territorial seas together with the right of transit passage through straits used for international navigation, notably the Fair Isle Channel and the North Channel, both of which fall within UK territorial limits. Any navigational controls applying to vessels exercising such rights must be submitted to, and be agreed by, the International Maritime Organisation (IMO) as part of their routeing measures under the SOLAS Convention. They must be able to meet criteria laid down by the IMO. IMO routeing measures can be based on safety considerations and on the protection of the marine environment. These controls can apply within, and beyond, the territorial sea where appropriate.

THE DUTY OF DISCLOSURE

The issue of Disclosure revolves around the following considerations:

- How much information is conveyed by the Shipper to the Carrier, the Ship's Master, and hence the Authorities at the Port of destination;

- The accuracy of the information conveyed to the above.

Disclosure affects information pertaining to several elements of the maritime framework. These are:

- The Vessel;
- The Crew;
- The Cargo;
- Cargo Insurance;
- Passengers;
- The Marine Environment.

Certain legal areas are also covered by the element of disclosure. These include:

- SOLAS;
- Carriage of Goods at Sea.

The Hague Rules, modified by the Hague-Visby Rules, confirmed the need for a shipper of goods to provide accurate information to a carrier concerning two main issues, these being the description of cargoes, as well as their nature (i.e. hazardous or dangerous), which could affect the safety of the vessel and its crew, and would thus affect the issue of damages resulting from accidents pertaining to the latter. The Hague-Visby Rules consolidated such information in the issuing of Ocean Bills of Lading and Sea Waybills, and the consequent responsibilities upon each party involved in the raising of such documentation. The new UNCITRAL Convention (**A/CN.9/WG.III/WP.39**) adds a specific duty and obligation upon shippers to provide the information that carriers need to comply with state regulations. Article 27 of the Convention Document states the Shipper's obligation to provide information, instructions and documents to the Carrier in advance of the loading of the cargo aboard ship. The draft Convention continues by dealing with the Shipper's liability for breach of the duty to supply information required by the Carrier to satisfy government requirements. The view, recorded in UNCITRAL Report **A/CN.9/552**, is that the Shipper's liability should be based upon fault, except for situations covered by Subsection (b) of draft Article 27 of the UNCITRAL Convention. In the same way that Carriers are subject to absolute duties of compliance, demanding more than simply the exercise of reasonable care in providing information to the relevant authorities, so Shippers (and their Agents) must accurately and completely provide Carriers with the relevant information concerning their cargoes.

If the information provided by the Shipper to the Carrier is incorrect or inadequate, then in consequence, the information provided by the Carrier to the Authorities at the Port of Destination must equally be incorrect or inadequate. A practical example of this is the description in Cargo Manifests of Consolidated or Grouped Cargoes in Less-than-Full Containerloads (LCLs) as "Said to Contain…" or "FAK – Freight of all Kinds". In this way, the whole issue of Marine Reporting and Controls may itself be severely compromised. The US CT-PAT (Customs-Trade Partnership Against Terrorism) scheme has forbidden the use of such terms, and requires the Shipper to accurately describe and account for the cargoes loaded aboard all ships destined for any US Seaport. Such erroneous or vague information such as FAK or other generic information used to describe LCL shipments can, at very least, result in the submission of false Declarations to the Customs Authority of Destination. To a greater degree, it could also compromise the validity of the Cargo Insurance Policy or even the Marine Insurance Policy covering the vessel itself under the principles of *Uberrimae Fidei* (in Utmost Good Faith). At worst, it could lead to a severe compromise of most national security or even some form of catastrophe befalling the vessel and even the Port of Arrival, or perhaps the marine environment adjoining the Port. This issue is covered in greater detail later in the study.

CHAPTER FOUR

REPORTING REGIMES

The principle of and requirement for marine reporting is embodied in both the 1958 territorial sea convention and the 1982 UN Convention of the Law of the Sea. It is equally embodied in the legal right of any coastal State to exercise control over its territorial sea, and requires any vessel entering that part of the sea, with an intention of passing through a limited stretch of waterway such as a strait, or entering a port, to declare its intentions of passage and to declare its identity. Failure to do so could result in the vessel concerned being intercepted by vessels belonging to the national authorities of the coastal State into whose waters the vessel has entered. Therefore, adequate advance notice of arrival is required from the vessel in the case of entry into port. In the case of passage through a strait, the vessel must notify the national authorities concerned of its intention to pass through the strait, and its intention to adhere to a specific designated shipping lane where deemed appropriate.

PORT INFORMATION

Every seaport needs to know about the vessels entering and leaving the port at any time. The main reasons concern requirements for the following activities:

- Vessel Berthing;
- Cargo Handling;
- Vessel and Cargo Clearance;
- Specific requirements for dangerous or Hazardous Goods;
- Vessel and Cargo Security;
- Port State Controls.

Information is generally conveyed to the Port Authority, in particular the Harbourmaster and the Port Administration, by the Shipping Agents who receive prior information concerning the vessel and its cargo well in advance of the vessel's arrival. Unless the vessel is carrying dangerous or hazardous goods, the agent is only required to report the vessel's arrival to the port a few days before the vessel actually arrives, although in many cases a schedule of vessel arrivals is created some time in advance of the vessel's actual arrival. Where hazardous or dangerous cargoes are concerned, the vessel is required by regulation to report in to the port at least 24 hours in advance of arrival so that adequate provisions may be made for the unloading of such cargoes from the vessel at a suitable location. In cases where there are many vessel movements into and out of port each day, then a detailed schedule of all vessel movements for a specific week will be required in order to facilitate an organised control schedule well in advance of the arrival of specific vessels, so that suitable berthing and unloading space may be arranged.

The first authority to be notified of a vessel's arrival is the port authority. The Harbour Master is responsible for all inward and outward vessel movements as far as the port is concerned, and must know in advance which vessels are likely to arrive within a specified period, usually the space of seven days or more. In many cases, schedules of vessel arrivals and departures are known by the port authority a month in advance of their actual arrival, but there are also many occasions when the Harbourmaster only ascertains the arrival of a vessel some hours before its actual arrival, and requests further information about the vessel from its agents at the port. This anomaly occurs quite frequently despite the various safety codes issued by both the International Maritime Organisation (IMO), the national maritime administration (The MCA in the case of the UK) and the port authorities themselves. However, in most cases, the port agents submit information to the harbourmaster well in advance of the arrival of a vessel, in order to ensure that all necessary procedures are taken to ensure the vessel's safe arrival and berthing, especially where the carriage of bulk, dangerous or hazardous cargoes is involved.

The information received by any port from any vessel is complex, although it may be used by different parties. In general, such information includes:

- The vessel's intended destination;
- The port of departure;
- The nature of the vessel (Passenger/Cargo);
- The size of the vessel;
- The flag of the vessel;
- The ownership of the vessel;
- The Nature and Identities of the crew;
- The Nature of the cargo (Cargo Manifest);
- Passengers (Passenger Manifest);
- Estimated Time of Arrival.

All this information builds up a picture of any vessel sailing within or into UK territorial waters, but it will only be privy to a specific port, i.e. the port of arrival. Once that information has been received, it will be used by a variety of authorities and organisations. These may include:

- The Port Authority;

- Health & Safety Authorities;
- HM Customs & Excise;
- Ships' Agents and Brokers;
- Freight Forwarders.

As the information is somewhat specific in its nature and subject to the Data Protection Act, it will not and cannot be disseminated to other parties not included in such activities unless absolutely required, e.g. in the case of dangerous or hazardous goods, where Coastguards or Port Health Authorities may require such information in the interests of the safety of the public. Indeed, certain information pertaining to the reporting of cargo may not directly reach the Port Authority unless the cargo is hazardous or dangerous, in which the Port Authority needs to know specific details about the cargo and the ship as laid down in the various pieces of maritime legislation and regulations.

THE MARITIME & COASTGUARD AGENCY (MCA)

The UK Maritime and Coastguard Agency has a long history, its Coastguard arm having originally been associated with the Royal Navy, as was HM Customs & Excise. At one time, the Coastguard function was part of the overall function of HM Customs & Excise, but the 1856 Coast Guard Act transferred responsibility for Coastguard operations from HM Customs & Excise to the Admiralty. The Coastguard organisation remained a separate function until the 1990s, when efficiency drives firstly made HM Coastguard a government executive agency, and eventually merged the organisation with the Marine Safety Agency in 1998 to form the Maritime and Coastguard Agency (MCA), with its headquarters located in Southampton. As well as the Southampton HQ, other Coastguard Centres are located around the UK on a regional basis, with the addition of mobile teams able to answer distress calls in specific areas as and when required.

The function of HM Coastguard has always been to monitor the UK Coastline for accidents or other problems pertaining to vessels and mariners, but this has now been integrated within the larger overall remit of the MCA in the controlling of UK Shipping. Unlike its North American counterparts, however, it has a more limited role in the regulation and monitoring of the UK Coastline. It has no powers to control international vessel movements, other than through the enforcement of the Traffic Separation Scheme (TSS) in the Strait of Dover, monitored and enforced by the CNIS located at Dover. However, it does have the powers to board, search and arrest vessels of UK nationality on suspicion of illegal maritime activities as long as it has enough evidence of such activities.

However, under the review by the IMO of Large Passenger Ship safety, a recent report conducted by the MCA has defined a GIS (Geographic Information System)-based Decision Support System for Maritime Search and Rescue (SAR), along with the Search and Rescue (Helicopter) Project. The GIS-based Decision Support System assessed the capacity of the Coastguard

Authority to deal with a mass evacuation of Large Passenger Ships, such as Cruise Liners, in the event of a fire or accident involving the vessel, involving the SAR capabilities of the MCGA as well as the ability and capacity of MCA personnel to respond to and deal with the incident concerned.

The primary functions of the MCA are concerned with the following areas:

- Inspection of vessels through its Marine Surveyors;

- Investigation of potential breaches of Merchant Shipping Legislation, especially the COLREGS, through the Enforcement Unit at Southampton;

- The CNIS Marine Reporting facility at Dover;

- Search and Rescue (SAR) activities involving the use of helicopters and lifeboats to answer emergency calls;

- Maritime Safety and Pollution Prevention, with controls maintained over the pollution of inshore waters as a result of chemical or hydrocarbon spillage from marine vessels;

- The Publication of Shipping Legislation Directives and other Bulletins concerning the safety and management of vessels, cargoes and crews;

- The monitoring of coastlines from the Regional Centres for the purposes of the protection of surfers, swimmers and the users of small marine craft;

- Accident prevention and monitoring, undertaken by means of regional Centres;

- Investigation of Accidents and Wrecks, undertaken by the Marine Accident Investigation Branch (MAIB).

Although the Coastguard Service uses helicopters as part of the Search-and-Rescue role, the fleet of Sea King helicopters used for Search and Rescue purposes is owned by a private commercial company – Bristows – and is contracted by HM Coastguard for its own use in the SAR role. The Coastguard helicopters are based on the South Coast of England and in the Hebridean Islands off the North-West Coast of Scotland. Alongside the HMCG operational activities, the Royal Air Force and Royal Navy have their own Search and Rescue (SAR) Helicopters based in various parts of the UK, the Royal Navy's SAR bases being located at RNAS Culdrose, Cornwall, and HMS Gannet at Prestwick Airport on the Clyde Coast in Scotland. Although the primary function of the RAF and Royal Navy SAR services is to deal with military emergency operational activities, their roles are also designed to dovetail with those of the Coastguard Service given the collaborative and common nature of all Search-and-Rescue activities. Indeed, the MCA is now leading initiatives in the creation of a national Search and Rescue framework, combining the roles of all emergency services involved in such activities in an overall partnership, and dealing with all incidents arising on land, sea, or in the air.

Where the US and Canadian Coastguards have the power – and actively exercise it – to intercept, board, search and arrest vessels deemed to be or suspected to be violating maritime territorial controls, the UK Coastguard Authority has similar powers, but does not use them to the same degree as their North American counterparts – powers of search and arrest are equally maintained by the Admiralty under the scope of the Royal Navy, and to a certain extent, HM Customs & Excise. To a lesser degree, so too do regional Police Constabularies, especially those in Scotland as defined under the scope of Scots Law. Even the Royal Navy to a large extent tends to distance itself from the tasks of the defence of national territorial waters in favour of a more global maritime presence, other than its role in protecting the Economic Exclusion Zone defined by the 200-mile limit with regard to fishing grounds. It should be pointed out that Canadian Coastguards are somewhat more reluctant to adopt the same active preventive measures as their southern neighbours, preferring to take on a role more akin to their UK counterparts wherever possible.

However, the Channel TSS regime provides a more enforceable role by the CNIS part of the MCA to the extent that a rogue vessel operating within the confines of the Channel may be monitored by the CNIS Coastguards and reported to the national authority of its flag. Even to this extent, the MCA cannot simply board a vessel within the TSS regime purely because it is violating the COLREGS Rules pertaining to the TSS regime. In reality, the role of HM Coastguard is limited to monitoring the UK's Coastline and co-ordinating activities pertaining to marine incidents, accidents and the rescue of mariners, along with the Royal Navy and RAF Search and Rescue (SAR) Helicopters and the lifeboats of the RNLI. Further policing is carried out form the air by the RAF's Coastal Command aircraft, as well as the RAF Fighter Squadrons based in the Northern part of the UK. HM Coastguard has a regionalised operational structure, with Marine Inspectors based in most major seaports for the purpose of examination of vessels whilst in port, and HMCG Offices situated in regional locations along the UK Coast. From these offices, teams of personnel can be deployed to patrol coastlines where required, and to co-ordinate emergencies as they arise.

The only part of HM Coastguard involved in the physical aspect of Marine Reporting and monitoring is that of the Channel Navigation Information Service (CNIS), based at the Channel Coast just outside Dover, ensuring that the mandatory reporting requirements for vessels passing through the Strait of Dover are upheld and maintained. This is also the only part of the Coastguard which can physically enforce the discipline of shipping movements, given the fact that it has the power to report and refer for prosecution vessels not obeying the Traffic Separation Scheme Regulations. However, the MCA, along with its European counterparts, is becoming involved in the Consolidated European Reporting System (CERS) initiative, which is designed to consider and implement a more integrated Reporting System with particular regard to the reporting of hazardous and dangerous cargoes aboard vessel. The initiative is still in its early stages of negotiation at the time of writing, but collaborative work between the Maritime Authorities of all the EU Member States is being undertaken across the EU to pave the way for the implementation of the system over the next few years.

Further down the Channel, the MCA deals with all its operations from its headquarters base in Southampton, including investigations and accident reporting. In the event of an accident or catastrophe in the Channel, a report is immediately sent to SOSREP, the Secretary of State's Representative in the MCA for Maritime Salvage and Intervention, and a contingency plan to prevent or act against environmental pollution, such as oil spills, or major destruction is implemented. There is a national contingency plan available for maritime disasters in the Channel, and this is co-ordinated alongside the French national maritime authorities in the form of the "Mancheplan", designed to alert and activate either British or French authorities, or both, in the event of a major maritime catastrophe in the Channel, and which allows for both Search-and-Rescue (SAR) and Counter-Pollution activities. The actual gravity of the situation is assessed by the MCA's CPSOs (Counter Pollution and Salvage Officers), who decide upon how best to deal with the situation. In the event of vessels breaking down or in danger of foundering within the Channel region, there is the facility of ETVs (Emergency Towing Vessels), four of which are stationed at strategic points around the UK, and one of which is stationed at Dover, and is jointly funded by the UK and French maritime authorities. The Mancheplan was successful implemented for two separate disasters involving the vessels *Erika*, a petroleum tanker, and the *Ievoli Sun*, a chemical tanker which sank in the Cherbourg Traffic Separation Scheme some 10 miles off the Channel Islands. More recent involvement by the MCA concerned the foundering of the container vessel *MSC Napoli* in the Channel in 2007 and the freighter *Ice Prince* in the Channel in early 2008.

The National Contingency Plan (NCP), which is designed to act against major marine pollution from marine and offshore installations, comprises the following operational activities:

- Search and Rescue (SAR);
- Salvage;
- Clean-up at Sea;
- Clean-up of the Shoreline.

This plan should be activated once a marine accident has been reported to the MCA, especially where there is any risk of pollution from oil from within the stricken vessel. It allows for the co-ordination of all activities associated with SAR, Salvage and any ensuing clean-up activities, although the extent of the disaster may not necessarily be fully assessed at the time of the accident. In many cases, the true extent of the damage to the environment may only emerge some significant time following the disaster, in which time valuable resources have been identified and collected to deal with such an emergency.

EC DIRECTIVE 2002/59/EC

The first area of the maritime reporting regime to be addressed, and one which defines the need for maritime reporting, is the EC Directive **2002/59/EC** of the European Parliament and the Council of 27 June 2002, establishing a Community Vessel Traffic Monitoring and Information

System. This Directive replaced Council Directive 93/75/EC [Official Journal of the EC L208 of 05/08/2002], and was enacted in 2002. It was to pave the way for other maritime monitoring and control measures, although it is still somewhat limited in its overall scope.

The Directive 2002/59/EC was the result of part of the action taken in line with the EC Commission's second communication on maritime safety following the disaster involving the tanker *Erika*, and was known as the Erika II package. The main purpose of the Directive was to establish a Community Vessel Traffic Monitoring and Information system (VTMS), which was designed to help to prevent accidents and pollution at sea and to minimise the impacts of such accidents on the marine and coastal environment, and consequently on the economy, health and well-being of local communities. Its primary concern, as with other safety measures, has been the control over the carriage of dangerous and hazardous goods by sea, especially the bulk carriage of such commodities.

The VTMS Directive covers all vessels of 300grt and upwards, whether or not such vessels carry dangerous or hazardous cargoes as defined by the IMO IMDG (International Movement of Dangerous Goods) Code, except for:

- Warships;
- Fishing vessels, traditional ships and recreational craft less than 45 metres in length;
- Bunkers below 5000 tonnes.

However, no provision was made in the Directive to identify the cargoes of such commercial vessels, especially where bulk carriage is not concerned. This is still a major issue, and remains to be resolved, other than the reporting of cargo on board vessels at the time a vessel enters port. It should also be noted that the provisions of the VTMS Directive are the same as those referring to the use of AIS (Automatic Identification System) in all commercial vessels.

VESSEL REPORTING AND MONITORING REQUIREMENTS

The operator of a ship bound for a port of a Member State must notify the Port Authority of that port certain information at least 24 hours in advance, where this is feasible. The information concerned must include:

- Name of the vessel;
- IMO Identification Number;
- Type of Vessel;
- Total Number of persons on board;
- Port of Destination;
- Estimated Time of Arrival.

The Directive also stipulates that ships built on or after 1 July 2002 and calling at a port of a Member State must also be fitted with:

- An Automatic Identification System (AIS), plus
- A Voyage Data Recorder (VDR) system ("black box") to facilitate investigations following accidents.

Member States have until the end of June 2007 to provide themselves with appropriate equipment and staff to utilise the AIS and VDR information and until the end of June 2008 to co-ordinate their national systems with those of other Member States. The process of building up all necessary equipment and shore-based installations for implementing this Directive must be completed by the end of 2007.

NOTIFICATION OF DANGEROUS OR POLLUTING GOODS ON BOARD SHIPS

In respect of the carriage of dangerous, hazardous or polluting goods on board ships:

- The shipper is required to deliver a declaration containing certain information (correct technical names of the dangerous or polluting goods and the address from which detailed information on the cargo may be obtained) to the master or operator prior to taking the goods on board vessel;
- The operator, agent or master of a ship must also notify the general information, such as the identification of the ship and the information provided by the shipper, to the competent authority.

In many ways, the above measures have been incorporated in the new Consolidated European Reporting System (CERS), which was implemented by all EU Member States at the end of 2007, and which is described later in this text.

Monitoring of hazardous ships and intervention in the event of incidents and accidents at Sea

Member States which have been notified of the presence of hazardous ships (ships which have been involved in incidents or accidents at sea, have failed to comply with notification and reporting requirements, have deliberately discharged pollutants or have been refused access to ports) must transmit the information they have to the Member States concerned.

Member States must take all appropriate measures consistent with international law to deal with incidents or accidents at sea and to require the parties concerned (the operator, the master of the ship and the owner of the dangerous or polluting goods carried on board) to co-operate fully with them with a view to minimising the consequences of the incident.

In addition, the master of the ship must immediately report:

- Any incident or accident affecting the safety of the ship;
- Any incident or accident which compromises shipping safety;
- Any situation liable to lead to pollution of the waters or shore of a Member State;
- Any slick of polluting materials and containers or packages seen drifting at sea.

The Directive provides for the possibility of ships being prevented from leaving or entering port in the event of poor weather conditions and obliges Member States to set up places of refuge to accommodate ships in distress.

ACCOMPANYING MEASURES

Ships entering the area of competence of a vessel traffic service must comply with any IMO (International Maritime Organisation)-approved ships' routing systems, which cover sensitive areas, areas with a high maritime traffic density and areas dangerous for shipping, and must use the vessel traffic services provided. Member States must ensure that these facilities have the requisite human and technical resources to accomplish their tasks.

Member States will have to co-operate to ensure the interconnection and interoperability of their national information systems, in order to ensure that the requisite information on the ship or its cargo can be exchanged electronically at any time.

Each Member State must designate the competent national authorities, port authorities and coastal stations to which the notifications required by the Directive are to be made.

Full co-operation must be arranged between the Commission and the Member States with a view to the future development of the European monitoring, control and information systems for maritime traffic. It will cover the development of automatic communication links between coastal stations and port authorities, and extension of the coverage of the European monitoring system. Efforts must also be made to improve the management of shipping information, which is one of the tasks of the European Maritime Safety Agency (EMSA).

In order to ensure that the Directive is being implemented successfully, Member States must make regular checks on the operation of their information systems and must introduce a system of financial penalties to act as a deterrent against failure to comply with the Directive's requirements regarding notification and the installation and carriage of the necessary equipment.

The Directive, although far-reaching, has met with differing levels of compliance throughout the European Community to date, with only some of the maritime nations involved able to show full implementation. Other states are still in the process of implementing VTS systems in their ports and waterways, as highlighted later in this text, and in general there are areas concerning compliance, especially in terms of maritime reporting requirements, which at present fall significantly short of the requirements set out by the Directive.

The overall purpose of the text is to identify all the major issues surrounding the basis of marine reporting, and also to identify and propose possible solutions to these issues. It is appreciated that the whole subject area is extremely complex, and that there is no simple answer to all the problems posed. Equally, there is no set or pre-determined panacea for the purposes of resolution to these issues. The proposed solutions are variable, and refer to a set of different scenarios, each depending upon different geographical and political considerations. However, given a world of political uncertainty and an atmosphere of continued threats of terrorism and insecurity, the whole issue of maritime security and vessel reporting is paramount in the maritime sector as a whole.

POLICING THE TERRITORIAL WATERS

Access to websites concerning the UK territorial waters yields little more than subjects such as environmental issues. The question was asked of a variety of organisations concerning the responsibility for policing UK territorial waters, and it soon became apparent that there is no defined and predetermined cohesive policy for such activity. It is a strange fact that although UK national territory in terms of *terra firma* has a police force responsible for maintaining the rule of law and the whole process of law and order, this same policy does not exist with relation to offshore activities. The Royal Navy, when approached, stated that its defence policy does not as such include the control of territorial waters, although it does have vessels capable of carrying out such a role. The police forces admit that areas of the 3-mile limit falling within their jurisdiction are to an extent subject to their control, but they have no real resources capable of dealing with such matters, such as patrol boats. The Fishery Protection vessels are capable of patrolling the 200-mile limit Exclusion Zone, but their limited numbers mean that they can only observe specific areas of water at any time. There are still Customs patrol vessels which operate around national waters, but given their limited numbers, they rely more on intelligence to establish illicit activities, and are therefore limited in their geographic capabilities.

As such, there is therefore no cohesive policy relating to the policing of UK national territorial waters, although much of this responsibility is shared between the Royal Navy, HM Revenue & Customs, and the Fishery Protection Vessels. Equally, there appears to be no physical means of controlling shipping entering UK national waters from the point of view of maritime patrols, unlike the policy maintained by the US Coast Guard, where such preventive measures exist. The

UK's Maritime & Coastguard Agency (MCA) carries out its work on a land-based basis, with regional centres controlling all Coastguard and other maritime-related activities, although it has helicopters at its disposal for Search-and-Rescue (SAR) activities where required, alongside those of the Royal Air Force and Royal Navy. The RAF also uses a fleet of Nimrod reconnaissance aircraft for monitoring activities, but these facilities are used to submit reports on maritime activity rather than the physical interception of vessels. Such a lack of patrolling measures may render the UK to the greater risk of terrorist threat of attack or physical attack from the sea, or even the risk of a massive maritime disaster because of no advance warning or measure to avoid such an incident by maritime means.

The offshore oil and gas sector, the fishing sector, and the overall use of the Continental Shelf, is only one area of maritime concern. It is part of the whole subject of maritime reporting and controls, which embraces anything concerning how maritime vessels and their cargoes are monitored within the framework of international security and international law, which is the subject of this text.

To summarise, a vessel enjoys the freedom of navigation while it is one the high seas, and beyond any form of national territorial limits. As soon as it enters such territorial limits, it becomes subject to national rules and laws under the UNCLOS and the Territorial Sea Conventions. To this extent, it must declare its presence where required to do so, especially if certain conditions for its right of passage become prevalent, such as security or safety. In many circumstances, the vessel may still enjoy the right of innocent passage, as long as its condition and status are known by the national authorities close to its passage. However, it is often necessary for the vessel to submit a report to these national authorities in cases where it is passing through limited international waterways, or where it is approaching a port of destination. Because of the nature of such vessels or the cargoes they carry, such reporting requirements are becoming much more prevalent, and the regimes associated with these reporting requirements are equally becoming much more necessary and complex. It is therefore the duty of the master of the vessel to ensure that he has all the necessary information available concerning his vessel and its cargo to submit an appropriate report as and when required by the national authority concerned. In an age of increasing electronic surveillance, there is already a substantial amount of electronic information available in advance concerning any commercial vessel and its movement to warrant a full monitoring process by national maritime authorities in order to ensure the safe passage of that vessel or to require it to submit a report to the country requiring such information. Failure to submit such information could result in action being taken against that vessel by the national authorities if there is adequate reason to believe that any part of the UNCLOS is being breached.

CUSTOMS MARITIME CARGO REPORTING & CONTROLS

In the UK, HM Customs & Excise, the Government Department responsible for Indirect Taxation, merged with HM Inland Revenue in May 2005 to form an expanded Revenue Department called HM Revenue & Customs. Although the main activity of the newly-merged Department is the levying of national taxes, both direct and indirect, the other primary function still paramount in the Department's role is that of the economic defence of the realm from a maritime point of view.

Although the role of HM Customs & Excise (now HM Revenue & Customs) has changed somewhat over the recent past, owing to the progressive use of electronic procedures, the powers of the Department concerning the control over incoming and outgoing vessels has not. The Customs & Excise Management Act of 1979 gives Officers of the Department the power to intercept, board and search vessels as required in the course of their duties, especially in cases where they have reasonable grounds to suspect a breach of the C&E Management Act. Although the Waterguard (the waterborne means of Customs patrol found at most major UK seaports in the past) has largely disappeared in its original form, the waterborne function has not, with several modern vessels now used to combat waterborne smuggling around the UK coastline. The vessels are part of the Marine and Aviation Agency of HM Customs & Excise, and operate in various regional maritime sectors around the UK. The Officers on board these vessels have the power to intercept and board any vessel entering the 12-Mile Limit (as sanctioned by the 1979 CEMA) suspected of attempting to contravene the C&E Act in any way, especially concerning the smuggling of taxable or prohibited goods, such as Cigarettes, Drugs and Weapons. If such goods are found, not only may the crew of the vessel be arrested and the offending goods seized, but the vessel itself is liable to be impounded and disposed of by the Department.

Customs Controls are those controls exercised over the process of international trade with relation to specific control over the following areas:

- Imports of Goods (Personal or Commercial);

- Exports of Goods (Personal or Commercial);

- Illicit Trade, i.e. Smuggling;

- Prohibitions and Restrictions of the Import and Export of certain Commodities and Products;

- Trade Statistics;

- Duties and Indirect Taxes.

Customs controls are defined to start at the baseline defining the area of Internal Sea, and also pertain to control over ports, harbours and wharves which may serve the purpose of international trade. Every seaport must seek the approval of the national Customs Authority prior to becoming operational, and thus becomes a Customs Port. The Commissioners of Customs & Excise are empowered by Section 19 of the 1979 Customs & Excise Management Act to appoint any area of the United Kingdom as a Customs Port, and to appoint boarding stations for Customs Officers to board ships (originally known as the Waterguard), although with the changes in import and export procedures to allow for more electronic-based regimes, the facility for boarding ships has decreased to a bare minimum, if not zero, thus allowing for little or no waterborne Customs control over inward or outward shipping movements.

The ports comprise the "internal and territorial waters of Her Majesty's dominions" and extend inland up to the "mean high water line". The Commissioners also appoint "approved wharves" for the loading or unloading of cargoes (**Customs & Excise Management Act (1979) s.20**).

Customs Officers have a general power to board ships inside the limits of a Customs Port (s.27). They may have access to every part of a ship, and any goods found concealed or undeclared are liable to forfeiture and seizure, along with the ship itself on certain occasions, especially where the illicit trade in drugs is concerned (s.28). A ship which is constructed or adapted or simply used for the purposes of concealing or smuggling goods may itself be forfeit and seized by Customs Officers in UK waters (s. 88), generally by way of securing the "writ of assistance" to the ship's mast.

A Report must be made by every ship, other than Authorised Regular Shipping Services such as Cross-Channel or North Sea Ferry Services, arriving at a Customs Port from any place outside the UK, or vessels carrying uncleared goods (i.e. goods not in UK/EU Free Circulation and thus Duty-Paid) brought in that vessel from any place outside the United Kingdom (s.35), including Third-Country (i.e. non-EU) goods which have crossed the European Union under Community Transit (CT) conditions (i.e. undeclared up to the point of entry into the UK). The Notice of Arrival (Form C13 as used in the UK) must be made by the ship's agent and submitted to Customs prior to the ship's arrival in port. This is often accompanied by the Notice of Arrival issued by the agent to the port authority to confirm the arrival of a vessel at port, in order to confirm berthing and unloading arrangements made between the agent and the port authority. The Ship's Report, Importation and Exportation by Sea Regulations 1981, **SI 1981/1260**, amended by **SI 1986/1819**, specify that a report (The Customs Cargo Report – CUSCAR, generally comprising the Ship's Cargo Manifest) must be made immediately to a boarding officer if he requests it. Otherwise, the report must be made within 3 hours of the ship reaching her place of unloading or loading, or within 24 hours after entering the limits of the Customs Port if she has not then reached that place. There must be no interference with goods after the ship has come within UK internal waters until a report is made. On arrival, a ship must immediately be brought to the boarding station, unless public health regulations require her to be taken to a mooring station pending examination and clearance to dock. Goods imported by sea must be landed at an approved wharf. If chargeable or dutiable goods are unloaded from ship without payment of the appropriate duties and taxes, or prohibited goods are imported, or imported goods are concealed or otherwise not correctly declared, they are liable to seizure and forfeiture (s.49). With the move from manual to electronic import declarations, however, there is little evidence of Customs landing or import controls at the port, as there is intense pressure on the Port Authorities to ensure that containerised consignments are moved from the port to an inland destination as quickly as possible following unloading from the ship, especially given the limited space available at the port for the detention or storage of goods.

No ship may depart from a port on a voyage to an eventual destination outside the UK unless clearance has been obtained. A Customs Officer may board a cleared ship while she is still in UK waters, and require documentary production of her clearance. A ship departing from a Customs Port must bring to at a boarding station if required (s.64). Consignments for exportation and stores must be loaded at an approved wharf and must be correctly declared, using the New Export System (NES) electronic procedures. The ship can only be cleared for departure once the Customs CHIEF Computer has given clearance for all goods declared for export to be loaded aboard vessel and those goods correctly loaded and recorded on the Ship's Cargo Manifest, including manifests concerning the shipment of consignments to the North Sea Continental Shelf.

Although it is accepted that a regime exists for Customs Cargo Reporting in line with the requirements laid down by the 1979 Customs & Excise Management Act, the information contained in such Reports may not necessarily be sufficient to satisfy the Customs CHIEF (Customs Handling of Import & Export Freight) Computer or Officers perusing such details. Containers unloaded from aboard ship will be classified in either of two categories – FCL (Full Container Load) containing cargoes pertaining to one single Importer – or LCL (Less-than-Full Container Load) containing a variety of consolidated or grouped cargoes pertaining to a variety of Importers. Whereas an FCL Container load will define the exact nature of the cargo contained therein, which can then be easily defined and declared by the Clearing Agent, an LCL Container Load will simply be defined to HM Customs & Excise as "Groupage" or FAK (Freight of all Kinds). At the point of Reporting, it will thus be impossible for the Examining Officer, or the CHIEF Computer, to define exactly the nature of each consignment carried within the Container until such time as the Clearing Agent makes the individual Customs Import Entry Declaration for each deconsolidated consignment. By this time, the Container may well have left the Port for a determined inland destination, and will not have been examined by an Officer of HM Customs & Excise other than if it has been subjected to an X-Ray examination at the Port, in which case a full out-turn of all consignments may be required by a Customs Officer. Given this lack of control, there is no certainty that an Officer would pick up any irregular details pertaining to cargoes such as the illegal import of drugs, firearms, weapons of mass destruction or even illegal immigrants.

The issue of the exemption of Authorised Regular Shipping Services from Customs Reporting Regimes (**JCCC Papers (04)10 & (04)27, HM Customs & Excise 2004**) gives rise to anomalies in the reporting of cargoes, as it is very likely that such vessels are not only carrying goods of EU Origin but also consignments under Community Transit (CT) Customs control, i.e. goods which are not in EU Free Circulation and are hence uncleared. They may also be carrying consignments on a consolidated basis, i.e. consignments grouped together in one consolidated trailer load, and for which there is only brief summary details referring to the consolidation, and not necessarily for each individual grouped consignment. There is a clear need for Customs to know what such consignments are and where they are to be cleared through Customs controls, as National Revenue is at stake. There is a significant risk that since Vessels pertaining to Authorised Regular Shipping Services (including Ferry services from Norway such as the sailings of DFDS and Fjord Line into the River Tyne) are not required to report into Customs prior to or upon arrival at a UK Customs Port, such cargoes will not themselves be reported to Customs in an adequate form to enable Customs to establish the nature and status of such consignments. In one case, however, an anomaly exists concerning the DFDS sailings between Gothenburg (Sweden) and the UK via Kristiansand (Norway), as the voyage is essentially an intra-EU sailing with a non-EU intermediate stop added in. The rules applying to such Authorised Services also apply to those sailings between Norway and Denmark, also operated by DFDS and Fjord Line. Indeed, there could also be the risk that if the Vessel concerned were carrying consignments or passengers of a nature deemed a threat to national security or the economic security of the nation, these contents could pass unnoticed into national territory without any form of verification or checks given the nature of the voyage within EU waters.

However, the fact that because a vessel sails within EU Territorial Waters between ports of two member states does not imply that the information pertaining to its cargoes automatically is passed from the despatching party to the receiving party. Although electronic facilities enable a Seller to communicate with a Buyer concerning the consignment of goods to be shipped, as far as commercial documents such as Invoices or Packing Lists are concerned, this information does not necessarily correspond with that contained on Loading Lists or Ship's Manifests, or even Bills of Lading or Waybills, which generally reflect upon the information contained in the former sets of Documents. Indeed, it is very likely that the information contained on either of these latter documents exists only in abbreviated form, and may prevail in a greater sense with the advent of electronic Bills of Lading presently being introduced under the revisions to the Carriage of Goods at Sea Acts and the Hague-Visby and Hamburg Rules. Hence the inability of HM Customs & Excise to maintain full controls over the information submitted by Shipping Agents or Shipowners pertaining to Customs Cargo Reporting, despite the requirements for Vessels other than those operating on Authorised Regular Services to submit Reports to the Customs Authority prior to or upon arrival in a UK Port. This scenario shows that although information pertaining to cargoes may be known by the Trader, be it Import or Export, it is not necessarily known or communicated by either Freight Agents, NVOCCs (Non-Vessel-Owning Common Carriers), Port Agents, Liner Agents, Shipowners or Customs Officials, despite the rules laid down by the Carriage of Goods at Sea Acts of 1971 and 1992 pertaining to the responsibilities of Shipowners, Shipping Agents and the Masters of Vessels. This would also suggest the possibility of a vacuum in information transparency and accessibility as far as the carriage of goods on the high seas is concerned. Hence the urgent need to review the level and detail of cargo information pertaining to any vessel sailing into or within the confines of EU Territorial Waters, especially as such information may pertain not only to the Insurance principle of *Uberrimae Fidei* (Utmost Good Faith) but also to issues of national security which could be prejudicial to the wellbeing or security of the national state.

It has come to the point that because of the reduction in the personnel resources of HM Revenue & Customs (the Department created as the result of the merger between HM Inland Revenue and HM Customs & Excise) concerning the maintenance of adequate physical controls at many UK Seaports, the Department has requested certain UK Port Authorities to report activities which may be deemed to be suspicious, irregular or untoward in any way. Furthermore, the resource reductions have resulted in HMRC centralising its import/export control operations in regional centres, at a distance from the seaports, and only sending officers to examine containers when deemed necessary. All import and export declarations are now submitted electronically to central Entry Processing Units rather than to a Port-based EPU. However, the Port Authorities themselves are under severe pressure to ensure that all consignments are moved swiftly out of the confines of the port and onwards to their respective inland destinations. The limitations posed by the summary information the Port Authority itself may receive from an incoming vessel imply that it is not possible for the Port Authority to inform HM Customs & Excise concerning the movements of every vessel and the nature of its cargo, especially when it is the individual Shipping Agent or the Freight Clearing Agent which receives the information pertaining to the cargo to be cleared through Customs. Indeed, HM Customs & Excise places more reliance on the Freight and Shipping Agents and the Importers to declare information pertaining to each cargo rather than the Seaport itself. Furthermore, information pertaining to arrivals into and departures from a specific port is limited to that port alone; no other port in the UK or the EU is able to gain access to such information, as the present reporting system only takes place between the vessel and the port concerned.

Given the freedoms enjoyed by the Member States of the European Union in moving goods within the Community, as long as consignments originate within the EU, there are no controls concerning their movement. This implies that an EU-registered ship sailing from, for example, a Port on the Baltic bound for a UK Port will require no Customs controls given the assumption that its cargoes originate within the EU and are thus not subject to Customs declarations. However, it should be noted that the vessel concerned may carry cargoes originating outwith the EU, e.g. from Russia or elsewhere. Unless that cargo is individually reported as being in separate containers or trailers, or the vessel itself is registered outwith the EU, the cargo may not be declared to the CHIEF Customs Computer when it arrives at the UK Port. The underlying risk is that undeclared cargo may "slip through the net" on arrival in the UK and may either be misdeclared or not declared at all, thus posing a substantial risk to not only the national revenue and hence the economic wellbeing of the nation but also may pose a threat to national security if it were subsequently discovered that the cargo was of a weaponry or chemical nature. As the level of Customs presence at the UK Ports has diminished, so the risk and threat to national security of unsolicited and undeclared imports has increased.

Only if cargoes are declared at the point of entry into the distant EU State under Community Transit (CT) status, and are then shipped via the EU Port of despatch to the relevant UK Port, will the consignment be declared on the Ship's Manifest to HM Customs & Excise at the point of arrival at the UK Port. In this way, a full Import Declaration can be made, and the consignment properly discharged out of Customs control.

The export element of Customs control, especially with regard to maritime movements, has become more automated and electronic with the implementation in 2002 of the NES (New Export System) means of export declarations, although there is still the requirement for the submission of the full cargo manifest to Customs by the Ship's Agents prior to the vessel being cleared by Customs for sailing. In this respect, the cargo manifest is based on the issuing of Marine Bills of Lading for each consignment, coupled with the raising of NES Export Declarations by the

Clearing Agent / Freight Forwarder. However, the submission of each set of documents rests with different parties, as the following summary shows:

- The Cargo Manifest is submitted to Customs by the Ship's Agents or the Port Agents;
- The NES Declarations are submitted by the Freight Agents;
- The Bills of Lading are raised by the Carrier (The Shipping Line).

The Bills of Lading are submitted by the Shipping Line to the Freight Forwarder responsible for arranging the shipment, and copies may also be held by the Ship's Agent, who submits the Cargo Manifest on behalf of the Line to Customs. Cases arise where there is uncertainty over who is responsible for the loading of cargo aboard vessel, owing to the absence of a specific INCOTERM in the contract of delivery, with the result that in some cases Bills of Lading are not submitted to a freight agent, and consequently no cargo manifest is submitted concerning the specific consignment to Customs. Customs are therefore unaware that the consignment in question has been loaded aboard vessel, and consequently has not been correctly declared. In the case of hazardous or dangerous cargoes, this failure to correctly record and declare a consignment could prove disastrous in the event of an accident aboard vessel or a collision, as a trader, i.e. the exporter or importer, could ultimately be held liable for the consequences of such an accident. A further consequence of a failure to correctly declare a consignment to Customs is that the trader is liable for VAT on the value of the consignment and equally a civil penalty on the grounds of a false declaration being made to Customs.

It is worthwhile noting the following procedure concerning the issue of NES Export Declarations since the procedures involved influence how quickly the vessel can be cleared by Customs for departure:

- The NES Pre-Shipment Advice Declaration (PSA) is entered into the CHIEF Customs Computer and a Declaration Unique Consignment Reference (DUCR) for the individual consignment is raised;

- The computer acknowledges the Declaration and clears the consignment for movement to the Port of Loading;

- The Consignment arrives at the Port and the Declaration Unique Consignment Reference (DUCR) is input into the CHIEF Computer;

- The CHIEF Computer selects a clearance route for the Consignment:

    a) **Route 6 Electronic Clearance without Examination;**
    b) **Route 1 Documentary Check;**
    c) **Route 2 Consignment Examination**

- Upon satisfactory checks being made, The CHIEF Computer clears the consignment for loading aboard vessel;

- The Departure Message is sent to the Agents signifying that the vessel is ready to depart;

- The Final message is sent to the Agents signifying that the vessel has sailed and that the cargoes have left UK and EU waters.

In all instances of loading aboard vessel, it is imperative that all steps are taken to ensure that all cargoes are correctly entered on Shipping Documentation so that correct Export Declarations can be raised and submitted to Customs in advance of the cargo being loaded aboard vessel, as well as the cargo manifest being submitted to Customs prior to the vessel's departure. Theoretically, failure to correctly declare a cargo to Customs could result in the refusal by Customs to allow the loading of the cargo aboard vessel, although in reality there are few physical checks of export cargoes made at the port owing to a lack of physical resources and manpower on the part of Customs at the port, thus allowing the port authority to carry out loading formalities without physical Customs checks on the consignment concerned.

With the transfer of most reporting mechanisms to electronic means, the structure of the maritime reporting regime with regard to Customs controls has also changed. Although Customs still maintain control over all seaports, there is no longer the same degree of physical presence of Customs Officers at many seaports. The CHIEF Customs Computer relies on the details of the Export Consignment in the form of the DUCR to ensure that the correct details of each consignment have been entered into the computer by the exporter or, more likely, the freight agent. However, in cases where the consignment is shipped Ex Works (EXW) and especially in a groupage arrangement, the exporter is very unlikely to see a copy of the Export Declaration, and in many cases, a DUCR may not be raised by the clearing agent as the consignment is part of a larger consolidated consignment arranged by the overseas buyer, and thus the only declaration raised at export will be the Master UCR which covers the whole LCL groupage container load. In this respect, the details shown on the declaration will show the agent/consolidator as the exporter, and hence their VAT details will be entered, rather than those of the individual exporters whose consignments are contained in the consolidation. In this respect, there is no compliance for each exporter, and this not only distorts statistical information pertaining to export consolidations, given that the Customs Authority places full responsibility for an export at the door of the exporter, but also masks and distorts information concerning the true contents of the container at the time of export. Such omissions contravene US Customs regulations under the CT-PAT initiative, and also compromise safety regulations concerning the carriage of cargoes by sea, especially concerning the nature of the FAL 2 Cargo Manifest and its requirements under the IMO FAL Convention.

As previously mentioned, most of the administrative and documentary control activity is conducted from distant Entry Processing Units and centralised control functions elsewhere in the country. Actual port-related activities are conducted on the basis of officers travelling to a port when required, for example in cases of random checks made on passengers disembarking from cruise liners or container scans. Otherwise, all declarations for cargoes, ship's stores, passengers and crews are being transferred to electronic facilities, and the procedures for these declarations are detailed as follows.

IMPORTS/ARRIVALS

The vessel notifies the port of its impending arrival. The Cargo Manifest (in its IMO electronic UN/EDIFACT CUSCAR format) is submitted electronically by the Port Agents representing the Shipping Line to the CHIEF (Customs Handling of Import & Export Freight) computer. The Port Agents also submit the IMO FAL Forms detailing the following information:

- Ship's Stores still on board vessel (INVRPT);
- Crew Lists and Effects;
- Passenger Lists.

Based on this information submitted electronically, an Officer may decide to travel to the port to board a vessel and examine the details pertaining to the crew.

One system which has facilitated the electronic submission of the Cargo Manifest is FCPS, an electronic Cargo Processing System originally developed by the Port of Felixstowe in the 1980s under the Maritime Cargo Processing (MCP) banner. It facilitates the submission of the cargo manifest to the Port Authority and Customs to enable Customs to select in advance containers which require examination or scrutiny upon unloading from the vessel. It also enables the Port Authority to move containers from the vessel in a short space of time and facilitate Customs and Port clearance by the freight forwarders or clearing agents by streamlined means, as the system also facilitates electronic import clearance direct to the CHIEF Customs Computer. However, the system still relies upon the accuracy of the information supplied on the cargo manifest, and this information may not be sufficient enough to show exact details of every cargo contained in any container, especially groupage/consolidated LCL container loads. Only that information supplied as a result of the information which is also used for the purpose of the issuing of a Bill of Lading will be found on the cargo manifest. This information may be insufficient for Customs purposes, and may result in greater numbers of containers being selected for scrutiny by Customs at the port of arrival.

The Freight Agents submit electronic online Import Declarations directly to the CHIEF Computer, which sends back an acknowledgement along with the calculation of Import Duty and VAT in the form of an Entry Acceptance Advice. Each Import Declaration represents the cargo in each container which may be detailed on the CUSCAR Cargo Manifest.

The drawback of the increase in tonnage and size of the new Super Post-Panamax container vessels (of the size of 8000 – 10000 TEU) means that the Cargo Manifest for each vessel becomes larger, with the risk that the computer systems required to analyse the information therein require updating to cover the increased volume of information or may take some time to absorb all the information contained therein. It is also the case that in many cases, the containers listed on the cargo manifest with only be detailed as groupage or consolidated loads, without defining the exact details of each individual cargo within the consolidation. Given the sheer volume of container information in each manifest, it is too cumbersome a task for the Customs Computer to analyse each cargo at the time the manifest is submitted, although containers are selected at random for scanning and examination at the port. Any cargo examined as a result of the container scan is only scrutinised based on an individual declaration submitted by the clearing agent which was identified by the CHIEF Computer on a Route 2 (full examination) basis.

In theory, the Marine Bill of Lading issued for every consignment should equate with the details on the cargo manifest, although for consolidations there are two types of Bill of Lading – the Master Bill of Lading and the House Bill of Lading. In many cases, especially under Ex Works (EXW) consolidation conditions, the Master Bill of Lading is issued for the full consolidation (assuming that the whole container load is destined for the same buyer), but the House Bills referring to each individual consignment therein may not necessarily be issued to the buyer as the whole container load is to be delivered to the Buyer's premises. The House Bills should be issued, however, for the prime purpose of declaration to the Customs Authority at the point of import, since a declaration must be submitted to Customs for each consignment within the container.

EXPORTS/DESPATCHES

In the same way that all import declarations for maritime cargo have been rendered electronic, so too have export declarations for maritime cargo and ship's stores. Electronic initiatives driven by the EU have resulted in many EU countries implementing electronic export declaration procedures, and the UK implemented its own electronic export regime, the NES (New Export System) in 2002 for all seafreight export declarations. The CUSCAR Cargo Manifest is submitted electronically by the Port Agent to Customs in advance of the vessel being loaded, especially in the case of shipments destined for the US, where Cargo Manifests must be submitted to US Customs officers based in the UK 48 hours prior to the vessel's departure under the US CT-PAT initiative. The NES Export Declaration is submitted to the Customs CHIEF Computer as a Pre-Shipment Advice (PSA) once the cargo is ready for shipment (usually no more than 24 hours before the consignment is due to be loaded aboard vessel), and this declaration is acknowledged by the Computer. Once the consignment has been loaded aboard the container and reaches the port of loading, another message (The Arrival Message) is entered by the Agent into the CHIEF computer stating that the consignment has arrived at the port and awaits clearance instructions. The CHIEF computer issues the appropriate message (Route 6 Automatic Clearance / Route 1 Documentary Check etc.) for the export consignment in question. Once the consignment has been cleared by the CHIEF computer, the consignment is loaded aboard vessel and a Route 7 Departure Message is issued by CHIEF. A further Route 8 message clears the vessel to sail, and departure is completed. At this point, the Marine Bills of Lading for each export consignment are issued to the party arranging the shipment.

The same electronic initiative which controls inward IMO FAL declarations is also used for outward movements. The Suppliers of Ship's Stores must also submit electronic declarations based on the UN/EDIFACT Inventory Report (INVRPT) for all Ship's Stores loaded aboard vessel prior to its departure. These declarations can be submitted electronically online in the same manner that inward Ship's Stores Declarations are submitted at the time of the arrival in port of the vessel. Thus, the electronic arrangement of Customs Export Declarations is as follows:

- NES Export Declaration (Exporter/Freight Forwarder/Port Agent);
- IMO FAL Form 2 Cargo Manifest (CUSCAR);
- IMO FAL Form 3 Ship's Stores Declaration (Ship's Master, Supplier or Agent).

However, given that an IMO Ship's Stores Declaration requires a signature by either the Ship's Master or the Agent, there is still the need for a hard copy to be made available to a Customs Officer where required. The same is true of both the FAL Form 2 Cargo Manifest and the NES Declaration. A hard copy of the Export Declaration plus supporting Departure Messages must be kept by the Exporter for presentation to a Customs Officer where and when required for VAT zero-rating or Excise suspension purposes.

Despite the increasing reliance on electronic means of reporting and declarations for Customs purposes, there is still a requirement for documentary evidence supporting any electronic declaration. This means that all parties involved in either import or export maritime activities must maintain a set of documentary records relating to every shipment. These requirements are based on liability for either VAT or Excise Duty, and require the supplier of anything loaded aboard vessel, be it exporters or Ship's Chandlers, to show proper accurate documentary evidence of everything loaded aboard vessel for compliance and control purposes.

THE CARGO DOCUMENTARY APPROACH

Previous sections dealt with the overview of documentation as part of the maritime reporting mechanism. A more detailed approach is now required in order to assess how cargoes in particular are declared, with reference to both the IMO FAL Form 2 and the Marine Bill of Lading, as the two forms relate to each other.

THE CARGO MANIFEST

Whereas the IMO FAL Form 2 is an overall cargo declaration (now covered by the CUSCAR regime) as well as being a summary of all cargoes carried aboard a vessel, the Marine Bill of Lading is an individual declaration and a documentary description of a specific cargo consignment, usually in a container, and also represents a specific cargo detailed in the Cargo Manifest. A specimen representative example of the IMO FAL Form 2, along with its electronic replacement, is shown in the Appendices following the text. An example of an Ocean (Marine) Bill of Lading is also shown in the Appendices.

The Cargo Manifest in either its manual or electronic format, is produced by the Port Agents prior to the loading of the vessel. In the case of the US-led CT-PAT initiative, this is a legal requirement for all consignments to be exported to the United States since 2002, for the purposes of the presentation of the cargo manifest to US Customs Officials at the port of loading at least 24 hours prior to the vessel being loaded. Thus, for export purposes, a comprehensive reporting system exists, assuming that all consignments within a container are correctly detailed on a Bill of Lading, although anomalies pertaining to this accuracy of information are detailed in the following section. In the case of an FCL, this may be so, whereas in the case of an LCL Groupage Load, there is every possibility that only a generic description is given on the Master Bill of Lading, which will also refer to and be referred to by the FAL 2 Cargo Manifest.

A further issue concerning the information supplied on a Cargo Manifest concerns the mixture of non-EU and EU consignments carried on various vessels. The EU Authorities have decreed that the issuers of the cargo Manifest may voluntarily include details of EU-originating cargoes alongside details of non-EU cargoes on vessels which are moving between two or more EU Member States. Although this can include deep-sea container vessels, it is more likely to refer to short-sea container vessel services where the vessel may be part of a feeder service to link in with a deep-sea container service, or may simply be operating on a service between various EU ports independently of any feeder service. Such services also include Authorised Regular Operators, who operate Ro-Ro Ferries in areas such as the North Sea and the Baltic Sea. Although the information they provide is more abbreviated and does not require the same detailed information as that supplied by deep sea operators or charter services on the grounds of the frequency and regularity of their sailings, there is still the need for a manifest covering all trailer and container loads aboard vessel for each sailing, as the vessel may carry both EU-originating cargoes, or at least those cargoes deemed to be in EU Duty-Paid Free Circulation, as well as non-EU cargoes not in Free Circulation, i.e. those cargoes under Community transit status, on which Import Duty still has to be paid, or cargoes transiting the European Community territory en route for a non-EU destination. The EU-originating cargoes should be covered by a T2L Document. This document allows the consignments under this document EU treatment by the Customs authority when they are unloaded at the EU port of destination.

These cases can be represented by the following matrix categorisation:

EU-ORIGINATING CONSIGNMENTS	NON-EU CONSIGNMENTS (FREE CIR)
DUTY PAID (T2L)	DUTY PAID
NON-EU CONSIGNMENTS	NON-EU CONSIGNMENTS
DUTY TO BE PAID ON ARRIVAL AT PORT	COMMUNITY TRANSIT – LEAVING EU

THE BILL OF LADING

A Bill of Lading has more distinct functions than does a Cargo Manifest. Whereas a Manifest gives overall details of a set of cargoes, which can then be summarily scrutinised by the Customs Authority for the purpose of examination of a specific cargo or the container in which it is located at the port, a Bill of Lading will be used for the purpose of an Import Customs Declaration, and may be scrutinised by a Landing Officer of the Customs Authority for details with relation to the assessment of Import Duties and Taxes, which cannot be undertaken with a Cargo Manifest. Furthermore, the Bill of Lading has three distinct functions which do not relate to a Cargo Manifest. These functions are:

- Document of Title (Ownership of the Consignment);
- Evidence of Contract of Carriage;
- Receipt by the Carrier for the Consignment.

In these respects, the Bill of Lading is a legal document and can be used as collateral in the contract of sale, as well as proof of responsibility for the carriage of the shipment. In this respect, it may be used as legal evidence where a Cargo Manifest cannot. In cases where a Non-Vessel-Owning Common Carrier (NVOCC), i.e. a shipping company which owns or leases containers but does not operate its own maritime vessels, issues Bills of Lading, the Bill will represent a Slot Charter, i.e. a transaction where the NVOCC has chartered space aboard a vessel owned by another shipping line for the purposes of shipping several containers to an overseas destination. In this case, there will not only be a Bill of Lading issued by the NVOCC, but also a further Bill of Lading issued by the Carrier with respect to the containers owned by the NVOCC which will be passed from the Carrier to the NVOCC. In this respect, it should then be possible to trace every container carried by a container vessel with respect to the owners of the containers and hence the consignments loaded aboard each container. In reality, containers aboard vessel may be owned by various different NVOCC owners, as well as containing varying degrees of information pertaining to their respective loads. Given the increasing size of container vessels along with their capacity to carry larger numbers of containers (>8000 TEUs), the relative facility to trace each container is becoming more complex and increasingly less straightforward, especially when it is admitted that the sheer quantity and volume of information held on a cargo manifest relating to such vessels is resulting in the manifest becoming more unmanageable, even in its CUSCAR electronic format. Imagine, therefore, that for every container loaded aboard such a vessel, there are even more Bills of Lading to raise, and that infers more time being spent in raising such documents. Hence the increasing burden of work placed upon the companies, especially shipping agencies, issuing both Bills of Lading and Cargo Manifests every time a container vessel sails, and equally the risk of inadequate information being input to complete both a Bill of Lading and a Cargo Manifest, resulting in a failure on the part of the vessel's master to be fully aware of the consignments aboard vessel, let alone the risk of failure to fully report these cargoes to the port of arrival.

There is a clause at the bottom right of the Bill, stating that the Goods are "**Received by the Carrier from Shipper in apparent good order and condition [unless otherwise noted**

herein]", i.e. that the Carrier bears no responsibility for loss or damage to the consignment prior to receiving it at the appointed place. The Bill of Lading is issued following the departure of the vessel from the port of loading, thus proving, especially in the case of a Shipped On Board Bill of Lading, that the consignment was confirmed as having been loaded aboard vessel. This confirmation is supported by the evidence of an Export Declaration to Customs, followed by a series of electronic messages confirming not only loading of the consignment aboard vessel but also the clearance of the vessel by Customs and its subsequent departure.

MARINE ACCIDENT REPORTING

Murphy's Law, however humorous, tells us that if anything can go wrong, it will. This is quite definitely true of the Marine sector, given the hazards associated with the movement of vessels within limited spaces of water. Accidents or incidents such as near misses frequently occur, despite the stringent Collision Regulations (COLREGS) applied to all international shipping movements worldwide. The whole issue of marine accidents or incidents concerns not just the accident or incident itself, but the reporting of such an event to the relevant authority.

If an accident occurs, it is reported to the local Coastguard, which will take immediate action to attend the scene. In certain cases, the accident may require the services of the local Search-and-Rescue (SAR) facilities, but in most cases, the vessel may have been damaged and will require assistance to the local port. In more extreme cases, the vessel may be grounded or even sink, and salvage operations will be required.

The Marine Accident Reporting systems include:

- MARS (Marine Accident Reporting System), operated by the Nautical Institute;
- HM Coastguard Accident Reporting.

The MARS system allows the confidential reporting of accidents or incidents, such as near-misses, without the fear of litigation, and the purpose of the system is to learn lessons form such incidents in order to avoid similar incidents in the future. The Reporting system required by HM Coastguard, however, may result in the matter being referred to the Marine Accident Investigation Branch, a division of the Department of Transport, for full investigation. Certain cases, such as the recent grounding of the vessel *Jackie Moon*, have resulted in criminal prosecutions against the Ship's Master.

The Merchant Shipping Regulations of 2005 pertaining to Accident Reporting have been revised, and now refer not only to commercial shipping but also to pleasure vessels, which therefore require all vessels of a pleasure or leisure nature to report any relevant incidents in the same way that would be applicable to commercial vessels above a tonnage of 300grt. These Regulations are set to enter force in mid-2005, and replace the Accident Reporting Regulations of 1999.

HAZARDOUS OR DANGEROUS CARGOES AND THE IMDG CODE

The Safety of Lives at Sea (SOLAS) Regulations concern the requirements by Ship's Masters and Shipowners to ensure that all necessary Health and Safety Regulations pertaining to the Crews of Ships are maintained and obeyed. On ships carrying general commercial cargoes or passengers, these Regulations refer to general practice under normal commercial activities, but on ships whose cargoes are primarily of a hazardous or dangerous nature, then the regulations become more stringent. Furthermore, the Regulations pertaining to the reporting of such vessels to shore-based authorities are equally more stringent. Ships carrying such cargoes are not only obliged by Regulation to report to the British and French Authorities under the Channel Navigation Information System (CNIS), but they are also required by law to report to the Port Authority of their destination prior to arrival at the port, so that appropriate measure can be taken to ensure their safe berthing and unloading, as well as their safe passage into national waters.

Cargoes subject to such requirements are:

- Hydrocarbons (i.e. Petroleum);
- Liquefied Natural or Petroleum Gas;
- Other Liquefied Gas;
- Chemicals;
- Explosives.

In the case of bulk cargoes carried at sea, this requirement is clearly evident, since the quantities of such cargoes carried in any vessel could result in catastrophic disasters should an accident occur either at sea or in port. The disasters pertaining to the ships "Erika" and "Prestige" proved such a scenario – the oilspills resulting from the "Erika" disaster on the French Coast proved extremely damaging to the coastline, as did previous disasters resulting from the grounding of the tankers "Torrey Canyon", "Amoco Cadiz" and "Erika". Other international disasters include the grounding of the tanker "Exxon Valdez" off the Alaskan Coast some years ago, with the resulting destruction of the local marine environment.

In the case of hazardous cargoes carried in containers alongside more general cargoes, the same risks exist although in reduced form. However, given the documentary regimes requiring the issuing of Dangerous Goods Notes for the carriage of such cargoes coupled with the interests of the insured parties concerning such marine ventures under the insurance principle of *Uberrimae Fidei* (Utmost Good Faith), the Master of the Ship and the Shipowners should be well aware of the risks of carrying such cargoes on board vessel. Indeed, there are strict rules within the framework of the Law of Carriage of Goods at Sea (**Carriage of Goods by Sea Act (1971)**) and the Hague/Visby Rules (**Art IV, Rule 6**) concerning where and how on board ship such consignments must be stowed, and the liability of the carrier for such cargoes. Under the rules of Marine Reporting, all ships carrying any kind or quantity of Dangerous or Hazardous Goods must report to the Port of Destination prior to arrival at the Port. However, certain cargoes are declared to Customs, the Carriers and the Insurers in such a fashion as to disguise their true nature, either because of the risk of the liability of higher Insurance Premiums or because of the desire of their owners to hide their true nature from national authorities. The Buyer or the Seller of such consignments has a Duty of Disclosure to inform the Carrier of the full and true nature of the cargo being carried, although there are occasions when this duty is not exercised. It is also stated in the Hague/Visby Rules, **Art IV Rule 6**, that if cargoes of a hazardous or dangerous nature are carried without the prior knowledge of the Carrier, if the Carrier discovers their true nature they may destroy or land the cargo at any place and hold the owner of the cargo liable for damages or expenses incurred in such action. However, if the Carrier is unaware of the nature of the nature of such cargoes and fails to report the vessel's movement to the Port of Destination in advance under the Hazardous Goods rules, then the Carrier may be held liable for not informing the Port Authority accordingly and running the risk of endangering the Port, its personnel and other vessels in the vicinity.

For the purposes of Ro-Ro carriage of hazardous or dangerous consignments, there are equally strict rules set out in the CMR Convention of 1956 (**Articles 6(f) and 7**), concerning the exact details to be included in the CMR Consignment Note and the duties and responsibilities of the shipper when both notifying the carrier of the nature and description of the consignment, especially its classification under the IMDG Code, and the liabilities incurred should the cargo be damaged or cause damage to the vessel while in carriage. In this respect, it is the express duty of the shipper to inform the carrier of the nature of the consignment so that adequate provisions may be made for the safe stowage of the consignment in either a container or a trailer aboard vessel in a position which is likely to minimise the risk of damage to the container, trailer or the vessel itself, as well as minimising the risk of compromise or prejudice to the ultimate safety of the vessel and its crew.

The transport of Dangerous and Hazardous Goods is covered by the IMDG (International Maritime Dangerous Goods) Code, which has been adopted by the IMO. For classification and definition purposes, the IMDG Code is divided into 7 Parts contained in Volume 1:

- General Provisions, Definitions and Training;
- Classification;

- Consignment Procedures;

- Construction and Testing of Packagings, International Bulk Containers, Large Packagings, Portable Tanks and Road Tank Vehicles;

- Transport Operations.

Volume 2 contains Sections on:

- Dangerous Goods List;

- Limited Quantities exceptions;

- Proper Shipping Names;

- Glossary of Terms;

- Index.

Application of the Code is mandatory, but it also contains provisions of a recommendatory nature which are stated in Chapter 1.1 of the Code.

Although the IMDG Code applies in general to ships carrying bulk cargoes of a hazardous or dangerous nature, it also applies to vessels carrying more general and varied containerised cargoes, amongst which may be cargoes of a dangerous or hazardous nature. The Code also refers to the responsibilities of agents and traders in ensuring that cargoes are correctly described and declared to the Shipping Line prior to loading aboard vessel. The need exists, therefore, for agents and traders trading in hazardous or dangerous goods to be equipped with an up-to-date copy of the IMDG Code at all times, to allow for changes in the Code as well as for the overall purpose of compliance with the regulations pertaining to the carriage of dangerous goods by sea.

Under the rules of Marine Reporting, all ships carrying any kind or quantity of Dangerous or Hazardous Goods must report to the Port of Destination prior to arrival at the Port, usually 24 hours in advance of the vessel's arrival at port, in order to allow for special provisions for the berthing and unloading of the vessel upon its arrival at port where hazardous or dangerous cargoes are concerned. However, certain cargoes are declared to Customs, the Carriers and the Insurers in such a fashion as to disguise their true nature, either because of the risk of the liability of higher Insurance Premiums or because of the desire of their owners to hide their true nature from national authorities. The Buyer or the Seller of such consignments has a Duty of Disclosure to inform the Carrier of the full and true nature of the cargo being carried, although there are occasions when this duty is not exercised. It is also stated in the Hague/Visby Rules, **Art IV Rule 6**, that if cargoes of a hazardous or dangerous nature are carried without the prior knowledge of the Carrier, if the Carrier discovers their true nature they may destroy or land the cargo at any place and hold the owner of the cargo liable for damages or expenses incurred in such action. However, if the Carrier is unaware of the nature of the nature of such cargoes and fails to report the vessel's movement to the Port of Destination in advance under the Hazardous Goods rules, then the Carrier may be held liable for not informing the Port Authority accordingly and running the risk of endangering the Port, its personnel and other vessels in the vicinity.

The transport of Dangerous and Hazardous Goods is covered by the IMDG (International Maritime Dangerous Goods) Code, which has been adopted by the IMO. The IMDG Code was developed as a uniform international code for the transport of dangerous or hazardous cargoes by sea, and was designed to cover such matters as packing, container traffic and stowage, with particular reference to the segregation and isolation of incompatible substances, where the potential contact of such substances could lead to severe accidents or could prejudice or compromise the safety and security of the vessel and her crew.

The development of the IMDG Code dates from the 1960 Conference of the Safety of Life at Sea, which recommended as its outcome that Governments should adopt a uniform international code for the transport of dangerous and hazardous cargoes by sea to supplement the regulations contained in the 1960 International Convention for the Safety of Life at Sea (SOLAS), which eventually became a full set of international regulations in 1974. A resolution adopted by the 1960 Conference stated that the proposed Code should cover such matters as packing, stowage aboard vessel and container traffic in general, although in 1960, container traffic was still in its infancy, the first containers having been carried by maritime means in 1956 along the East Coast of the USA. The full IMDG Code, resulting from a working group of the IMO Maritime Safety Committee which began to prepare the Code in 1961, was adopted by the fourth IMO Assembly in 1965, although since its adoption it has undergone many changes, both in appearance and content, to maintain pace with the ever-changing needs of industry as well as the overall maritime transport of goods, especially with the ever-increasing use of sea containers to transport cargoes worldwide.

Amendments to the Code originate from two sources. These are:

- Proposals submitted directly to the IMO by member states;

- Amendments which are required to take account of and provide for changes to the United Nations Recommendations on the Transport of Dangerous Goods, which set the basic requirements for all transport modes.

Amendments to the provisions of the UN Recommendations are made on a two-yearly cycle, and approximately two years after their adoption by the UN, they are adopted by the authorities responsible for regulating the various transport modes, which in the case of the UK is the Department for Transport (DfT). In this way, a basic set of requirements applicable to all modes of transport is established and implemented, thus ensuring that difficulties are not encountered at intermodal interfaces, such as the transport of containers by both sea and road, and equally the transport of cargoes by trailer using both road and sea means, especially where Ro-Ro maritime transport is involved.

The application of the IMDG Code (now Amended Version 2006), is mandatory, but it also contains provisions of a recommendatory nature which are stated in Chapter 1.1 of the Code. The classification of a cargo into its applicable category according to the provisions of the IMDG Code is the direct responsibility of the shipper or consignor, regardless of who is arranging the shipment according to the International Terms of Delivery (INCOTERMS), or by the appropriate designated competent authority where specified in the Code. This Code can include a Freight Agent, where that agent has been specifically empowered as the competent authority by the shipper or consignor/consignee.

Although the IMDG Code applies in general to ships carrying bulk cargoes of a hazardous or dangerous nature, it also applies to vessels carrying more general and varied containerised cargoes, amongst which may be cargoes of a dangerous or hazardous nature. The Code also refers to the responsibilities of agents and traders in ensuring that cargoes are correctly described and declared to the Shipping Line prior to loading aboard vessel. The need exists, therefore, for agents and traders trading in hazardous or dangerous goods to be equipped with an up-to-date copy of the IMDG Code at all times, to allow for changes in the Code as well as for the overall purpose of compliance with the regulations pertaining to the carriage of dangerous goods by sea.

The ship owner or operator will only accept and handle dangerous goods by prior written arrangement, and then only on the express condition that the shipper provides a full and adequate description of the cargo to be shipped. If this arrangement is accepted, a special stowage order, often referred to as a dangerous goods form, will be issued which indicates to the master of the vessel that the cargo conforms to the prescribed code of acceptance laid down by the ship owner or operator. The shipment will not take place until a special stowage order, which is the authority for shipment, has been issued by the ship owner or operator, given that the dangerous or hazardous cargo must be stowed in a specific location as far from the vessel's accommodation quarters as possible. Furthermore, the shipper must fully describe and classify the cargo, and ensure that it is correctly packed, marked and labelled. This can be achieved through the services of a freight forwarder.

Before dangerous goods can be authorised for shipment, the following information is required:

- Name of sender/consignor;

- Correct technical name of the dangerous/hazardous goods to be carried;

- Class of dangerous/hazardous goods, as given in the IMDG Code;

- Flashpoint (if applicable);

- UN Number to identify the substance;

- Details of outer packing;

- Details of inner packing;

- Quantity to be shipped in individual packages and in total;

- Additional information for radioactive materials, explosives and consignments in bulk (e.g. tank containers, road tankers etc.).

The Dangerous Goods authority form will have a reference number and will also show the sailing details, including the ports of departure and destination for which the consignment is authorised, plus the following details:

- The hazard class;
- UN Number;
- Labels;
- Key number (in case of emergency);
- Any special instructions.

On the arrival of the goods at the port of loading, the consignment and the authority to ship are submitted to the master of the vessel for ultimate approval prior to customs clearance and loading, although in reality, the customs export declaration will have been submitted in advance of the consignment being despatched to the port of loading. The Dangerous Goods Note (DG Note) issued for the consignment must also be completed, along with a Container Vehicle Packing Certificate, and these documents must accompany the goods.

SHIP ROUTEING AND TRAFFIC SEPARATION SCHEMES (TSS)

The practice of following predetermined routes for shipping originated in 1898 and was adopted, for reasons of safety, by shipping companies operating passenger ships across the North Atlantic. Related provisions were subsequently incorporated into the original SOLAS (Safety of Lives at Sea) Convention. The 1960 SOLAS Convention referred to ships' routeing measures in busy shipping areas on both sides of the North Atlantic, and Contracting Governments undertook the responsibility of using their influence to induce the owners of all ships crossing the Atlantic to follow recognized routes and to ensure adherence to such routes in converging areas by all ships, so far as circumstances permitted.

Meanwhile, the analysis of casualty statistics was showing that collisions between ships were becoming a worrying cause of accidents, especially in congested waterways. In 1963, the Liverpool Underwriters Association reported 21 collisions responsible for total losses of ships, compared with a five-year average of 13.8. A report on tanker hazards presented late in 1963 to the United States Treasury concluded that most accidents were due to human error, with speed in congested waters a principal cause. The report stated that there were too many diverse "rules of the road", the width of navigable channels had generally not kept pace with the increase in sizes and tonnages of vessels, and not enough was being done to use modern communications.

At the same time, the Institutes of Navigation of the Federal Republic of Germany, France and the United Kingdom had begun a study on improving safety measures in congested areas, such as the English Channel. The group came up with a series of proposals, including the idea that ships using congested areas should follow a system of one-way traffic schemes, like those being used on land. Traffic lanes of this type were already in use on the Great Lakes of North America. The proposals were favourably received by the Maritime Safety Committee of IMO (then IMCO) in 1964 and governments were urged to advise their ships to follow the routes suggested by the group.

The IMO's responsibility for ships' routeing is also enshrined in SOLAS Chapter V, Regulation 8, which recognizes the Organization as the only international body for establishing such systems, while Rule 10 of the COLREGs (Collision Regulations) prescribes the conduct of vessels when navigating through traffic separation schemes adopted by IMO. The responsibilities of the IMO are also determined under the United Nations Convention on the Law of The Sea (UNCLOS), which designates the IMO as "the competent international organization" in matters of navigational safety, safety of shipping traffic and marine environmental protection. In 1977 the Assembly authorized the Maritime Safety Committee (MSC) to adopt Traffic Separation Schemes (TSS) on the Organization's behalf, in order to speed up the procedure (the MSC normally meets twice a year, the Assembly only once every two years).

Governments of coastal States intending to establish a new vessel routeing system, or amend an existing one, must submit proposed routeing measures to the IMO Sub-Committee on the Safety of Navigation (NAV), which will then evaluate the proposal and make a recommendation regarding its adoption. The recommendation is subsequently passed to the MSC for adoption. As well as traffic separation schemes, other routeing measures adopted by IMO to improve safety at sea include two-way routes, recommended tracks, deep water routes (for the benefit primarily of ships whose ability to manoeuvre is constrained by their draught), precautionary areas (where ships must navigate with particular caution), and areas to be avoided (for reasons of exceptional danger or especially sensitive ecological and environmental factors). Ships' routeing systems and traffic separation schemes that have been approved by IMO, are contained in the IMO Publication, *Ships' Routeing,* a thick volume, which is updated when schemes are amended or new ones added.

The publication includes **General Provisions on Ships' Routeing**, first adopted by IMO in 1973, and subsequently amended over the years, which are aimed at standardizing the design, development, charted presentation and use of routeing measures adopted by IMO. The provisions state that the objective of the principle of ships' routeing is to improve the safety of navigation in converging areas and in areas where the density of traffic is great or where freedom of movement of shipping is inhibited by restricted searoom, the existence of obstructions to navigation, limited depths or unfavourable meteorological conditions".

The following definitions summarise how a Traffic Separations Scheme is designed to function:

The **Traffic Separation Scheme (TSS)** is a vessel routeing measure aimed at the separation of opposing streams of maritime traffic by appropriate means and by the establishment of traffic lanes.

A **Traffic Lane** is an area within defined limits in which one-way traffic is established. Natural obstacles, including those forming separation zones, may constitute a boundary **separation zone or line**, which is a zone or line separating traffic lanes in which ships are proceeding in opposite or nearly opposite directions; or separating a traffic lane from the adjacent sea area; or separating traffic lanes designated for particular classes of ship proceeding in the same direction.

A **roundabout** is a separation point or circular separation zone and a circular traffic lane within defined limits.

An **Inshore traffic zone** is a designated area between the landward boundary of a traffic separation scheme and the adjacent coast

A **recommended route** is a route of undefined width, for the convenience of ships in transit, which is often marked by centreline buoys along a **deep-water route.**

The **deep-water route** is a route within defined limits which has been accurately surveyed for clearance of sea bottom and submerged articles.

A **precautionary area**: an area within defined limits where ships must navigate with particular caution and within which the direction of flow of traffic may be recommended.

An **area to be avoided** is an area within defined limits in which either navigation is particularly hazardous or it is exceptionally important to avoid casualties and which should be avoided by all ships, or by certain classes of ships.

Traffic separation schemes and other ship routeing systems have now been established in most of the major congested shipping areas of the world such as the Strait of Dover, the Malacca Straits, the Strait of Gibraltar and the Öresund, and the number of collisions and groundings in these areas has been dramatically reduced.

At the point of entering a traffic separation scheme in a limited waterway such as an international Strait, vessels passing through the Strait are assigned shipping lanes according to their size, speed and type, so as to ensure that vessels containing hazardous or dangerous cargoes are kept separate from those carrying conventional, non-hazardous loads. They must maintain that lane throughout their passage of the Strait, and must not deviate from their course. They are monitored by the national authority of the coastal State overlooking the Strait throughout their transit, and must ensure that all relevant information concerning their identity and cargo is communicated to the national authority concerned at the time of transit.

Weather conditions can also affect a ship's navigation, and in 1983 IMO adopted resolution A.528(13), *Recommendation on Weather Routeing,* which recognizes that weather routeing, the principle by which ships are provided with "optimum routes" to avoid bad weather, can aid safety. It recommends Governments to advise ships flying their flags of the availability of weather routeing information, particularly that provided by services listed by the World Meteorological Organization.

CNIS REPORTING

In 1966, the Institutes of Navigation in the UK and West Germany published a report proposing maritime traffic separation schemes in a number of geographical areas, and in June 1967 a Traffic Separation Scheme (TSS), the first of its kind in the world, was established and implemented in the Straits of Dover, between the UK and France. This pioneering initiative, based on the principle of separate designated shipping lanes for both directions of passage, led to a significant reduction in the number of collisions between vessels on opposing courses through the Strait. However, at the time, observance of the scheme was purely voluntary, but in 1971 a series of accidents in the Channel led to calls for immediate action. In the most serious incidents, the tanker *Texaco Caribbean* collided with a freighter off the Varne shoals, and during the following night, the wreck of one of the vessels was struck by the freighter *Brandenburg*, which also sank. Some six weeks later, the freighter *Niki* struck the wreckage and sank with the loss of all 21 people on board at the time. As a result, the IMO's Maritime Safety Committee (MSC) meeting of March 1971 recommended that the observance of all Traffic Separation Schemes in operation should be made mandatory, and this recommendation was adopted by the IMO Assembly later the same year. The Traffic Separation Scheme in the Straits of Dover thus became the first mandatory traffic scheme from 1971. The following year, in 1972, the Conference which adopted the Collision Regulations (COLREGs) also made the observance of traffic separation schemes mandatory.

The Strait of Dover became the world's first IMO-approved Traffic Separation Scheme (TSS) in the 1970s, and was the first scheme to implement full radar surveillance. The Channel Navigation Information Service (CNIS) was introduced in 1972 to provide a full radio and radar safety service for all shipping in the Dover Strait, and is jointly operated by the UK and French Authorities from the Dover Maritime Rescue Co-ordination Centre (MRCC) and CROSS Gris Nez in France.

The Strait of Dover is one of the busiest shipping lanes in the world today. It handles a wide variety of ships passing each way through the Strait each day, as well as the frequent sailings of passenger and vehicle ferries across the Channel from the European Continent to the UK and vice versa. All maritime traffic passing through the Strait is directed into a series of tightly-controlled shipping lanes under the Traffic Separation Scheme (TSS) for both directions, with eastbound shipping traversing the French side of the Strait, and westbound traffic traversing the English side of the Strait. The means of controlling these maritime movements is undertaken by the English and French Coastguards within the scope of the CNIS (Channel Navigation Information System) maritime reporting mechanism, and this system is maintained by both authorities from each side of the Channel, with, in principle, information on vessel movements passed from each authority to the other where appropriate.

Unlike other areas of the UK coastline, the Strait of Dover is an area which limits the expanse of water between UK and Continental shores. Because of the limited distances between the UK and France (some 19 Miles between the Foreland and Cap Gris Nez), it is impossible to enforce the normal limits imposed by the provision of the Territorial Sea, i.e. the 12-Mile limit. At this point, only the 3-Mile Limit applies insofar as national Territorial waters are concerned, and the waters within the Strait are monitored by both the UK and French Coastguards.

All ships passing eastwards through the Strait, on the French side of the Channel, must report to the French Coastguards at the CROSS Gris Nez location, and ships passing westwards, on the UK side, must report to CNIS Section of the Maritime and Coastguard Agency (MCA) at the Foreland, overlooking the Port of Dover.

Mandatory Reporting in the Channel itself has only existed since 1999, mainly as a result of the need to monitor maritime traffic following the disaster resulting from the grounding and destruction of the tanker *Erika* off the French Coast. Prior to this, the MAREPS (Marine Reporting System) existed as a voluntary regime, but following a series of marine accidents it was decided to implement a mandatory Marine Reporting System to ensure that every vessel passing through the Strait of Dover reported to either of the national Authorities, depending upon its direction of sailing. The IMO Sub-Committee on the Safety of Navigation at its 46th Session in July 2000 approved a mandatory Ship-Reporting system for the whole of the Channel from the Western Approaches opposite the French Lighthouse at Ouessant (Ushant) up to the existing controls at the Strait of Dover. The system, called MANCHEREP (Channel Reporting), would oblige ships above 300grt to give all information about themselves, including their identity and cargo, to coastal authorities. This system would complement the existing systems of the ship-reporting systems at Ouessant (OUESSREP), implemented in 1996, and the Pas-de-Calais Reporting system at Cap Gris Nez (CALDOVREP), implemented in 1999.

Alongside the mandatory reporting regimes in place, the regime of Traffic Separation Systems (TSS), regulating the distances separating ships sailing in line up or down the Strait, has existed since 1977. Alongside the CNIS regimes using the Vessel Tracking System (VTS) technology, the AIS (Automatic Identification System) is also used to track and monitor the movements of vessels through the Strait subject to and adhering to the Traffic Separation Scheme (TSS), which can be viewed on internet AIS websites such as http://www.miu.com/ais, http://www.aislive.com or http://www.shipais.com portals. However, although AIS was made mandatory for all vessels by the end of 2004, it is still to a degree in its development stage concerning its use by many seaports.

Because of the nature of the International Collision Regulations (COLREGS) concerning Traffic Separation Schemes (specifically **Rule 10** of the **COLREGS**) in limited international waters such as the Strait of Dover, the CNIS Reporting System as applied over Maritime Traffic in the Strait is not only mandatory, but is also enforceable by law. Rule 10 of the COLREGS expressly states that vessels entering into TSS regimes must obey the Rules by maintaining their course and position within the Traffic Separation Scheme throughout the geographical area where it is enforced, and must not deviate from that course governed by the Scheme under any circumstances unless calling at a Port located within the area concerned. Instances have arisen where ships have failed to obey the Traffic Separation Scheme (TSS) rules, and their details have been intercepted by the CNIS office at Dover. A report is then sent to the MCA Enforcement Unit located at Southampton. Details of the rogue vessel concerned and the manner of breach of Rule 10 of the COLREGS are passed to the maritime administration of the vessel's flag state for appropriate action in cases where the vessel is not bound for either a French or UK port, and is simply passing through the Strait. The result is often that the master of the vessel concerned has been prosecuted by the appropriate court of law. Where the vessel is bound for a UK Port, the master may be arrested by the UK authorities and prosecuted under the terms of Rule 10 by a UK Court of Law, with the sentence often being a substantial fine.

The regulations concerning shipping movements through the Strait of Dover have resulted from not only the volume of traffic using the Strait but also the number of accidents and collisions which have taken place over the years. However, the Strait of Dover is not the only narrow strait of water separating two countries in Northern Europe – another is the Öresund, separating Sweden and Denmark. The Öresund, between Denmark and Sweden, makes an interesting comparison with the Strait of Dover, given that where there is a fully-controlled reporting in the Strait of Dover, there is no controlled reporting system in the same way for vessels passing through the Strait between the Kattegat, to the North, and the Baltic Sea, to the South. Although vessels arriving at Danish or Swedish Ports located on the Öresund must report in to those Ports, there is as yet no reporting system similar to the CNIS at the Strait of Dover. The issue of both the Öresund and the Storebaelt, the waterway passing entirely through Danish territory, is covered as a case study in greater detail in part three of this study.

The extent of the Öresund region covers the maritime area from Malmö and Copenhagen in the south to Helsingør (Denmark) and Helsingborg (Sweden) in the north, and thus covers the limits of the waters between Denmark and Sweden. Given the limit of distance between the two countries, there is no defined area of international water between both countries, and this has resulted in an agreement between the two countries concerning the definition of the contiguous zones encompassed by the Sound, and the rights and obligations of vessels sailing through the Sound in either direction. At its widest point, between København and Malmö, the Öresund is some 15 km across, allowing for a combined road and rail crossing in the form of a tunnel, and artificial island (Pebarholm) and a 7.8 km bridge. At its narrowest point, between Helsingør (Denmark) and Helsingborg (Sweden), it is less than 10 km across.

An AIS Chart also shows the position of all commercial vessels sailing within the region. It should also be noted that although the Öresund at its narrowest point, between Helsingør

(Denmark) and Helsingborg (Sweden), at the northern end of the Strait, is narrower than the Strait of Dover, there is now a VTS Reporting System, implemented by the Danish and Swedish authorities in mid-2007, requiring vessels to report to the Maritime Authorities on either side of the Strait depending upon their direction of sailing. The system used is more or less the same as that used on the Storebaelt (Great Belt) to the west of the Danish island of Sjaelland. There is therefore a form of Traffic Separation Scheme such as operates within the Strait of Dover, although less complex than that used in the Straits of Dover. The reporting system in operation concerns vessels reporting into a port of arrival within the Öresund region. Vessels transiting the Strait en route for a destination beyond the Öresund do not submit any form of report to either country bordering the Strait.

The matter is compounded by the fact that at its narrowest point between Helsingør, in Denmark, and Helsingborg, in Sweden, the Öresund is less than 10 miles in breadth. Indeed, such is the narrowness of the Strait at that point that there is no international area of waters between the areas bounded by national territorial waters on each side. Hence the perceived need for a mandatory reporting system obliging vessels passing through the Strait to report to either the Danish or Swedish Maritime Authorities depending upon their direction of sailing and the side of the Strait in which they are located.

MARINE REPORTING – 24 HOURS IN ADVANCE

The European Union published a Directive, 2002/6/EC in February 2002, followed by a Communication in May 2003 on the enhancement of Maritime Transport Security, including a Proposal for the Regulation pertaining to the enhancing of Ship and Port Facility Security, in line with existing regulations established by the IMO and SOLAS. Although the Proposal embraced much of the existing areas of concern relating to maritime security and marine reporting, especially concerning the security of ships and their crews, neither did it seek to integrate all the relevant reporting mechanisms, nor did it seek to grant further powers of maritime control to the Admiralty, Customs and Coastguard Authorities in the same way that the US and Canadian Governments have delegated such powers to their respective national authorities (**COM(2003) 229, Paragraphs 2.5 & 2.6**). However, the PROSECUR (PROcedure of SECURity) proposal contained in EU Commission Communication COM(2002) 233, also referred to in COM(2003) 229 allows for direct links and exchanges between the Ports and Customs Authorities and the Immigration Authorities responsible for checking people at the external borders under the scope of the Schengen Agreement of 1990 (**Paragraphs 15, 33 & 34**).

The present system of Marine Reporting in normal circumstances requires vessels to report to the port of arrival 24 hours in advance of their arrival, using both electronic means and IMO FAL Documents. This means that the vessel does not report to the national authority, unless it is carrying dangerous or hazardous cargoes, and even then the reporting mechanism is to a large extent on a voluntary basis and cannot necessarily be enforced other than for vessels entering U.S. territorial waters under the Automated Manifest System (AMS), where the reporting mechanism is mandatory. Failure of the vessel to report into the U.S. Authorities, in particular

U.S. Coastguard, can result in the vessel being refused entry into the U.S. Port in question. For deep-sea vessels approaching EU waters, the 24 hour rule implies that the vessel is approaching UK / EU waters from out in the international high seas, and is shortly to enter the 200-mile zone. From this point, it heads toward the 12-mile and 3-mile limits respectively. In reality, the vessel's Agent will report the vessel's impending arrival to the Port of destination with any information relating to the vessel and its cargo.

For vessels sailing from within the EU, this system is less effective. Given that the greatest distance across the North Sea, for example between the UK and Norway or Sweden, allows for around 20-24 hours, the vessel is effectively reporting into the UK port at the time of its departure. Only in the case of sailings to the UK from Spain, Portugal and the Baltic Sea, would the vessel be reporting into the UK port while it was in mid-voyage. However, as stated earlier in the text, the need to report cargoes in the case of intra-EU sailings is not as necessary a requirement at present as is the need to report cargoes and the nature of the vessel arriving from a non-EU source, e.g. Canada or the United States, as the vessel may well be operating under the scope of the Authorised Regular Operator initiative.

It should be pointed out at this stage that under the UN Convention of the Law of the Sea as it stands, a vessel is not required by law to report in to a national authority, especially given the rights of Innocent Passage, as long as it displays its national flag and other identification markings. Only if a specific rule or agreement exists with particular countries concerning reporting requirements will a vessel be required to report in to a national authority, for example the CNIS in the Strait of Dover. Indeed, there appears to be no form of national regulatory control over shipping passing through the North Channel, between Northern Ireland and Scotland, which may be classed as being national territorial waters and thus subject in their entirety to UK national controls. The original MAREP (Marine Reporting System) used in the Channel, was entirely voluntary, and could not be enforced by either the French or UK Maritime Authorities.

One advantage of the 24-hour rule is that if there is a requirement for HM Customs & Excise to be present at the time of berthing of the vessel, they are able to arrange teams to carry out any examinations required at the port concerned. However, given the sparse nature of such teams around the UK, HM Customs & Excise relies heavily on intelligence reports, as well as the good offices of the port authorities to inform them of any irregular activities concerning the arrival or seaward activities of any particular vessel.

However, should a vessel deviate from its course to another port because of problems or weather conditions, further reports are required to inform the new port of arrival of its deviation in course. This may lead to confusion or at best hurried arrangements at the port of arrival to receive the vessel, as well as the need to ensure that onward transport is arranged for cargoes or passengers. At present, there appears to be no means of disseminating information throughout the UK or EU port system to allow for sudden deviations by vessels, or at least to warn other ports in the case of major hazards or potential incidents pertaining to dangerous cargoes.

If there is a problem with passengers, e.g. terrorism or, more likely, accidents at sea, casualties or fatalities, HM Coastguard is informed and appropriate action can be taken to effect evacuations or rescues, along with the services of the RNLI Lifeboats. It should, however, be noted that such incidents will be reported to HM Coastguard as a matter if urgent necessity and not as a matter of general policy. Other than incidents of such kinds, HM Coastguard does not involve itself in Marine Reporting other than the CNIS activities undertaken at Dover, unlike its US and Canadian counterparts, which insist upon receiving information about every vessel approaching and sailing through waters close to the North American coastline. Equally, unlike the US and Canadian Coastguards, the UK Coastguard regime has no powers of arrest; these are left in the hands of the Admiralty. However, HM Customs & Excise does still have the resources to arrest or seize vessels in UK waters in the form of the vessels and teams used by its Marine Agency wherever they are required, although due to the relatively small number of these vessels, they cannot be sent to every seaport at once, hence the value of intelligence in locating a suspect commercial vessel or pleasure craft.

In these respects, the 24-hour Reporting rule is extremely limited in its effectiveness. It allows for certain information concerning a vessel and its contents to be received on a limited basis but does not strictly allow for action to be taken in the event of potential problems such as accidents or terrorist threats. Much can happen in the space of 24 hours, and the present system risks rendering the UK or the EU vulnerable to various kinds of potential problems. Indeed, the 24-hour rule has hitherto not prevented marine accidents from occurring, such as oilspills, collisions, groundings and wrecks on the EU shoreline. These disasters still occur from time to time regardless of procedures taken by vessels to submit reports to their port of arrival.

CHAPTER FIVE

CONVENTIONS, CODES AND CONTROLS

THE COMITÉ MARITIME INTERNATIONAL (CMI)

The Comité Maritime International (CMI), formally established in 1897, is the oldest international organisation in the maritime field worldwide. Its foundation followed that of the International Law Association (ILA) by several years, and indeed the CMI was seen as being a descendant of the ILA. However, the CMI was the first international organisation to be concerned exclusively with maritime law and related commercial practices. Its origins date back further than 1897, and stem from the efforts of a group led by Belgian commercial and political people who came together in the early 1880s to discuss and to put before the newly-founded ILA a proposal to codify the whole body of maritime international law. It had been acknowledged and accepted for some time that the courts of admiralty and maritime law were courts of international law, and in the 1860s the first international codification of the principles of General Average (the basic principle of marine insurance) was drawn up in London, and this culminated in the ILA conference of 1890 that adopted the first **York/Antwerp Rules** relating to damage caused to both vessels and cargo, and the subsequent remedies and means of compensation for such damage. These Rules have been subsequently amended and reviewed on many occasions, with the most recent amendments being in 1994.

Following two failed diplomatic international conferences in Antwerp and Brussels in the 1880s concerning attempts to internationally unify the various codifications of maritime law, the CMI was formally organised as direct outgrowth of these two conferences. The ILA decided not to continue with such codification, and it was eventually agreed by the ILA that those interested in pursuing such a goal should form a separate body whose purpose would be to continue with this task. The agreement with the ILA was announced in a circular letter from the Comité Maritime International dated 2 July 1896. From this it may be deduced that the embryonic CMI already existed in an initial form, however limited, prior to its formal establishment in 1897. The letter conveyed the decision that the CMI would promote the establishment of national associations of maritime law, and would ensure a structured relationship between these associations. It also stated that each national association should be composed of lawyers, mercantile and insurance interests, and that its goal should ultimately be the unification and codification of international maritime law.

The CMI was established in Antwerp, Belgium, by several eminent Belgian figures, most of whom were involved in the maritime sector from a legal and insurance aspect, and these were joined by other figures from the Belgian Government, the judiciary and legal profession, shipowners, average adjusters, and insurance and commercial figures, all of whom signed a second circular letter in August 1896. This letter suggested that there should be formed a "Belgian Association for the Unification of Maritime Law". The same people who were to form the Association were also to form the first Bureau of the CMI.

The Belgian initiative was soon followed by organising efforts in other countries. The CMI's founders were joined by people from other countries who were actively working to organise national maritime law associations, and all these figures convened in Brussels in June 1897 to formally establish the CMI as the parent international organisation to continue the effort to unify the world's maritime laws and to adopt a constitution for the CMI. Representatives of 8 nations attended the meeting, this first international conference of the CMI led directly to the formation of several new National Member Associations (NMAs).

The original failed conferences of the 1880s also laid the foundation for the partnership between the Belgian Government and the Comité that resulted in the series of "Brussels Diplomatic Conferences on Maritime Law". These conferences adopted the many conventions and protocols drafted by the CMI over more than 80 years, and were held between 1910 (Collision and Salvage) and 1979 (Hague-Visby / SDR). The CMI Liverpool Conference of 1905 adopted a resolution requesting the Belgian Government to convene an international conference to examine the Comité's draft conventions on collision and salvage, and so the first Conférence Diplomatique de Droit Maritime (Diplomatic Conference on Maritime Law) took place in 1910, concerned primarily with issues of Collision and Salvage.

The Constitution was eventually drawn up, setting up the number of both Titular Members (9 per country) and delegates of NMAs (6 per NMA). It also established a "Bureau Permanent" as the interim governing body of the CMI to function between Conferences. Conferences were to be held once every year, but such conferences were also to fulfil the role of a general assembly and thus were not solely limited to the debate and adoption of drafts and resolutions. Between 1899 and 1955, the numbers of Titular members were increased to 10 per country, and in 1955, the Madrid Conference adopted the constitution which allowed for one or more Vice-Presidents, one or more Secretaries-General and Secretaries and a Secretary for Administration, as well as the President, Treasurer and one delegate from each NMA. An Administrative Council was added, and was given most of the functions originally assigned to the Bureau Permanent. To date, the number of International Conferences has declined, only convening every 3-4 years. Because the administrative structure of the CMI eventually became too unwieldy and unmanageable, the 1972 Antwerp Conference was devoted to reforming the constitutional structure of the Comité, and the Administrative Council and Bureau Permanent were replaced by an Executive Council composed of the CMI Officers and 6 representatives elected by the Assembly. The International Conference was itself replaced by an annual General Assembly of the NMAs. A further Constitution was adopted at the 1992 Genoa Assembly, and effectively completed the restructuring of the CMI, as well as creating two new categories of membership and clarifying a third, namely the category of Consultative Membership, which brings the CMI into closer working relationships with other international organisations such as the United Nations and the IMO. However, certain roles of the CMI have been effectively removed from the organisation's function and transferred to other bodies. With the formation of the Legal Committee of the International Maritime Organisation (IMO) in 1968 following the *Torrey Canyon* disaster and resulting pollution, the IMO began to take over from the Government of Belgium the role of organising diplomatic conferences in the field of maritime law. However, this did not bring the preparatory role of the CMI to an end, although it may not be appreciated how much the work has been carried out by the International Sub-Committees and subsequent Conferences of the Comité in order to compose the initial drafting of every convention considered by the IMO Legal Committee except the 1969 Intervention Committee and 1973 Protocol and the 1996 HNS Convention.

In addition to its continuing work on maritime conventions, the CMI is involved in the formation and maintenance of codes of maritime and related commercial practice. In 1990 the CMI adopted uniform rules for SeaWaybills, and for most of its existence the Comité has been custodian of the York/Antwerp Rules for the adjustment of General Average, which were recently revised by the CMI at its 35th International Conference in Sydney in 1994. The Comité was also responsible for much of the law relating to the carriage of goods at sea, including the updated laws contained in the Hague-Visby Rules of 1968, which, in the case of the UK, became part of the Law contained in the Carriage of Goods by Sea Act (COGSA) of 1971. The Comité is presently working with UNCITRAL (United Nations Committee on International Trade Law) on standards for Electronic Document/Data Interchange (EDI) which covers the Electronic Bill of Lading. There is also the possibility of the CMI co-ordinating the work of a number of non-governmental international organisations in a study for UNCITRAL of the issues involved in the structuring of a comprehensive convention on maritime transport which could have a scope far beyond that of any of the past conventions. The 1972 Constitution declared the object of the Comité to be the unification of maritime and commercial law, maritime customs, usages and practices. The 1992 Constitution broadened the scope of activity of the Comité to cover maritime law in all its aspects, including the CMI's work carried out on the legal status of offshore mobile craft involved in oil exploration and production beneath the high seas.

THE INTERNATIONAL MARITIME ORGANISATION (IMO)

The International Maritime Organisation (IMO), the division of the United Nations (UN) charged with the control of maritime affairs, is based in London, and oversees all aspects of maritime activity, ranging from the management, security and safety of vessels to marine pollution, the marine environment and maritime cargo security. It is recognised that the ownership and management chain surrounding any vessel, its movements and what it carries can embrace many countries, considering that most vessels spend their economic life moving between different countries and hence many different national jurisdictions and maritime regimes, often far from their country of registry. Indeed, the nationality and ownership of the vessels may differ radically, with the vessel being registered in a location completely different from the headquarters of the organisation owning it. Equally, the cargo it carries may originate in so many countries, it is almost impossible to apply a specific regime to that cargo once it is being carried on the high seas. There has therefore been the need for a long time for a regime and structure of international standards to regulate shipping, which can be adopted and accepted by all the world's maritime countries. The first maritime treaties date back to the 19th century, including the introduction of the universally-accepted Load Line (The "Plimsoll Line", invented by Samuel Plimsoll). Later, the disaster of the liner *Titanic* in 1912 gave rise to the first international safety of life at sea convention – later consolidated as the SOLAS (Safety of Life at Sea) Convention, still the most important international Treaty addressing maritime safety.

The Convention establishing the International Maritime Organisation (IMO) was adopted in 1948, and entered into force in 1958. Until 1982, it was known as the IMCO, the Intergovernmental Maritime Consultative Organisation. The IMO as an organisation met for the first time in 1959. Its main task has been to develop and maintain a comprehensive regulatory framework for shipping and its present remit includes safety of vessels, environmental concerns, legal matters, technical co-operation, maritime security and the efficiency of shipping. It is based in London, in the UK, and comprises 167 Member States and three Associate Members. It comprises an Assembly and a Council, comprising 32 member states elected by the Assembly, which acts as the governing body. There are also several specialised Committees and Sub-Committees, which are as follows:

- Maritime Safety Committee (Safety at Sea);

- Marine Environment Protection Committee (Marine Pollution);

- Technical Co-Operation Committee (Implementation of Technical Measures);

- Legal Committee (Legal matters within the scope of the Organisation);

- Facilitation Committee (Reducing the formalities and simplifying the documentation associated with the flow of international maritime traffic, especially concerning vessels entering or leaving ports and terminals).

These Committees are the focus for the technical work to review and update existing legislation or to develop and adopt new maritime-based regulations, with meetings attended by maritime experts from Member Governments, together with those from interested intergovernmental and non-governmental organisations. The result is a comprehensive body of international conventions, supported by a large number of recommendations governing and concerning every aspect of shipping. There are measures aimed at the prevention of accidents, including standards for vessel design, construction, equipment, operation and manning. Key Treaties include SOLAS (Safety of Lives at Sea), first agreed in 1960, which was the first most important of all Treaties dealing with maritime safety. The SOLAS was further enhanced and reviewed in 1974, and it is this version which provides the basis for all international maritime safety standards used today, the latest standards including the removal of all combustible substances and materials from the interiors of commercial vessels as part of the SOLAS 2010 regulations. The MARPOL (Marine Pollution) convention for the prevention of pollution by ships was later agreed, following the disastrous wreck of the *Torrey Canyon* tanker off the Isles of Scilly in 1967 and the subsequent oil pollution of the nearby coastlines as a result of the oil spillage from the wreck, estimated at 120,000 tonnes of crude oil. The result was the International Convention for the Prevention of Pollution from Ships, 1973, as modified by the later Protocol of 1978 relating thereto, and referred to as MARPOL 73/78. This convention covers not only oil spillage and pollution but also pollution by chemicals, goods in packaged form, sewage, garbage and general waste, and air pollution, including that caused by emissions from the engines of marine vessels. This was followed by the STCW Convention on standards of training for seafarers.

There are also measures concerning distress and safety communications, one notable result of which was the establishment of the Global Maritime Distress and Safety System (GMDSS), which was adopted in 1988, was phased in from 1992 and became fully operational in 1999. The International Convention on Search and Rescue (SAR) was initiated in the 1970s, which eventually established the International Mobile Satellite Organisation (IMSO), which has greatly enhanced the provision of radio and other messages to ships. There is also the International Convention on Oil Pollution Preparedness, Response and Co-operation. Further measures include the establishment of Compensation and Liability Regimes, including the International Convention on Civil Liability for Oil Pollution Damage, the convention establishing the International Fund for Compensation for Oil Pollution Damage, and the Athens Convention covering liability and compensation for passengers at sea. Two treaties were adopted in 1969 and 1971, enabling the victims of oil pollution to obtain compensation much more easily and quickly than had hitherto been possible. Both treaties were amended in 1992 and again in 2000, in order to increase the limits of compensation payable to the victims of pollution. A number of other legal conventions have been developed since then, most of which concern liability and compensation issues.

Inspection and monitoring of compliance with all the relevant Conventions and Regulations are the responsibility of all the Member States of the IMO, but the adoption of a Voluntary IMO Member State Audit Scheme is expected to play a key role in enhancing the implementation of IMO Standards. The International Maritime Organisation also has an extensive technical co-operation programme, which identifies needs among members whose resources are more limited, and matches them to assistance, such as education and training. The IMO has also founded three advanced level Maritime Educational Institutes in Malmö in Sweden (The World Maritime University – WMU), Malta, and Trieste, Italy.

THE IMO FAL CONVENTION

The original Convention on the Facilitation of International Maritime Traffic was agreed by all the governments subscribing to the International Maritime Organisation (IMO) in 1965, and has remained in force ever since. Its purpose is to simplify and reduce to a minimum the formalities, documentary requirements and procedures on the arrival, stay in port and departure from port of all commercial ships engaged in international voyages. It refers in general to those ships and shipping lines not included in the schedule of Authorised Regular Operators, i.e. those shipping lines involved in Ro-Ro short sea operations within European waters, and also excludes warships and pleasure vessels, i.e. yachts.

The Convention refers to the summary declaration to the Port Authority and to the national Customs Authority of the following details:

- Cargoes;
- Crew's effects;
- Crew members;
- Passenger Lists;
- Ship's Stores;
- General Declarations;
- Maritime Declarations of Health.

The purpose of the regime is to enable both the port of arrival and the Customs Authority to assess the contents of the ship without the need to scrutinise in minute detail the ship once it arrives, and thus to clear it through all relevant national controls in the shortest time possible.

In the **General Declaration**, which must be dated and signed by the Ship's Master or the Shipping Agent, the information required by the appropriate authorities is as follows:

- Name and Description of Vessel;
- Nationality of Vessel;
- Registry details;
- Tonnage details;
- Master's name;
- Name and address of Vessel's Agent;
- Brief description of cargo;
- Number of crew;
- Number of Passengers;
- Brief details of voyage;
- Date and time of arrival or departure;

- Port of Arrival or Departure;

- Location of vessel in the port.

The FAL 2 **Cargo Declaration** for arrival purposes contains details of the ship and the Ship's Master, as well as the ports of arrival and departure, and details of both the cargoes and Shipping Documents, e.g. Bills of Lading, as well as the destination of any cargo remaining on board following the unloading of cargo at the port in question. For departure purposes, the Declaration must contain details of the cargo loaded aboard, and details of all the Shipping Documents, e.g. Bills of Lading, associated therewith. Cargoes of Hazardous or Dangerous Goods should be included, but should also be declared separately on specific declarations.

The **Crew Declaration** details the crew and their respective ranks and positions.

The **Passenger Declaration** details the names and addresses of all passengers aboard ship, their point of embarkation and point of disembarkation.

The **Maritime Declaration of Health** provides information required by Port Health Authorities concerning the state of health of all persons aboard vessel, be they crew or passengers, during the voyage and on arrival at port.

The Cargo Declaration, Crew Effects Declaration and Ship's Stores Declarations are subject to scrutiny by the national Customs Authority, and allow Customs Officers to board ship while in port and verify the details of the Declarations. It should be pointed out that all vessels while in Port are subject to Customs controls, and thus may not leave port without Customs clearance.

The Convention also allows for facilities by the port to clear cargoes and passengers off ships, and to ensure that all clearance formalities are conducted as swiftly and efficiently as possible, in order to avoid unnecessary delays.

It should be noted that the IMO FAL Declarations for the Crew of a vessel do not substitute and are not substituted by the formalities laid down by either the IMO ISPS Code or national Customs Import Declaration requirements, but are complementary to them, thus resulting in additional bureaucracy for vessels and port authorities alike. Although the element of security is contained in both regimes, there are different levels of security applied depending upon the specific regime required. It would appear that with the introduction of the ISPS regime, the Shipping Lines, Agents and Port Authorities have become increasingly embroiled in greater amounts of administration in dealing with the respective FAL and ISPS regimes, and this has inevitable led to an overlap in the requirements of each regime.

The FAL Forms are still generally completed in manual format, although the initiative now exists to translate all the Forms into electronic format using EDI (Electronic Data Interface) technology. In a booklet published in 2001 (**FAL.5/Circ.15, February 2001**), the IMO recommended that the

FAL regime be converted into electronic transmission by vessels and agents using the EDI regime, which was also being introduced into other reporting facilities, especially Customs Declarations. It was decided that all the FAL Forms could be transmitted in electronic format using EDI, and that other documents of a manual nature could be dispensed with by the appropriate public authorities. The EDI system would allow for the download and derivation of a hard copy format of the appropriate FAL Form, which could be stored on computer for record purposes, and printed off when required as documentary evidence.

The Electronic Declarations are designated in UN/EDIFACT format as follows:

- **FAL Form 1** - IMO General Declaration (CUSREP);

- **FAL Form 2** - IMO Cargo Declaration (CUSCAR);

- **FAL Form 3** - IMO Ship's Stores Declaration (Inventory Report Message – INVRPT);

- **FAL Form 5** - IMO Crew List (PAXLST);

- **FAL Form 6** - IMO Passenger Declaration (PAXLST);

- **FAL Form 7** - IMO Dangerous Goods Manifest (International Forwarding and Transport Dangerous Goods Notification Message – IFTDGN).

It should be noted that there is no EDI equivalent of the FAL Form 4, the Crew's Effects Declaration. Also, the FAL Forms 5 and 6 have been integrated as one single Crew and Passenger List, simply referring to all persons aboard vessel, crew and/or passengers.

The CUSCAR Cargo Manifest, presented by the Shipping Line or the Agents to Customs at the time of the Ship's arrival in Port, is seen as a major issue by Shipping Lines, Customs and Coastguard alike, because of its sheer bulk. It may be transmitted separately from the FAL summary form, but is seen by many as an encumbrance rather than an advantage. The brief summary of the Cargo Manifest as a FAL Form 2 does not detail all cargoes in depth, and the Ship's Manifest has always been seen as a separate document, issued by the Shipping Line to the Ship's Master at the time of sailing. With the introduction of the new, huge Super Post Panamax Container Vessels of the size of 7,000 TEU (Twenty-Foot Equivalent Unit) plus (at present 8,000 TEU+ vessels are being constructed and introduced into service), the sheer volume of information provided on the cargo manifest is in many cases too much for the average computer to cope with, and even in ZIP format, provides problems in terms of download and analysis of cargo information. A further problem emerges concerning the information provided per container, where consolidated groupage cargoes are described in the Bill of Lading as "Said to Contain…" or "Freight of all Kinds", statements outlawed by the United States for Import purposes. This scenario leaves wide open the possibility of omissions in information presented to Customs, Coastguards and Port Authorities concerning each individual cargo, especially where cargoes of a dangerous or hazardous nature are concerned. These issues are addressed in a later section of Part II of the study. Customs in the UK has already admitted that it is unable to fully scrutinise all details of the existing CUSCAR manifests for several reasons:

- It leaves all Import Declarations to the Trader, i.e. the Importer, or the Clearing Agent;
- It prefers to ensure that all cargoes leave the port of import as quickly as possible;
- It cannot distinguish cargoes based on a consolidated entry in the manifest;
- There is too much information to digest from the present reports from the large container ships.

With the increasing passing of responsibility for the accuracy of Customs Declarations to the trader or the agent, it would appear that Customs are no longer able or even willing to spend vast amounts of resources in examining cargo manifests, and would only scrutinise details on a purely random basis, or on the grounds of prior information referring to the suspect nature of a specific container. Indeed, most examinations of containers at the port by Customs are conducted through the container scans undertaken on a random basis. The cargo manifest will be transmitted to the port authority and hence derived and downloaded in theory by the various agents clearing import consignments carried by all incoming ships. In reality, most import clearances are still undertaken by the clearing agent based on the clearance instructions given by the importer in the form of specific documentation, such as Invoices, Packing Lists and Bills of Lading.

ISPS

As shown in this paper, Maritime Security encompasses a variety of issues, but refers in different ways to different aspects of the Maritime Sector. In order to enhance Maritime Security for both vessels and ports, through amendments to SOLAS Chapters V and XI, the IMO introduced in 2002 the International Ship and Port Facility Security (ISPS) Code, which came into force in July 2004. Alongside the implementation of the Code, International Ship Security Certificates (ISSCs) are issued to each ship able to satisfy the Maritime Security conditions laid down by the IMO. Other technical co-operation and co-operative work is being carried out with other UN Organisations such as the International Labour Organisation and the World Customs Organisation.

Chapter XI of the SOLAS has been split into two Sections, XI-1 and XI-2. The newly-created Section XI-2 deals with Special Measures to enhance Maritime Security, and includes a requirement for ships and shipping companies to comply with the ISPS Code. Chapter V of SOLAS also made the requirement for all vessels over 300grt to install the AIS facility, now compulsory in all such vessels. These requirements form a framework through which ships and port facilities can co-operate to detect and deter acts which pose a threat to maritime security, although the regulatory provisions do not extend to the actual response to security incidents, or to any necessary clear-up activities following such an incident.

The ISPS Code deals with the following activities:

- Enabling the detection and deterrence of security threats within an international framework;

- Establishing roles and responsibilities;

- Enabling the collection and exchange of security information;

- Providing a methodology for assessing security;

- Ensuring that adequate security measures are in place;

- Gathering and assessing information;

- Maintaining communication protocols;

- Restricting access; preventing the introduction of unauthorised weapons, etc;

- Providing the means to raise alarms;

- Implementing vessel and port security plans, and ensuring that training and procedural drills are properly conducted.

In practice, the ISPS Code requires all ships to have a recognised and competent Security Officer, as well as a recognised Security Office in each Shipping Company, including its address and contact details. The Master of the Ship must report all necessary security details, including details of its complement and identification, to the Port Authority upon or prior to arrival at the port of destination. Action Checklists are maintained by both the Port Authority and the Vessel concerning such security measures, although these do not include the monitoring and inspection of cargoes other than the mandatory reporting of hazardous or dangerous cargoes.

VESSEL TRAFFIC SERVICES (VTS)

Traffic Separation Schemes (TSS) and other ships' routeing systems can be integrated with a **Vessel Traffic Service (VTS)** system, which is defined and intended as a service designed to improve the safety and efficiency of vessel traffic and to protect the marine environment. VTS may range from the provision of simple information messages to ships navigating in certain areas, such as the position of other marine traffic or meteorological hazard warnings, to the extensive management of marine traffic within a port area or a waterway.

Generally, ships entering a VTS area report to the authorities, usually by radio, and may be tracked by the VTS control center, usually located at or close to a port. Ships must keep watch on a specific VHF radio frequency (set at specific Channels, such as Channel 11 or 15) for navigational or other warnings, while they may be contacted directly by the VTS operator if there is risk of an incident or, in areas where traffic flow is regulated, to be given advice on when or where to proceed. The VTS operator watches a computer screen monitor to monitor the vessel's movement as it enters or exits the river or estuary channel, along with the movements of other vessels in the vicinity.

Traditionally, the master of a ship is made responsible for a ship's course and speed, assisted by a pilot where necessary, especially when navigating in confines such as rivers or estuaries. Originally, ships approaching a port would announce their arrival using flag signals, but with the development of wireless radio in the late 19th century, radio contact became more important. However, the development of radar (from the acronym RADAR – Radio Detection and Ranging) during World War II made it possible to accurately monitor and track shipping traffic. The world's first harbour surveillance radar was inaugurated at the Port of Liverpool, England, in July 1948 (although it is claimed that a basic system was operating on the Isle of Man immediately prior to this) and in March 1950, a radar surveillance system was established at Long Beach, California, the first such system in the United States.

The ability of the coastal authority to keep track of shipping traffic by radar, combined with the facility to transmit messages concerning navigation to those ships by radio, therefore constituted the first formal VTS systems. The value of VTS in navigation safety was first recognized by the International Maritime Organisation (IMO) in Resolution A.158 (ES.IV) *Recommendation on Port Advisory Systems* adopted in 1968, but as technology advanced and the equipment to track and monitor shipping traffic became more sophisticated, it was clear guidelines were needed on standardising procedures in setting up VTS. In particular, it became apparent that there was a need to clarify when a VTS might be established and to allay fears in some quarters that a VTS might impinge on the ship's master's responsibility for navigating the vessel.

As a result, the IMO adopted Resolution A.578 (14) *Guidelines for Vessel Traffic Services* in 1985, which stated that VTS was particularly appropriate in the approaches and access channels of a port and in areas having high traffic density, movements of noxious or dangerous cargoes, navigational difficulties, narrow channels, or environmental sensitivity. The Guidelines also made clear that decisions concerning effective navigation and manoeuvring of the vessel remained the responsibility of the ship's master. The Guidelines also highlighted the importance of pilotage in VTS and reporting procedures for ships passing through an area where a VTS system operates.

The revised *Guidelines for Vessel Traffic Services, including Guidelines on Recruitment, Qualifications and Training of VTS Operators,* were adopted as Assembly Resolution A.857(20) in November 1997. The Guidelines update and expand on the now revoked resolution A.578 (14) and are associated with a new SOLAS regulation V/8-2 on VTS.

Vessel Traffic Services were not specifically referred to in the International Convention for the Safety of Life at Sea (SOLAS) 1974, but in June 1997 the IMO's Maritime Safety Committee adopted a new Regulation 8-2 to Chapter V (Safety of Navigation), which sets out when VTS can be implemented. The regulation states that VTS contribute to the safety of life at sea, safety and efficiency of navigation and the protection of the marine environment, adjacent shore areas, worksites and offshore installations from possible adverse effects of maritime traffic. National governments may establish VTS when, in their opinion, the volume of traffic or the degree of risk justifies such services. However, it is stipulated by the IMO that no VTS system should prejudice the "rights and duties of governments under international law" and a VTS system may only be made mandatory in sea areas within a State's territorial waters. The regulation entered into force on 1 July 1999.

The process of vessel and port interface concerning information given at the time the vessel enters or leaves port revolves around the use of Vessel Traffic System (VTS) reporting. There is a need for every vessel, whether leaving or entering port, or transiting through international channels restricted in width, to make its existence known to other vessels in the vicinity and hence identify itself, especially as dictated under the EU Vessel Traffic Monitoring Directive (VMTD), 2002/59/EC, and incorporated in the UK Vessel Traffic Monitoring and Reporting Regulations of 2004. For this reason, most major ports and stations overlooking international Straits operate an electronic Vessel Traffic Monitoring System, and several VHF channels are open for the purposes of radio communication between the Port Control regime and the vessel itself. Computer graphics are used to display the position of a particular vessel at any time during their approach to or departure from the port itself, and these graphics illustrate the ship's position relative to other ships in the vicinity, and its projected course.

The VTS regime is categorised in 4 levels:

- **Information** (The vessel displays its position, by AIS and Radar Identification);

- **Contributory** (The vessel physically reports into the Port);

- **Navigational Assistance** (The Port VTS Controllers offer guidance to and advise the ship of its position in relation to other Ships and Navigation through Channels);

- **Traffic Organisation** (Orders are given to each ship to alter course or to navigate to its berthing location).

It should be noted that the Port can advise a ship to alter course to take specific action, but the Port cannot order a ship to take action. Any navigational decisions must still be left to the Ship's Master or the Pilot in charge of the ship while entering or leaving port.

SOLENT AND PORT OF SOUTHAMPTON VTS

An illustration of how a typical VTS system operates can be found in the example of the Solent and Port of Southampton VTS system, covering the whole of not only the Port of Southampton but also Southampton Water and all the other ports, wharves and jetties located thereon, plus the areas covering Portsmouth (both commercial and naval activities) and the Isle of Wight. Incidentally, Southampton is also the Headquarters of the Maritime and Coastguard Agency, so there is every reason to assume that the MCA would want to ensure that maritime reporting regimes are properly undertaken close to home.

In this case, VTS has been used to great effect. The Port of Southampton uses a VTS system which controls not only Southampton water, but also the Solent. This is required because of the complexity of shipping movements throughout the area, considering the following activities:

- Deep Sea Container vessels;
- Chemical and Hydrocarbon Carriers;
- Cruise Liners;
- Short Sea Ferries;
- Isle of Wight ferries;
- Warships out of Portsmouth.

The VTS system is operated primarily by the Port of Southampton, but accounts for all shipping in the area other than simply what is departing from or arriving at the Port of Southampton, including oil tankers using the Fawley facility, and the vessels serving both Portsmouth and the Isle of Wight and thus local to the Solent.

The Port of Southampton is one of the largest ports in the South of England, and ranks alongside the Port of Felixstowe in the volume of container traffic handled. It is also home to Cunard Line, now part of the US-owned Carnival Corporation, which owns the liners *Queen Elizabeth*, *Queen Victoria* and *Queen Mary 2*, which are both based at Southampton. The waters used by vessels out of Southampton are illustrated in the following chart, which also shows the navigation channels used by the vessels. The restrictions in width and depth of the channels in Southampton water should also be noted, and to what extent great care is required when negotiating these waterways.

From the above chart, a more detailed version of the previous chart, the complexity of vessel movements in and around the Solent and Southampton water can be deduced, without needing to physically track each movement using either the VTS or AIS systems. The very location of the Channels shows the need for such controls, given the daily volume in vessel traffic. This is borne out by the AIS image below of the same area, showing the complexity of vessel traffic movements within the Southampton Water and Solent areas, and outwards into the adjacent reaches of the Channel.

The AIS image identifies vessels in the area, but does not allow for contact to be made with those vessels. Rather, it provides a passive monitoring image of the movements of each vessel over a specified period of time. The VTS system allows not only for the image of vessel movements in the area, but also provides for an active monitoring system facilitating contact with the vessels concerned using the appropriate VHF Channel frequency.

An example of a VTS monitor display is shown in the diagram below for the Solent and Southampton Water. Note the Channel depths and the various markers positioned throughout the channels, and compare these markers with the channel markings and depths shown on the first illustrated chart of the area. The difference is that, where the previous chart was based on a manual format, the following chart is based on electronic format and can therefore be used by both vessels and land-based control rooms for traffic monitoring purposes. On the electronic version, updates can be input on a regular basis, unlike the need to completely reprint manual versions. Such systems thus allow the VTS operator to monitor the vessel's movement along a channel, and to identify courses appropriate for the safe navigation of that vessel. Where the channel narrows and becomes more restrictive, there is a greater need for the close monitoring of the vessel concerned, especially as it will be pursuing a course allowing for safe passage away from other vessels in the vicinity. The VTS Operators on shore are able to communicate with any of the vessels shown on the diagram using the appropriate VHF Channel, and can guide them through the channels as well as enabling them to maintain course with relation to other vessels in the vicinity. Information for mariners concerning maritime conditions can also be obtained from the VTS system using the appropriate VHF Channel.

The VTS system enables the shore-based operator at the Port of Southampton to closely monitor and regulate all commercial maritime traffic anywhere within the scope of the VTS system, although such regulation is still seen as advisory, rather than mandatory. The master of the vessel may still take decisions based on their own perception of their course and location, regardless of the information conveyed by the VTS operator. The main function of the system, however, is to endeavour to control maritime traffic in the area in much the same way that an air traffic control system controls aircraft movements into and out of an airport. The VTS operator may not be able to engage visual contact with a vessel for some time, as the vessel is well out of range, hence the need for the extensive radar coverage of the area as shown in the diagram below of the VTS scope for the Southampton, Portsmouth and Isle of Wight areas.

FORTH VTS

The above system concerning the VTS system in the Southampton area can be compared with a similar system used in the Firth of Forth by the Forth Ports authority. The system used by Forth Ports was a uniquely-designed system designed to encompass all shipping activities in the whole of the Firth of Forth, from the Port of Grangemouth, Scotland's largest port, at the western extremity of the Firth, along the Firth to the Port of Rosyth, which handles both naval vessels, cruise ships and the Ro-Ro service operated from Rosyth to the Port of Zeebrugge in Belgium, and thence to the Port of Leith, adjacent to the City of Edinburgh. Other, smaller ports such as Burntisland and Methil, are located further down the Firth, on the south coast of the kingdom of Fife. The eastern extremity of the VTS system is at a line between Tantallon Castle, to the east of North Berwick on the east Lothian Coast, to Fife Ness, the most easterly extremity of the kingdom of Fife. Particular hazards are the two Forth Bridges, and several islands, particularly Inchkeith and Inchgarvie, located to the east of the bridges, and the Isle of May and Bass Rock, located on the north and south sides respectively in the entrance of the Firth of Forth.

The Forth VTS system is controlled from the Port of Grangemouth, and deals with all shipping entering any of the above ports. The AIS system, which is not based in the region itself but on the overall satellite system, monitors marine traffic in the Firth, but only on a passive basis given the status of the vessel's AIS equipment at the time. However, the system only monitors these movements, and does not provide an interactive communication with the vessel. The user of the AIS monitoring system can therefore only monitor the movement of a specific vessel with relation to other vessels in the vicinity, but cannot intercept those vessels in any way.

THE PRINCIPLE OF THE VTS SYSTEM

As explained later in this text, the Automatic Identification System (AIS) simply monitors marine traffic from a distance on a general basis and relies on the activation of the AIS equipment of each individual vessel. The signal generated by the vessel's AIS transponder is picked up by electronic equipment on other vessels and shore-based establishments, including any computer linked to the internet-based AIS websites. The VTS system, however, operates through a series of communication and electronic links between the shore-based operator and the vessel. The vessel's transponder transmits a signal via satellite, which is in turn linked by electronic means to both the VTS monitoring system and the AIS system.

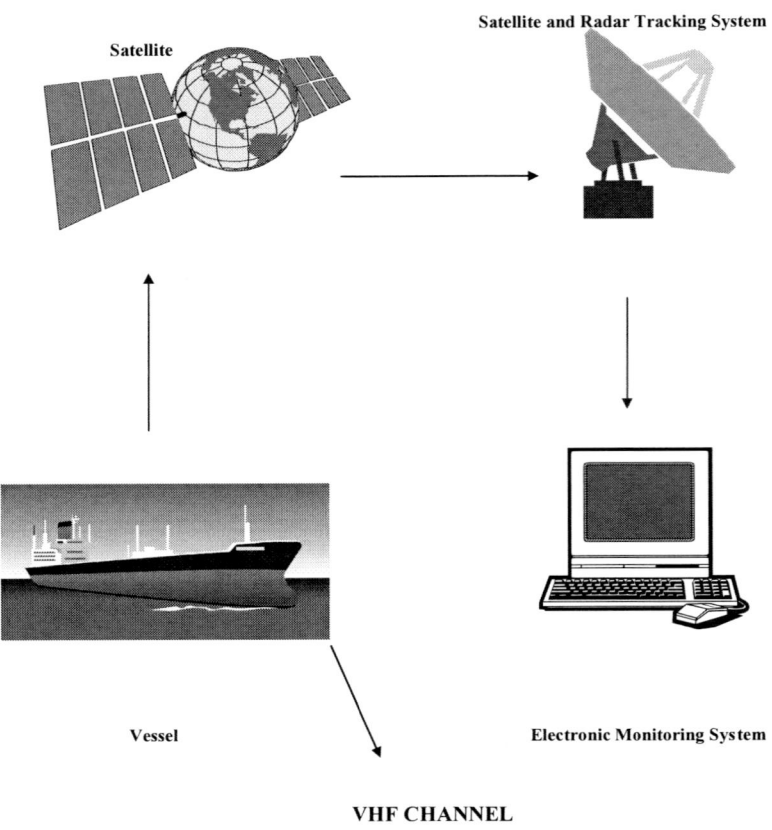

VHF CHANNEL

A Typical VTS System

The position of the vessel is logged in the VTS system and is shown on the monitor screen of the Operator Workstation in the VTS operations room. The AIS system also picks up the vessel's position and shows it on the AIS monitor, along with the vessel's identification characteristics. The operations room VTS can translate the information to a simulator or other systems as required. The system is supported by the communications system using specific VHF frequencies, allowing the shore-based VTS operator to communicate with the vessel's master to verify speed, course, and any other information required to ensure the safe arrival of the vessel at port or its departure from port and exit into the open sea. The system also allows the masters of various vessels to maintain contact with each other as well as with the VTS operator while sailing within the VTS-controlled area.

However, not every port uses or is equipped with VTS facilities, on the grounds of simplicity of navigation through channels on the approach to the port, or because the port is not deemed large enough to necessitate the use of VTS. The lack of such control systems makes vessel reporting activities less efficient and inevitably means that less control may be exercised over vessel movements within the vicinity. Furthermore, the lack of VTS facilities in some areas means that there may be a lack of communication between vessels sailing within such waters, especially where Port Controls are concerned. It becomes more evident that with the number of vessels, both commercial and pleasure, plying both international seas and territorial waters, as well as their increasing size and, for that matter, the maritime synergy between all types of commercial and leisure vessels, there is a greater need for the implementation of VTS facilities in every UK port to allow for greater controls over maritime traffic movements close to all UK ports. In the case of the Vessel Traffic Monitoring Directive, such reporting systems are mandatory for larger ports and those with restricted channel access.

What has become evident is that despite a rigorous maintenance of Collision Regulations (COLREGS) as well as clearly-defined Rules of the Road, accidents still occur within territorial waters, and these are often avoidable if systems such as VTS were more widely used, especially by not only the ports themselves but also by small and pleasure craft hitherto not covered by the regime. At present, VTS is largely limited to commercial vessels and does not generally apply to pleasure craft such as cruisers and yachts, although on the larger pleasure cruisers VTS may be installed for safety purposes. It is, however, becoming increasingly essential that small craft of the leisure variety, as well as other marine craft under the 300 gross registered tonnage threshold used for more commercial purposes such as fishing, should report into ports where commercial activity takes place. It is clear that the presence of such craft can impose as much of an obstacle or inconvenience to larger commercial ships as those craft exceeding 300grt, and that such movements can result in severe accidents occurring where incorrect sailing and navigation procedures were not obeyed or carried out, thus contravening the Rules laid down by the 1996 Merchant Shipping Act as well as the VTMD and in more general terms by the International COLREGS.

While VTS operates between ports and vessels within the boundaries of waters close to the port jurisdiction, that boundary will refer to a finite area a certain distance from the coastline. VTS does not operate in open seas, and therefore cannot apply where ships are in open waters. Should an incident between two or more vessels occur outside the geographical jurisdiction of the VTS regime, the port cannot be seen as being in control of such a situation, and therefore has no control over the consequences of any such incident.

A further limitation of the VTS system is that it refers to vessel traffic management insofar as movement within designated shipping lanes is concerned; it does not refer in any way to the vessel's cargo nor its passenger or crew complement. Thus if an incident or accident occur within the jurisdiction of the VTS regime, the nature of the vessel's cargo or the stowage of that cargo aboard vessel will not be questioned or investigated unless it were found that incorrect stowage of cargo, particularly of a hazardous or dangerous nature, were found to have contributed in some way to the resulting catastrophe, especially of an environmental nature. And since there is no perceived direct correlation between the nature of the cargo and the handling of the vessel by its crew, the two issues remain mutually exclusive, unless the accident or collision contributed in some way to the damage to the cargo aboard vessel and hence to a potential environmental catastrophe. A recent case of the collision of a vessel with a support of the Road Suspension Bridge over the Storebaelt in Danish waters highlighted the fallibility of the VTS system. For some reason, the VTS system failed to foresee and identify a navigation problem aboard the vessel which led to the collision. However, this is an infrequent case. In general, the VTS regime gives the port or national maritime authorities a reasonable amount of control over shipping movements in the area, and enables the authority concerned to maintain contact with vessels passing through the area at any time.

AUTOMATIC IDENTIFICATION SYSTEM (AIS)

The Automatic Identification System (AIS) is an electronic system enabling an observer to view and track the movements of several vessels at any one time projected on a computer screen. It can thus be used by shipping lines and cargo operators to track the movements and locations of vessels carrying specific cargoes. The vessel's identification, direction, speed and heading may be monitored throughout a period of time, and by clicking the computer mouse on a particular vessel, its identification information can be accessed immediately. Manoeuvring and other accurate navigation information can also be accessed simultaneously, and can be related from both ship and shore to other vessels in the vicinity. The AIS is a shipboard broadcast system which acts as a transponder, operating in the VHF Maritime Band, capable of handling well over 4500 reports per minute and updates as often as every 2 seconds, and which can be accessed by ship and shore alike.

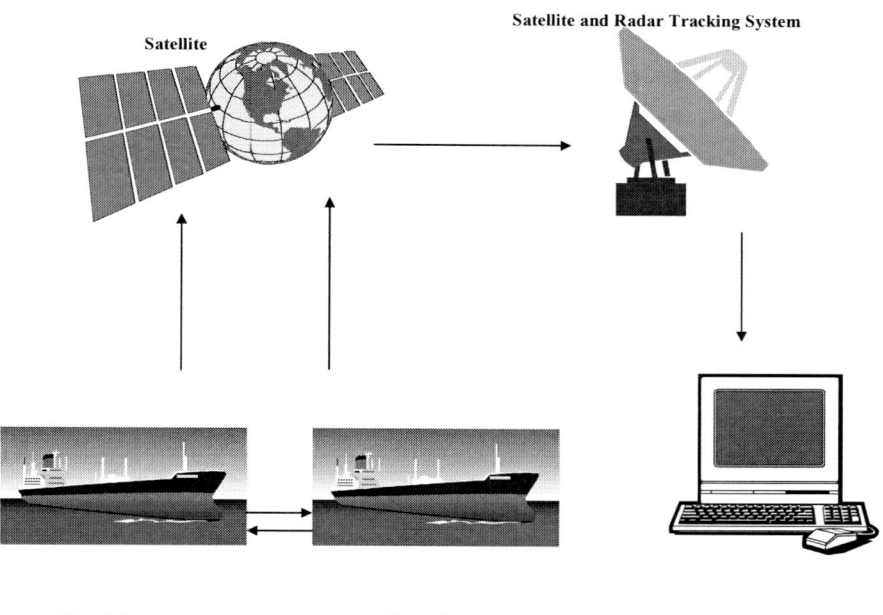

A Typical AIS System

AIS transponders automatically broadcast information, such as their position, speed and navigational status, at regular intervals via a VHF transmitter built into the transponder. The information originates from the vessel's navigational sensors, generally its Global Navigation Satellite System (GNSS) receiver and gyrocompass. Other information, such as the vessel name and VHF call sign, is programmed when the equipment is installed and is also transmitted regularly. The signals are received by AIS transponders fitted on other vessels or on land-based systems, such as VTS systems. The information received is displayed on a monitor in the form of data (as on the vessel's bridge equipment) or as graphical format on a shore-based (or vessel-based) computer or chart plotter, showing the positions of the other vessels in a manner similar to a radar display.

The information broadcast includes the following sequences and information:

Every 2-12 Seconds depending upon the vessel's speed or every 3 minutes if the vessel is at anchor:

- The Unique Referenceable Identification Number of the Vessel (MMSI Number);
- Navigational status, including "At anchor", "Moored" and "Under way using Engine";
- Rate of turn – Port or Starboard, up to 720 degrees;
- Speed over ground, between 0 and 102 knots in steps of 0.1 knots;
- Position accuracy (exact latitude and longitude);
- Course over ground relative to North;
- True Heading and Course over Ground - 0-359 Degrees;
- Time Stamp – the exact time the information was generated.

Then, every 6 minutes, the following "static" information is transmitted on the Class A AIS system:

- The Vessel's Unique Identification Number (MMSI Number);
- IMO Number;
- International Radio Call sign;
- The Name of the Vessel;
- Type of Ship;
- Dimensions of Ship to nearest metre;
- Location on ship where reference point for position reports is located;
- Type and location of position fixing device or antenna (GPS to undefined);
- Draught of Ship;
- Destination;
- Estimated Time of Arrival at Destination.

Voyage-related information such as draught, cargo, destination, ETA and route plan is generally manually entered and updated by the bridge team, although in most cases the details of the cargo are not included in the information provided.

The AIS system allows for the monitoring and tracking of the vessel by electronic means from the moment it leaves port throughout its voyage, or at least through the part of its voyage which can be monitored by the system, which in theory is the whole voyage as long as the vessel has its transponder system switched on throughout the voyage. The movement of the vessel generally shows up on the computer monitor screen as a red line trailing behind the vessel, showing a series of red dots which signify the points at which information concerning the vessel's movement was transmitted and received. As long as the transponder is switched on and activated, the AIS system allows the vessel to be identified while it is still moored in port. In some ways, the system bears certain similarities to the satellite-based Global Positioning System (GPS) used by most if not all the global commercial and military maritime sector. AIS systems are being implemented on both vessels and ports, as well as with the CNIS at Dover, in accordance with the 2004 Vessel Tracking and Monitoring Directive, and is proving extremely useful in tracking and monitoring vessels on their voyages.

Although AIS has been a mandatory measure for all commercial vessels since the end of 2004, its functions are still somewhat limited. The system is now required to be installed in every merchant ship over 300grt, and is being used by many ports, with other ports in the process of developing and installing the system for their own use. However, at present, the system only allows for the vessel to be identified concerning its general characteristics such as name, IMO Registration Number, Dimensions, tonnage, flag and owner. The AIS Website identifies all such vessels shown within the monitoring scope of the website areas and accesses not only their identification information but also pictures of the vessel where available, enabling the viewer to establish the nature of the vessel and to deduce its function. However, cargoes and contents of each vessel recorded on the system are not included in the information provided.

However, ships under 300grt are not yet included on a mandatory basis in the system, nor are leisure craft such as yachts and pleasure-cruisers, although initiatives exist to extend the use of AIS to smaller vessels. This may be seen as a major issue, since much of the marine activity around the coastlines of both the UK and the European Union concerns the movements of both small commercial craft and leisure craft, both coastwise and internationally. To this extent, there is a vacuum in the information available concerning the relationship between the movements of merchant ships and the movements of leisure craft, especially in cases where the movements of the latter may be seen as encroaching upon the movements of the former. Furthermore, AIS applies to merchant ships – it appears not officially to refer to Warships or Submarines of any national Navy which, in any case, are not subject to commercial maritime traffic requirements other than passage through certain International Straits such as the Strait of Dover and the Öresund between Sweden and Denmark.

Warships and other vessels used by Government Departments involved in maritime protection such as fisheries may be fitted with AIS, in order to monitor the movements of other vessels, especially fishing vessels. Fishing vessels used in deep waters are already fitted with passive AIS, enabling them to detect other vessels in the vicinity without displaying their own position. In the interests of fishery protection, particularly in the areas bounded by the European EEZ, such fishing vessels are monitored by the fishery protection vessels of each EU maritime nation, in order to enforce the maintenance of strict fishing quotas laid down by the EU as part of the Common Fisheries Policy. Those fishing vessels deemed to be contravening the quota regulations may be boarded, arrested and escorted to the nearest port. In this respect, AIS may be used for governmental monitoring purposes as well as general monitoring within the commercial sector. It should also be noted that vessels used by government agencies for these purposes will often have their own AIS systems switched off for some of the time, to avoid being detected by commercial vessels for a variety of reasons, especially those relating to security. Naval vessels, Customs vessels and Fishery Protection vessels fall into this category, as they are operating at sea on activities relating to matters of national security, and require a level of secrecy as part of their operations.

Information pertaining to the movements of commercial vessels is available to all parties with access to computerised facilities. The AIS Internet website allows anyone with an interest in any particular vessel located in a specific area included on the internet-based facility to access information pertaining to its whereabouts at any point in time. Specific AIS websites can be found at:

http://www.lloydsmiu.com
http://www.aislive.com
http://www.aisliverpool.org.uk

These websites can be accessed by online registration of the person with their e-mail address and brief description of their activities and/or occupation. Once registration has been completed, the viewer may access a whole variety of worldwide locations included in the AIS Web Portal. The AIS Liverpool website only covers UK maritime territory, but is still very comprehensive in its scope, affording a significant view over all vessel movements around the UK coastline. It is also free of charge to users, and offers a wide range of access to related maritime links.

However, as a security measure, certain of the AIS websites are divided into two formats:

- General information (website free of charge);
- Specific information (website payable by subscription).

Unlike the AIS Liverpool website, the other free-of-charge website versions do not give specific details of ships, on the grounds that the users will be of a more amateur nature, and will not be using the system for professional reasons. Such users are also not seen to be verified for security purposes, and thus cannot gain access to specific information on vessels and their true position at the time of access of information. The information provided on the free website portal thus takes into account a delay of some 2 hours in the vessel's position between the reporting of its position and the time its location is shown on the AIS display.

The payable website displays up-to-date information of a more accurate nature, although in reality this information may still be slightly out-dated by up to 2 minutes. However, the exact information relating to the vessel's identity and nature may be accessed on the payable website, thus allowing the user (usually a maritime professional or a national authority such as Coastguards or Customs) to access up-to-date information on the vessel, its route and its identification details.

The reasons for the selective dissemination of information refer to the misgivings expressed by the IMO concerning the security of AIS information. At its 79th session in December 2004, the Maritime Safety Committee of the IMO agreed that, in relation to the issue of freely-available AIS-generated vessel information and data on the world wide web (WWW) internet systems, the publication on the web or elsewhere of AIS data transmitted by vessels could be detrimental to the safety and security of vessels and port facilities, and was undermining the efforts of the IMO and its Member States to enhance the safety of navigation and security in the international maritime transport sector. The Committee condemned what it saw as "the regrettable publication on the world-wide web, or elsewhere, of AIS data transmitted by vessels, and urged member governments, subject to the provisions of their national laws, to discourage those who make available AIS data to others for publication on the world-wide web or elsewhere from doing so" (source: www.imo.org).

Hence the decision taken by both Lloyd's Intelligence Unit and Lloyd's Register Fairplay to restrict detailed information to paying subscribers to their respective systems. The AIS Liverpool ShipAIS system remains free, but on the proviso that users maintain discretion concerning their use of vessel information provided on the system.

The AIS website at http://www.shipais.com shows, as well as up-to-date details of all shipping located in all UK maritime areas, details of vessel movements in considerable detail, including a tracking device to show the historical movements of vessels over the previous hours. It also has links to other European AIS websites for various locations, including the Netherlands, Sweden and Norway.

The AIS System can be used to target a specific vessel and shows its IMO details, dimensions and tonnage, as well as its active status at the time of perusal (i.e. Moored, At Anchor or Under way using Engine). For vessels under way, their course and speed will be shown, along with their destination. The AIS System allows for the monitoring of the vessel's course and position while the vessel is within the domain of the AIS area covered on the website.

There are three categories of AIS equipment which can be installed aboard vessel. These are:

- **Class A**, which is compulsory for all commercial shipping and base stations on land;
- **Class B**, which is a scaled-down version for use on small or pleasure craft, or craft on which AIS Class A is not compulsory, and does not require a skilled operator;

- The **'receiver-only'** set, which listens in to the AIS frequency, allowing the operator to display AIS-transmitting vessels on to an electronic chart without transmitting the receiver's own position. This system is also used by the Fishery Protection vessels for reasons of security.

Such information is without doubt a useful tool to any authority or individual seeking to monitor the movements of vessels within the geographic scope of the AIS domain, and is a valuable tool alongside the existing monitoring controls used by Authorities such as the CNIS facility at Dover or Port Authorities. It is to be assumed that most users of the AIS website system are doubtless quite innocent in their motives for information access, and are either shipping enthusiasts or maritime professionals. However, the ease of use of the system and its availability to the public at large may render the movements of vessels monitored within the AIS website domain vulnerable to the less-than-honourable attentions of such people whose nature and motives for accessing the AIS website may be somewhat deceptive and undesirable, such as terrorists or the traffickers of illegal contraband. Crews of vessels, ship-spotters, marine enthusiasts, port authorities, national authorities and commercial organisations are one thing; international terrorists and the traffickers of illegal goods and immigrants are another. Internet access is available to all, but there is a need to monitor the usage of such systems in order to ensure that the motives of the user are justifiable and are for purely benevolent or professional purposes, as well as maintain the integrity of the Data Protection Act. Although in principle the nature of the system is admirable, insofar as it provides instant access to information pertaining to the movements of all applicable participating vessels, it is not totally watertight and secure in that it allows access by anyone registered on the website to maritime information pertaining to all such vessels, and nor is it sufficiently far-reaching in providing total information pertaining to not only information concerning the vessel itself but also the nature of its contents, be they passenger or cargo. And, as pointed out by various users, the information contained on the database is not always completely accurate, either because of delays in the transmission of information or because of inaccurate data on the vessel itself.

It should be noted that, in some ways, AIS is a historic tracking device. The history of vessel movements can be shown on a graphic display, and this in turn can be used to show a succession of vessel movements within a given scope of maritime activity. Although the system does not relate to a vessel's sailing plan or even its contact with maritime authorities, a good picture can be derived concerning how any vessel may be tracked throughout a segment of its voyage.

The other advantage of the system is that it denotes the types of vessels in the area, shown by the colour schemes depicting each type of vessel. In theory, any area covered by an advanced and detailed AIS system will therefore show the historic movements of all commercial vessels within a given timeframe, enabling the operator to track all movements in that area and thus derive sailing patterns for all such vessels. Certain other shipping line websites, such as ACL, enable the shipper to track each of the ACL vessels while they are in transit.

Other AIS sites, such as AIS Holland (www.aisholland.com), enable the shipper or vessel operator to identify and track vessels entering and leaving the Maas/Rijn estuary at the port of Rotterdam. Given the density of traffic activity and relative congestion within the Rotterdam waterways, it can be seen just how necessary a vessel tracking and monitoring system is in the area, both for port control purposes as well as for commercial tracking and monitoring purposes.

The use of AIS was incorporated in the SOLAS as Regulation 19 in **SOLAS Chapter V – Carriage Requirements for Shipborne Navigational Systems and Equipment**, and set out the navigational equipment to be carried vessel, according to the type of vessel concerned. In 2000, the IMO adopted a new requirement, as part of a revised new Chapter V, for all ships to carry AIS systems capable of providing information about the vessel to other vessels and to coastal authorities automatically. The regulation also allows flag States to exempt ships from carrying AIS equipment when those vessels are to be taken permanently out of service within two years following the date of implementation, i.e. up to the end of 2006. Performance standards for AIS were adopted in 1998.

The regulation requires that AIS must:

- Provide information as detailed previously in the section automatically to appropriately-equipped shore stations and other ships;

- Receive automatically such information from similarly-fitted ships;

- Monitor and track ships;

- Exchange data with shore-based facilities.

The regulation applies to all vessels built on or after 1 July 2002 and to vessels engaged on international voyages constructed before 1 July 2002, according to the following timetable:

- Passenger ships, not later than 1 July 2003;

- Tankers, not later than the first survey for safety equipment on or after 1 July 2003;

- Vessels, other than passenger ships and tankers, of 50,000 grt and upwards, not later than 1 July 2004.

An amendment adopted by the Diplomatic Conference on Maritime Security in December 2002 stated that ships between 300 grt and 50,000 grt were required to fit AIS equipment not later than the first safety equipment survey after 1 July 2004 or by 31 December 2004, whichever date was to occur earlier.

For the shipper and the shipping line, vessel tracking is a requirement in an age of heightened security. There is a need at all times to know a vessel's location, as well as its date of departure and its estimated date and time of arrival at the port of destination. Considering also the needs of the shipper, this device also enables the shipper to plan shipping movements and cargo deliveries, in order to plan production scheduling and order fulfilment. For the shipping line, the AIS device enables them to accurately track any of their vessels while in transit, and to guarantee vessel departures and arrivals to their customers at any time, thus also guaranteeing quality of overall service.

LONG-RANGE IDENTIFICATION AND TRACKING (LRIT)

The Long Range Identification and Tracking of ships had been debated by the 2002 IMO SOLAS Conference which had adopted Conference resolution 10 on early implementation of LRIT.

The initial purpose of long-range identification and tracking of ships is to enhance security for Contracting Governments, without undue impact to the security of ships, by providing vessel identity and current location information in sufficient time for a Contracting Government to evaluate the security risk posed by a ship off its coast and to respond, if necessary, to reduce the risk.

A robust international scheme for long-range identification and tracking of ships is an important and integral element of maritime security. An active and accurate long-range identification and tracking system also has potential safety benefits, most notably for maritime search and rescue. Accurate information on the location of the ship in distress as well as ships in the vicinity that could lend assistance will save valuable response time to affect a timely rescue.

The development of LRIT is a result of many discussions dating from February 2002, as part of the 'Security Package' developed in the aftermath of the terrorist attacks of 9/11, including extensive deliberations at IMO supported by two workshops on 'Global Tracking of Vessels' held by the International Association of Marine Aids to Navigation and Lighthouse Authorities (IALA).

Proposals for long-range identification and tracking of ships, as a means of enhancing maritime security, were discussed during the development of the special measures to enhance maritime security which were adopted by the 2002 SOLAS Conference. However, in view of the complexities involved it was recognized at an early stage that it would not be practically possible to complete the work by December 2002, so as to include appropriate provisions in the comprehensive maritime security measures which entered into force on 1 July 2004.

Following further research work, at the 80th session of the Maritime Safety Committee (MSC) of the IMO, the Working Group on Maritime Security held extensive discussions relating to proposed draft amendments to SOLAS to include a new regulation on long-range identification and tracking of ships (LRIT).

Other important issues on the MSC agenda include the adoption of proposed amendments to SOLAS relating to the provision of mobile satellite communication services in the Global Maritime Distress and Safety System (GMDSS), further development of goal-based standards and discussion of security and facilitation issues related to the carriage of containers by ships.

SOLAS regulation V/19-1 on LRIT entered into force on 1 January 2008 and applies to ships constructed on or after 31 December 2008 with a phased-in implementation schedule for ships constructed before 31 December 2008. The LRIT system is intended to be operational with respect to the transmission of LRIT information by ships as from 30 December 2008.

SOLAS regulation V/19-1 was adopted at the 81st session of the Maritime Safety Committee in May 2006, along with performance standards. As a result of this session, it was decided to introduce LRIT as a mandatory requirement for the following ships on international voyages:

- Passenger ships, including high-speed craft;
- Cargo ships, including high-speed craft, of 300 gross tonnage and upwards; and
- Mobile offshore drilling units.

The regulation, incorporated in SOLAS, and effective as from 1 January 2008, establishes a multilateral agreement for sharing LRIT information for security and Search-and-Rescue (SAR) purposes, amongst governments contracting to SOLAS. It allows flag States to protect information about the ships entitled to fly their flag, where appropriate, while allowing coastal States access to information about vessels navigating off their coasts.

The Long-Range Identification and Tracking (LRIT) system provides for the global identification and tracking of ships. The LRIT system consists of the shipborne LRIT information transmitting equipment, the Communication Service Provider(s), the Application Service Provider(s), the LRIT Data Centre(s), including any related Vessel Monitoring System(s), the LRIT Data Distribution Plan and the International LRIT Data Exchange. Certain aspects of the performance of the LRIT system are reviewed or audited by an LRIT Co-ordinator acting on behalf of all Contracting Governments.

LRIT information is provided to Contracting Governments and Search-and-Rescue (SAR) services entitled to receive the information, upon request, through a system of National, Regional, Co-operative and International LRIT Data Centres, using where necessary, the LRIT International Data Exchange. Each Administration should provide to the LRIT Data Centre it has selected a list of the ships entitled to fly its flag which are required to transmit LRIT information, together with other relevant details, and should update, without undue delay, such lists as and when changes occur. Ships should only transmit the LRIT information to the LRIT Data Centre selected by their Administration.

The obligations of ships to transmit LRIT information and the rights and obligations of Contracting Governments and of Search and rescue services to receive LRIT information are established in regulation V/19-1 of the 1974 SOLAS Convention.

LRIT is a Maritime Domain Awareness (MDA) initiative to allow member States to receive position reports from vessels operating under their flag, vessels seeking entry to a port within their territory, or vessels operating in proximity to the State's coastline. MDA offers a range of benefits, including security, environment and safety / search and rescue benefits. The basis of the LRIT system is that all ships will report their identity and position to a receiving authority every six hours using an automated system.

The LRIT system design is based on a multi-level receiving system (data centres) that report up to a central IMO data exchange. The receiving systems are referred to as LRIT data centres and can be as simple a small database connected to a satellite service provider to receive position reports and connected to the IMO data exchange for transmitting reports.

The position reports of the vessels are to be made available to other member States for purchase, whenever the vessel is within 1000 nautical miles of the purchasing member's coast, or when a vessel seeking entry to a Member State's port is a pre-determined distance or time from that port. IMO will establish a central data distribution plan that will facilitate the exchange of the position reports and will route reports based on each Member State's desire to purchase reports.

The initial operational concept provided an opportunity for member States to deploy one of three styles of LRIT data centre: a National LRIT Data Centre (NDC) to service their own flagged vessels only, a Regional LRIT Data Centre (RDC) or Cooperative LRIT Data Centre (CDC) that services two or more member States flagged vessels, or the International LRIT Data Centre (IDC). At the IMO Maritime Safety Committee session in October 2007 (MSC83) it was determined that the system could move forward towards implementation without the formation of an IDC, although discussions are ongoing regarding an IDC. The data flow is from a vessel, through the communications and application service provider, to the International Data Exchange (IDE) and then back out to the requesting contracting government.

The LRIT information ships will be required to transmit include the vessel's identity, location and date and time of the position, and this will be carried out electronically, although there is no interface between LRIT and AIS. Whereas AIS is a broadcast system, data derived through LRIT is available only to the recipients who are entitled to receive such information, and, as a result, safeguards concerning the confidentiality of such data have been built into the regulatory provisions of the LRIT regime. SOLAS contracting governments will be entitled to receive information about ships navigating within a distance not exceeding 1000 nautical miles off their coast. The LRIT will be installed as a matter of course on all ships constructed on or after 31 December 2008, with phased introduction on those vessels constructed before that date. This date has been fixed on the grounds that LRIT is scheduled to become operational on 31 December 2008.

LRIT equipment on board vessel must be capable of being configured to transmit the following minimum information set in an automatically generated position report (APR):

- The identity of the ship;
- The position of the ship; and
- The date and time of the position.

In addition, ship LRIT equipment must be able to respond to poll requests for an on-demand position report and must be immediately able to respond to instructions to modify the APR interval to a frequency of a maximum of one every 15 minutes. APRs will be transmitted as a minimum 4 times per day (every 6 hours) to a National Data Centre or to a Cooperative or Regional Data Centre nominated by the Maritime Administration / Flag Register.

As with AIS, the information provided by LRIT is limited. Furthermore, it may be assumed that the information provided by each relevant target vessel is up-to-date. Given that ships and their cargoes can be resold or re-chartered while in the middle of the voyage (as in the case of petroleum tankers), there is the risk that the information derived from the system may not be entirely correct. Furthermore, the system does not, in any case, include information on cargoes and passenger lists – these are still only contained in the vessel's manifests and may not necessarily be known to the entire crew, let alone the authorities of the governments contracting to the LRIT system. In any case, in the event of piracy or international terrorism, it is hardly likely that a terrorist is going to openly transmit information concerning a vessel's whereabouts if that terrorist has sinister designs on the purpose of the vessel's activities once it approaches port. In short, the LRIT system is still lacking in its function and does not contribute in a global sense to the overall requirements of an integrated maritime reporting system. It does not transmit the intentions of the vessel with regard to either its sailing plan or its intended port of arrival, or even its complement with regard to crew, cargo or passengers.

SMALL & LEISURE CRAFT

At present, Marine Reporting applies to commercial vessels, or at least vessels of a tonnage of 300 grt plus. However, the commercial sector based on such tonnages is not the only sector requiring a more vigorous Reporting regime. Along every coastline, there is a multitude of small craft sailing, from fishing vessels to pleasure cruisers, powerboats, yachts, dinghies and inflatable craft, not to mention jetski and other powered waterborne sports machines. These vessels pose just as major a hazard to commercial shipping as do commercial vessels, but are not covered at present by reporting regimes. Indeed, the level of marine experience held by the operators of such craft, especially the users of jetski craft, may well be much less than crews in charge of larger commercial vessels, given that the basic requirement for jetski operation and usage allows for no more than a brief operating course lasting one day provided by the makers of such craft. It is known in certain UK Ports that jetski users have a habit of "buzzing" certain car ferries on their way into and out of certain East Coast UK Ports, and have become a major hazard to such ferries as a result, often to the point of activities in the form of deliberate near-misses which directly contravene the International Collision Regulations (COLREGS) and Rules of the Road, especially as such craft appear not to be subject to the reporting requirements laid down by each individual Seaport, other than the requirements for the purposes of the reporting of incidents and accidents laid down by the Merchant Shipping (Amendments to Reporting Requirements) Regulations 2005, scheduled to enter force in May 2005. In the United States, the Department of Defense (DoD) and Department of Transport (DoT) impose tight restrictions on the control and use of such vessels around the US Coastline, and rigorous checks on vessels and their users are imposed as a result, as well as tight certification regimes for all vessel skippers, be they professional or amateur.

There are also controls exercised by Customs over the arrival and departure of pleasure craft to and from UK ports and harbours, although these controls are no longer as local and direct as they used to be. Any yacht arriving at a UK port is required to fly a specific flag bearing the letter "Q" at the time it enters a UK harbour from outside UK waters, and declarations must be submitted to Customs concerning the nature of the vessel, its nationality and any goods it is carrying, including stores used by the crew. In the case of the arrival of a non-EU vessel, the vessel's owner/skipper must complete a C1331 Form showing details of the vessel, its contents and the length of its stay in the UK. There is a copy to be submitted to Customs at the time of arrival of the vessel, and a further copy to be completed and submitted to Customs when the vessel is due to depart. These forms must be presented to the local or nearest Customs Office, despite the fact that given the shift to electronic means of declarations, most Customs Offices relating to a port are distant from the port itself and are often located many miles away. It is even unlikely that there will be any Officers available to inspect the vessel in question unless absolutely required, thus incurring a risk of inconvenience to the crew and skipper of the vessel concerned. Thus, direct reporting by a pleasure craft to the local authorities has become severely compromised as far as compliance is concerned, given that such vessels do not bear the same importance and priority as the larger commercial vessels.

There is a need, therefore, to include the sector of small and pleasure craft in the overall scope of Marine Reporting, as there are many occasions when such craft have proven a major hazard to other vessels, not only in the commercial sector but also naval vessels such as Submarines and surface Warships. In areas cloaked in secretive or restrictive defence activities such as in the upper reaches of the Firth of Clyde, from an area bounded by Brodick (Isle of Arran) to the west and Ardrossan on the Ayrshire Coast to the east, the last thing required by the Royal Navy is for one of its Nuclear Submarines to be approached by a craft containing people whose presence is not required for security reasons or which may be seen as a threat to the peace or the Defence of the Realm. Even in comparatively normal circumstances, small craft are often ill-equipped for a sudden change in the elements, and it is a regular occurrence for lifeboats of the RNLI to have to rush to the rescue of some unfortunate amateur mariner in distress as a result of a sudden change in sea conditions.

It cannot be expected that every craft venturing into inshore or offshore waters would be equipped for such purposes; dinghies and small yachts, as well as other small craft fitted with outboard motors are not suitable for such forms of technology, although larger yachts and pleasure cruisers are, and indeed are being fitted with forms of AIS Transponder and other technological navigation aids as part of their overall construction or refit. However, it is the duty of all mariners, especially those indulging in pleasure or amateur marine activities, to be aware of and even attend courses on the basics of navigation and the Rules of the Road, and to ensure that their activities do not place the lives of others or the safety of other vessels in danger. Many courses exist in the basics of marine activities and disciplines, and ensure that those venturing out in small vessels are proficient enough in such marine disciplines to handle such vessels, as well as to navigate them through local waters.

In the case of larger craft of the leisure and pleasure nature, as well as small commercial vessels such as light fishing craft and barges, there is the need to include such vessels in the Marine Reporting regimes, for both safety and security reasons. Such craft not only operate in inshore waters, but venture into international waters as well, especially in the cases of both the larger pleasure yachts or motor cruisers and fishing vessels. In many cases, their movements are less well controllable than those of larger commercial vessels, yet they pose the same problems and hazards in international waters as do their larger counterparts, and thus require the same amount of supervision as do larger commercial vessels. Indeed, in the fishing sector, there is a great requirement for the monitoring and control of such activities, especially by vessels belonging to or attached to the national fishery protection agencies, owing to the continual contravention of EU-imposed fishing quotas within national territorial waters, i.e. the EEZ, by a variety of fishing vessels of various nationalities. In cases such as larger fishing vessels, modern technological instruments are installed as a matter of course for the purpose of compliance with navigational requirements, including the use of passive AIS, but this is largely not the case for the smaller fishing vessels. Likewise, the larger pleasure cruisers and yachts are equipped with state-of-the-art navigational and communication aids, and will soon be equipped with the latest development of the AIS system, the scaled-down Class B system, which can be used by less experienced operators than those required to operate the Class A system, which is used on all commercial vessels. There is also a passive AIS receiver-only system, which enables the operator to listen in to the AIS frequency, allowing the display of all vessels in the vicinity on an electronic chart without the operator's vessel having its own position transmitted. However, the smaller and older pleasure craft are less likely to be equipped with such instrumentation unless the master of the vessel deems it necessary or appropriate to install such equipment. Eventually, it is likely that all pleasure craft destined for open waters will have to be equipped with some form of AIS system, in order to ensure that their position can be monitored at all times, especially for safety reasons.

A EUROPEAN MARITIME REPORTING SYSTEM

It would not be surprising to ascertain that the European Union, in implementing Directive 2002/59, establishing a Community Vessel Traffic Monitoring and Information System, also requested a Study into the feasibility of the creation of a full pan-European Maritime Reporting System. The main consideration in this exercise is the movement of Hazardous or Dangerous Goods, which is equally the prime mover behind most other marine reporting systems in operation. The principal objective of the Study was "to formulate recommended scenarios for the

EU to meet the objectives of all the EU Member States concerning the safety and efficiency of shipping in their coastal waters by developing and implementing an adequate maritime reporting system" (**Mare Forum 2000: The Shipping Risk Management Forum**).

The following secondary objectives were also formulated:

- The creation of an overview of the current status with regard to HAZMAT in the EU Member States, including organisational, legal and technological aspects;
- The identification of possible (feasible) options for the implementation of a European Maritime Reporting System (EMRS), based on the current status of reporting systems (HAZMAT, MAREPs), taking into account organisational, legal and technological developments;
- To formulate recommendations on the options to be preferred by the EU, by means of an analysis of:

    a) The implementation aspects (scenarios) of each identified option, taking into account local circumstances;

    b) The consequences of each identified option with respect to costs and benefits.

Several options were considered by the Consortium as a result of the Study, and varied in activity and complexity from doing nothing to a complete review of the existing system were reached by the Consortium responsible for conducting the Study.

These options were outlined as follows:

Option 0

Maintaining the present situation without any action by the EU. There would be no change to the present HAZMAT (Hazardous Materials) Directive, and the correct or perceived implementation of the Directive is a matter for each individual EU Member State and thus open to interpretation by each Member State. Co-operation between the relevant EU Member States would be organised by the Member States themselves, and would not refer to any central body for guidance. This option could ultimately lead to an incompatibility of Reporting Systems throughout the scope of the maritime sector of the European Union.

Option 1

Maintaining the HAZMAT Directive as the backbone for the EMRS, taking into account the results of the survey on the current status of its implementation. Where improvements are required, an action plan may be drafted to improve the Directive itself or the way it is implemented by Member States. The EMRS would thus consist of a modified HAZMAT implementation.

Option 2

An EMRS providing information enabling the Competent Authorities of Member States to take preventive action to avoid hazardous situations, individually or in co-operation with the Competent Authorities of other EU Member States. The implementation of an additional reporting system where vessels report their intentions, i.e. their Sailing Plan, to a Competent Authority *is not foreseen* as part of the EMRS. As with Option 1, the HAZMAT Directive is seen as being the essential basis for a future marine reporting system.

Option 3

An EMRS providing information enabling the Competent Authorities of EU Member States to take preventive actions in order to avoid hazardous or potentially disastrous situations such as accidents or collisions. To ensure more efficient co-ordination of this information, co-operation would need to take place in a Regional Co-Ordination Centre (RCC). Implementation of additional reporting whereby vessels report their Sailing Plan to a Competent Authority is not foreseen as part of this EMRS. The HAZMAT Directive would remain the backbone of this reporting system, but would require modification.

However, under this Option, more detailed information on the intended route of the vessel has to be obtained than is available at present under the present HAZMAT Directive, thus implying the need to modify the present Directive.

Option 4

This would be an EMRS providing information enabling the Competent Authorities of EU Member States to take preventive actions to avoid hazardous situations. Co-ordination of such actions would take place in a Central Co-Ordination Centre (European Co-Ordination Centre or ECC). However, as with the above, an additional reporting system where vessels report their Sailing Plan to a Competent Authority of the EU Member State is not foreseen as part of the EMRS. Again, the HAZMAT Directive would form the basis for this Option.

As with the previous options, more detailed information concerning the intended routes of the vessel would be required to enable the ECC to take any necessary preventive actions, thus implying a significant modification to the existing EU HAZMAT Directive.

Option 5

As Option 2, but where the implementation of an additional reporting system where vessels report their Sailing Plan to a Competent Authority *is* part of the EMRS. The Sailing Plan would be submitted by the Ship's Master.

This Option would also require significant modification to the existing HAZMAT Directive, especially as Sailing Plans can alter during the voyage owing to a variety of circumstances including delays or weather conditions.

Option 6

As Option 3, but where the vessel's Sailing Plan would be submitted to a Regional Co-Ordination Centre (RCC). The additional reporting system would be part of the EMRS.

Option 7

As Option 4, but where the vessel's Sailing Plan would be submitted to a European Co-Ordination Centre (ECC), and where an additional reporting system would be seen as part of the EMRS.

The following recommendations were also submitted by the Consortium:

- An EMRS where operators (Ship's Masters, Shipping Lines) notify dangerous, hazardous or polluting goods on board a vessel 24 hours in advance of entering EU coastal waters, and where masters of these vessels report their Sailing Plan and intentions at the same time;

- To use as definition for EU Coastal waters the total sea area covered by the regions where EU Member States are responsible fore providing Search and Rescue (SAR) operations;

- The information on the Sailing Plan of each vessel expected to arrive in EU Coastal waters could lead to a co-ordinated action between EU Member States which the vessel would pass, e.g. the UK and France (The Channel), or Sweden and the other EU Member States with coastlines on the Baltic Sea. The recommendation is to start with one Regional Co-ordination Centre for the Atlantic region;

- As long as transiting vessels (i.e. those vessels not bound for or leaving an EU Port but passing through EU territorial waters en route to another non-EU Port) cannot be obliged to report to a Competent Authority, they would be asked to co-operate *voluntarily*. The fact that their presence would be known to an EU Competent Authority would be a stimulating factor to this;

- AIS could be used as a source of information on actual ship positions, their speed and heading (which it now is – these recommendations were made in 2000, before AIS was implemented). It is recommended to use this information within the EMRS to check the information provided by the vessel's Sailing Plan submitted by the Masters of vessels within the AIS area;

- The 24 hours port notification, required by almost all EU Ports, can be used for checking the Sailing Plan submitted by the Ship's Master prior to entering EU waters;

- The drafting of a new Directive, integrating all previous Directives on Marine Reporting, in the same way that the proposed EMRS would be an *Integrated Reporting System*. In this way, all MAREPs used throughout EU waters should be integrated together with the implementation of additional reporting systems, thus ensuring the correctness of all Sailing Plans submitted to any of the EU Competent Authorities. This in turn would present a more efficient and accurate picture of all vessel traffic within EU territorial waters;

- A starting point would be the establishment of a Regional Co-ordination Centre for the Atlantic Region, and then merging other areas into this Regional Centre. However, if the preference was to establish RCCs in each region, the following MAREPs could act as checkpoints for the transition of vessels from one region to another:

- **Gibraltar** (Mediterranean/Atlantic Region);

- **Dover** (Atlantic/North Sea Region) – CNIS Reporting System;

- **Lerwick** (Atlantic/North Sea Region);

- **Great Belt (Storebaelt)** (North Sea Region / Baltic Region) – VTS System.

It is interesting to note that out of the above locations, three are part of the UK (although Gibraltar is a UK Dependency), and the other is in Denmark.

The criteria used for reporting purposes should also be harmonised, to either length of vessel or tonnage of the vessel.

To reduce the burden of reporting by the Master of a Vessel, all EU MAREPs should be using AIS as the means for identifying vessels, although in several cases, a VTS system is being implemented to provide more accurate and interactive reporting of information. If the Sailing Plan of the vessel is still valid, in that no deviation to the course of the vessel has occurred between the Estimated Time of Arrival (ETA) at MAREP and the Actual Time of Arrival at

MAREP, there would be no need for further reporting by the vessel concerned, as the MAREP would have obtained the required information from the Co-Ordination Centre.

It was admitted by the Consortium compiling the Study that their influence or power to demand an EMRS is limited. They could not insist upon receiving information or force Authorities or Shipping Lines to submit information concerning the vessel and its [potentially dangerous] cargo. Hence the fact that the next step envisaged by the Consortium was to engage in dialogue with the IMO to investigate the ultimate feasibility of the Project, and thence to secure support from the European Union itself, especially given the variety and depth of each individual Option available for implementation. The complexity of the Study would require significant consideration by the EU Authorities, as well as counting upon the willingness of each EU Member State to engage in the proposed European Maritime Reporting System (EMRS).

As with the other reporting systems in operation, the EMRS revolves around the reporting of Hazardous or Dangerous Cargoes. It integrates certain other national reporting requirements to a degree, but assumes the ability of all EU Member States to integrate their national HAZMAT reporting requirements under the overall EU requirements laid down by a modified and updated EU HAZMAT Directive. It does not *per se* cover reporting requirements for other general cargoes, nor does it cover the requirements laid down by the IMO ISPS Code. Indeed, it also operates independently of the AIS regime, which by its nature is worldwide in its scope. In this respect, there is still a divide between the overall issue of Marine Security and the more specific issue of the carriage of hazardous or dangerous cargoes.

The European Sea Ports Organisation (ESPO) compiled a response to the EMRS, available on the Internet, which, although welcoming the principle of such a reporting system, expressed doubts concerning its practicality and the likelihood that it would create additional bureaucracy over and above that affecting seaports under the present maritime security regimes. Areas of concern included:

- The monitoring of vessels transiting EU waters but not calling at an EU port (e.g. vessels transiting the Strait of Dover and the Öresund en route for Ports such as those in Norway or Russia);

- The recording of movements of all vessels within the scope of EU territorial waters;

- Clear distinctions to be made between the use of AIS and Voyage Data Recorders (VDRs);

- The transmission of data for container vessels, given the sheer volume of information given the increase in size of such vessels, and the ability of such vessels along with shipping lines, shipbrokers and freight forwarders, to transmit such information in its entirety using electronic methods such as Electronic Data Interchange (EDI);

- The need for the IMO to consider and approve such initiatives.

In December 2004, the European Commission stated that it would take legal action against the UK and seven other countries for failing to implement vessel traffic monitoring and information systems. The result is that at present the UK Maritime & Coastguard Agency is endeavouring to update its IT systems to allow for the new CERS (Consolidated European Vessel Reporting System) which is intended to address the issue of vessel monitoring throughout the maritime remit of the EU. The CERS is intended to harmonise all the present European vessel monitoring systems in order to prevent environmental disasters such as those caused in the wake of the ERICA disaster, and to create a pan-European system along the lines of the options shown previously.

However, the main thrust of the EU Commission's argument revolves not so much about the kind of system used, but the whole reason for using it. The Strait of Dover may be covered by maritime reporting systems, but elsewhere around the UK coast, there are no reporting systems in force. In particular, there are no reporting systems in use in the North Channel and the Firth of Clyde. This situation prevails despite the extensive frequency of maritime traffic through these areas, with relatively large volumes of shipping using all the aforementioned sea areas. All of these areas are located within UK national territorial waters, and yet none of them are covered by any form of VTS system, hence the challenge to the UK authority posed by the EU Commission.

As always, studies by trans-national working groups and Consortia are admirable, as is the anticipated creation of a supranational marine reporting regime, however limited in its scope. However, the issue of practicality and effectiveness remains. The main areas of concern are still the basis for such information and how it can be disseminated and transmitted with the least additional bureaucracy and inconvenience to all parties and authorities concerned. Equally, given the present existence of a whole series of administrative requirements for both vessels and ports, there is a clear risk that an additional regime of this kind would congest the reporting system to the point of overload and hence a complete breakdown in the system, or at worst a series of accidents and catastrophes caused by the failure of the system to be operated by each member state owing to its cumbersome burden on existing activities. In the event, the implementation by several EU maritime authorities of VTS systems in accordance with the EU VTMS Directive has, to a certain extent, fragmented the pan-European initiative, and rendered the idea of a fully-integrated Reporting system less practical on the basis of national controls over autonomous VTS reporting systems.

THE UK CONSOLIDATED EUROPEAN REPORTING SYSTEM (CERS)

The UK Consolidated Reporting System (CERS) is a new marine information management system which has been developed by the Maritime & Coastguard Agency (MCA) to meet, amongst other things, the UK marine reporting obligations under the provisions and dates indicated in the European Parliament and Council Directive 2002/59/EC.

- All ships of 300 gross tonnage and above, when bound for a UK port, are subject to a ship notification requirement prior to entry into port that applies at least 24 hours in advance of their arrival. If the voyage is less than 24 hours in duration, the report should be issued no later than the time of departure from the last port.

- All recreational craft of 45 metres length and over, when bound for a UK port are affected by a ship notification requirement, prior to entry into port, that applies at least twenty-four hours in advance of their arrival.

- All ships regardless of size, when carrying dangerous or polluting goods, either departing from or bound to a UK port are affected by the dangerous or polluting goods notification requirements.

The Regulations are the UK implementation of certain requirements contained in European Parliament and Council Directive 2002/59/EC and, in part, the international reporting requirements that apply in the event of an accident/incident at sea.

The Regulations introduced this new notification requirement, prior to entry into port, for ships of a nationality of any EU/EEA member state bound for a port located in an EEA (European Economic Area) State, with the exception of:

    a) Ships of less than 300 gross tonnage;

b) Warships, naval auxiliaries and other ships owned or operated by the Government of an EEA state which are used for non-commercial public service;

c) Fishing Vessels;

d) Traditional Ships;

e) Recreational Craft having a length of less than 45 metres.

A. Vessel Information

The owner, operator, agent or master of a ship is required to notify the authority of the port to which the ship is bound, of the following information:

a) Ship identification (Name, call sign, IMO identification number or MMSI number);

b) Port of Destination;

c) For a ship leaving a port in a member state: the estimated time of departure form the port of departure or pilot station, as required by the competent authority, and the estimated time of arrival at the port of destination;

d) For a ship coming from a port located outside the European Community and bound for a port in a Member State: the estimated time of arrival at the port of destination or pilot station, as required by the competent authority;

e) The total number of persons on board.

B. Cargo Information

a) The correct technical names of the dangerous, hazardous or polluting goods, the United Nations (UN) numbers where they exist, the IMO hazard classes in accordance with the IMDG, IBC and IGC Codes, and, where appropriate, the class of the ship as defined by the INF Code, the quantities of such goods and their location on board and, if they are being carried in cargo transport units other than tanks, the identification number thereof;

b) Confirmation that a list or manifest or appropriate loading plan giving full details of the dangerous, hazardous or polluting goods carried and of their location on the ship is on board;

c) The address from which detailed information on the cargo may be obtained.

The UK Maritime & Coastguard Agency (MCA) has incorporated the Consolidated European Reporting System (CERS) in its Merchant Shipping Notices in late 2007, replacing Merchant Shipping Notice **(MSN) 1784** with **MSN 1817** on the CERS for the following requirements:

1) Ship arrival and departure notifications, including additional requirements for ships carrying dangerous, hazardous or polluting goods (DPG); and

2) Reporting requirements in the event of an accident or incident.

MSN 1817 details the technical requirements applicable to vessels complying with the Merchant Shipping (Vessel Traffic Monitoring and Reporting Requirements) Regulations 2004, which amended the Merchant Shipping (Reporting Requirements for Ships Carrying Dangerous or Polluting Goods) Regulations 1995, and implemented the European Union (EU) Vessel Traffic Monitoring and Information System Directive 2002/59/EC. The Regulations are also part of the international marine reporting requirements which apply in the event of an accident or incident at sea.

The MCA has made provision for the reporting of such cargoes to be made electronically by e-mail or EDI/XML format, in line with other electronic reporting facilities, usually in the form of an attachment to an electronic message such as an e-mail. This can be done by the ship owner, operator or their appointed agent, and can be submitted on a 24/7 basis. The main issue concerning the provision of electronic submission purposes revolved around the Community Service Provider (CSP) computer system operated by specific ports, especially as many ports, especially in the UK, operate different CSP electronic systems. Vessels sailing to and from the Isle of Man or the Channel Islands are deemed to be sailing to or from non-EEA ports. The EEA is defined as being the European Union (EU), plus the countries of Iceland and Norway, which belong to the EFTA (European Free Trade Association) along with Switzerland and Liechtenstein, which are landlocked and do not have seaports in their national territory.

Although the CERS applies in particular to vessels carrying dangerous, hazardous or polluting goods, it does not replace the existing Regulations implemented in 2004 concerning the principal area of vessel traffic monitoring and reporting requirements. The CERS complements all existing vessel reporting regulations, and applies to specific conditions with relation to the carriage of dangerous or hazardous goods. These regulations should still be consulted alongside the new CERS Regulations with regard to vessel reporting requirements. Furthermore, the CERS Regulations assume that the master of any vessel concerned has full access to all information concerning the carriage and stowage of hazardous or dangerous goods on board the vessel. In cases of the carriage of bulk cargoes, this will not be an issue, but for the carriage of containerised cargoes, especially where consolidations and groupage consignments are concerned, the issue becomes more prevalent and may highlight problems concerning the availability of such information, especially where large deep sea container vessels are concerned.

THE EU ENTRY SUMMARY DECLARATION (ENS)

In order to improve the safety and security of its Member States, the European Union (EU) introduced in 2010 a mandatory advance notification requirement regarding the import, export and transit of goods, in addition to existing EU Customs regulations. The new requirements, which entered into force on 1 January 2011, have been laid down in various EU Commission Regulations known as *"The Security Amendment to the Community Customs Code"*, in particular EU Regulation **1875/2006**. They apply to all sectors of the shipping industry, and are in principle similar to the Advance Manifest (AMS) reporting system required by the US and Canada as a result of the C-TPAT (Customs & Trade Partnership Against Terrorism) initiative launched in the wake of the 9/11 tragedy.

For goods which are being imported, cargo information in the form of an ***Entry Summary Declaration*** **(ENS)** must be submitted in advance to the customs office at the first port of entry into the EU. For goods which are being exported, cargo information is also to be submitted in advance either in the form of a ***Customs Declaration for Export, Re-export or Outward Processing***, or if such a declaration does not apply, then in the form of an ***Exit Summary Declaration*** **(EXS)**. The time limits for submission of the required information differ depending on the cargo being carried and the nature of the trade. For deep-sea containerised shipments, e.g. from the Americas or Asia to the EU, the ENS must be lodged at least 24 hours prior to commencement of loading in each non-EU load port.

The carrier (shipping line) or its representative must declare cargo information in advance to the Customs office of first entry port in the form of an Entry Summary Declaration (ENS) when:

- Importing cargo into the EU from a non-EU origin;

- When containers are carried on board a ship following a non-EU voyage but which must be trans-shipped in a subsequent EU port. This would apply for instance to cargo loaded in the US and bound for the Middle East but trans-shipped in Antwerp;

- When cargo remains on board for carriage to other European or non-European ports (FROB).

As long as traders can show they have followed certain criteria, including their ability to demonstrate a transparent supply chain audit trail in terms of documentation and procedures, the individual customs administrations may waive the need for an ENS, provided that:

- They have access to all the necessary electronic information in the trader's records;
- They are able to carry out full risk analysis for safety and security purposes.

Operators which are based in the EU or have regional offices in the EU can apply for "Authorised Economic Operator" (AEO) status. The benefit to the operator of being awarded AEO status is a reduction in the amount of cargo information that needs to be submitted to customs at the initial stage of reporting, although more details are generally submitted later to Customs in the form of monthly reports. This status is essentially governed by the ability of the trader to satisfy supply chain security and transparency requirements, especially with regard to Customs and logistics compliance issues.

In each non-EU load port, the transmission must be carried out no later than 24 hours prior to start of loading to the vessel bound for an EU port. To comply with this regulation, the shipping line will require complete and correct shipping instructions. The documentation closing times will follow the same timelines as other "advance manifest" 24-Hour Rule locations such as USA, Canada or Mexico. They are stipulated in the marine carrier's booking confirmation.
Transmission of ENS is obligatory for all cargo discharged in an EU port (including trans-shipment cargo) as well as FROB cargo (Foreign Cargo Remaining on Board), i.e. cargo which is discharged in a port outside the EU after the vessel has called an EU port.

In many cases, the advance notification which is issued at the port of loading needs to be given by the ship operator, carrier or his representative, such as the ship's agent. At present there is no distinction within the regulations as to whether, in the case of a chartered vessel, the charterer or the owner is considered to be the operator/carrier for the purposes of submission of the required declarations. However, it is expected that the charterer will be defined as the operator/carrier under a time charter, and the owner will be the operator/carrier under a voyage charter party. In containerised shipping, a freight forwarder, or Non Vessel Operating Common Carrier (NVOCC), will normally issue the advance notice, although this can also be carried out by the shipping agency at the port of loading. However, in the case of submission by a freight forwarder or NVOCC, this submission can only be carried out with the ship operator's full knowledge and consent. In the case of combined transport operations where trucks are driven on to a ro-ro ferry, it is the duty of the haulage company, its representative or the truck driver, to submit the advance notification prior to arrival at the port of loading. With regard to vessel-sharing arrangements such as slot carrier agreements in the container trade, the declaration is to be issued by the carrier issuing the Bill of Lading rather than the ship operator.

If the information is submitted by a nominated third party, such as an agent or freight forwarder, the ship operator will still be held responsible if notice is not delivered in advance or on time, and this delay may result in a penalty being imposed. However, the third party will still be liable for the accuracy of the information provided. Regardless of who provides the advance cargo declaration, the responsible party must also provide their ***Economic Operator Registration and Identification Number*** (EORI), which is essentially the trader's VAT Number plus an additional set of digits, in the case of the UK "000". For example, if a UK-based trader's VAT Number is 123 4567 89, their EORI will be 123456789000. The use of an EORI has been mandatory within the EU since 1 July 2009. Once advance notice has been submitted, a confirmation will be issued containing a unique 18-digit number called a ***Movement Reference Number*** (MRN), used hitherto for Community Transit movements. The entire system is electronic, and therefore the person giving notice to Customs requires a computer system which can interface with the national Customs system. However, at the present time there is no system that is common throughout the EU capable of handling the new declarations, and for the present each Member

State retains its own national system. If the customer has their own EORI number available, the carrier will not accept a declaration to Customs to be made by any third party. All declarations which include a MRN (Movement Reference Number) are made by the carrier.

An exemption from the requirement to submit declarations for cargo being imported or exported may be granted for vessels trading purely between ports of EU Member States if certain specific criteria are met. Further exemptions exist for goods that remain on board a vessel whilst in the EU which are destined for a port outside the EU, and these do not need to be declared for export, even when loaded at a previous EU port. In addition, a vessel departing the EU and then calling at a foreign port before returning to the EU is not required to submit export documentation prior to departing from the first EU port. However, the cargo must be declared in an ENS before the vessel returns to the EU.

The information submitted in the various declarations is used by Customs to conduct a risk assessment of the cargo from a viewpoint of security and safety. As a result of this assessment, the cargo will then be classed as either risk type A, B or C, which in turn determines how the Customs authority will respond. For example, if the Customs office identifies a serious safety and security risk in relation to cargo to be loaded onto a deep sea container ship and classifies it as risk type A, it will issue a "*Do Not Load*" (**DNL**) or "*Customs Hold*" message preventing the carrier from shipping the cargo. **DNL (Do Not Load)** is the message returned by the EU customs office of first entry in receipt of the ENS in the place of an MRN. It means that analysis has been carried out on the declaration and that an unacceptable risk exists concerning the goods covered by the ENS declaration. This risk level may be further compounded by a lack of information entered on the cargo manifest with relation to details of the cargo. In the same way that the US and Canada outlawed the terms FAK (*Freight of All Kinds*) and "*Said to Contain…*", the ENS system allows for a similar level of controls applied to scrutiny of the Entry Declaration, hence the risk assessment carried out by the relevant EU Customs authority on each declaration.

The shipper is therefore required to submit an accurate and detailed set of shipping instructions to the carrier or their agent in order to facilitate an Entry Summary Declaration. The required data elements for the Entry Summary Declaration are:

- Full name and address of shipper and consignee;

- Full name and address of notify party where goods are carried under a negotiable "to order" B/L;

- Container number;

- Acceptable goods description (general terms for example "consolidated cargo", "general cargo", "Freight All Kinds", "Said to Contain", cannot be accepted);

- Minimally, the first 4 digits of the HS Commodity Code, although the 6-digit HS Code is recommended;

- Marks and Numbers of packages;
- Cargo gross weight (in kilograms);
- Seal number;
- UN Dangerous Goods Code and IMDG Classification Code, where applicable;
- Method of payment for transport charges in case of "Freight Prepaid" (CFR, CIF, CPT, CIP), for example payment in cash, payment by cheque, electronic credit transfer, etc.

The ENS will be sent to the Customs office of the first port of entry (first port of call) in the EU, and this Customs office will carry out a security risk assessment.

The advance cargo declaration (ENS) is sent electronically to the Customs Office of the first port of entry (first port of call) in the EU, and this Customs Office carries out a security risk assessment on the ENS, with the aim of identifying any potential serious safety and security risks.

The Customs Office of the first EU port of entry may identify 3 types of risks:

- Risk Type A: the Customs Office having identified a serious safety and security risk with the cargo to be loaded on board a Deep Sea container ship, will issue a "***Do Not Load***" (DNL) message resulting in the carrier not being allowed to load the relevant cargo on board the ship;
- Risk Type B: This refers to cargo posing a serious safety and security risk, or arousing suspicion of a security risk, and which will be intercepted and handled in the first EU port of entry;
- Risk Type C: In the event of the Customs Office having identified or suspected a safety and security risk, which is not considered to be serious, the cargo will be intercepted and handled in the EU port of discharge.

For **short sea** container traffic, e.g. Russia to the EU, apart from the following variations, the same information and procedures apply as above.

For short sea movements, in each non-EU load port, the transmission of the ENS Declaration must be carried out no later than 2 hours before arrival at the first port of entry in the EU.

Under such circumstances, there are only the following two risk types:

- Risk Type B = Interception of a suspicious shipment at the first port of entry;
- Risk Type C = Interception of a suspicious shipment at the port of discharge.

In this case, information about the ultimate shipper/consignee is not required in an ENS. If, however, an independent freight forwarder wants to file the ENS himself, i.e. instead of the ocean carrier, he will still require the consent of the ocean carrier to do so. Only in cases where the appointed agent of the ocean carrier, or the agency division of the ocean carrier, files the ENS will prior consent from the ocean carrier not be required.

In addition to submitting an ENS, an operator must also advise the national Customs authority of a vessel's arrival by the submission of an *Arrival Notification* (AN) by a means acceptable to the customs office in that particular Member State. The AN may comprise of a list of MRNs relating to the vessel, or what is termed an "Entry Key", which consists of information about the vessel and the cargo (e.g. mode of transport, the vessel's IMO number, expected date of arrival).

There are certain drawbacks with the new Entry Declaration system. Firstly, each national Customs authority in the EU still retains its own national control system, which, as explained earlier, may not be compatible with those of other national Customs authorities within the EU. This implies that information submitted in the form of an ENS to one Customs authority cannot necessarily be transmitted to other Customs authorities, especially in the case of the diversion of a vessel from one EU port to another port in another EU member state, owing to a perceived lack of compatibility in systems used by each authority.

Secondly, the information provided for each cargo as contained within the ENS is only transmitted to the Customs authority and not to any other national organisation. This means that any information deemed as being sensitive or prejudicial to national security may not necessarily be passed to other security authorities, such as other government departments, e.g. Defence or Interior. In this sense, the effectiveness of such information may be reduced, as it cannot be disseminated amongst the parties which ultimately may still have an interest in it, and thus leading to the risk of prejudicing national security interests.

Details of information are laid down in **Annex 30A** to Regulation **1875/2006**. Advance cargo declarations must be done electronically and the carrier is responsible for the timely electronic transmission of this ENS (one ENS per Bill of Lading), for the accuracy and completeness of information therein.

The required cargo information must be submitted to the Customs Office at the latest 24 hours before commencement of loading of the containerised cargo in each foreign port of loading on board the ship or 4 hours before the arrival of the vessel in the first EU port of destination for conventional or Ro-Ro cargo. The declaration applies to each non EU port of loading.

To comply with this regulation, the carrier will require from its customers complete and accurate shipping instructions 5 working days before loading on a vessel calling in Europe. The documentation closing time, included in the carrier's procedures, will be adjusted accordingly, following same guidelines as those enforced in other advance documentation 24-hour rule countries such as the US.

In case shipping instructions have not been received within the documentation closing time, then related bookings will be deferred onto the next vessel with no pre-advice and no appeal. In case containers do not arrive at the port gate and/or are not Customs cleared within the terminal closing date, then the whole related Bill of Lading/Booking will be deferred onto the next vessel and the shipper will incur, for all containers related to an incomplete Bill of Lading/Booking, the following expenses:

- Terminal quay rent/storage charges and/or plug-in;
- Terminal change of voyage costs;
- Booking transfer charge ("no show charge") and possible dead freight in peak season;
- Any other associated demurrage charges;
- A Customs fine from the European discharge or transit port for the "no show" of the declared cargo.

All expenses as resulting from loading denial as decided by European customs will be for full account of shippers.

CHAPTER SIX

ROLES AND RESPONSIBILITIES

MULTIMODAL INFORMATION AND THE INTERNATIONAL SUPPLY CHAIN

A key factor in deciding upon the transparency of information submitted through Marine Channels is the availability of information emanating from the Supplier of a consignment of goods, or, in the case of passenger liners, the agency booking the voyage on behalf of individual passengers. If the Supplier or the agency concerned does not convey accurate or detailed information to the Carrier, then it cannot be expected that the Carrier can in turn convey such information to the relevant authorities of the country of destination or even the port of arrival.

In the case of sea cargoes, the information flow within the Supply Chain commences at the door of the Exporter. In order to facilitate such a flow of information, there are 13 recognised International Terms of Delivery – the INCOTERMS – which are occasionally revised to account for changes in international market conditions or to clarify the varying degrees of risk and responsibility incurred by either the Seller or the Buyer in each of the stages of any international shipment. The very basic Term used by the Exporter is Ex Works (EXW), where the Exporter does no more than make the consignment ready for collection from the Exporter's premises by the Buyer. The Buyer takes total responsibility for the shipment right up to their own premises. It would be normal practice to expect the Exporter to inform the Buyer of the nature of the shipment by way of a Commercial Invoice or a Packing List.

However, in cases where the consignment from the Exporter is collected by a haulage company on behalf of the Buyer and transported to a point of consolidation for loading into a container, such information may well be absorbed into a more general description pertaining to the overall contents of the groupage container on the basis of an LCL shipment. Under such circumstances, it is more common to find the terms "Said to Contain…" or "Freight of all Kinds" (FAK) used, or even a general term applicable to the purposes of the consignment, e.g. "Automotive Parts". The fact that within such a consignment there may be a host of different commodities included does not figure in the description used on a Marine Bill of Lading. A more radical example is that of a consignment described loosely as "Cosmetic Products", which may contain commodities ranging from aromatic oils through soaps to lipsticks and nail varnish. However, the consignment may also include items such as nail varnish remover, which is classed as Hazardous Goods because of its flammable nature, but since the overall groupage consignment description made no mention of this, the specific commodity was overlooked and no specific Dangerous Goods documentation was issued for the nail varnish remover, despite the evident risk involved in the shipment of the consignment.

Groupage or Consolidation is one of the principal enemies of the accuracy of information pertaining to marine cargo reporting. Where the freight agent has accurate detailed knowledge of the consignment to be shipped, that information should be adequately transmitted via the carrier to the port of arrival, and any extra precautions required in the case of the reporting of hazardous goods will be taken. But if such information is not known, then such precautions cannot be taken and the result is a compounding of risks pertaining to both cargo insurance and the provisions for the handling of hazardous goods under the IMO Codes, especially under the IMDG and FAL requirements. In this respect, there is a clear need for the freight agent to be absolutely aware of the nature of the consignment at the time that consignment is loaded into the container, so that the correct information concerning the cargo can be passed to the carrier, i.e. the Shipping Line, prior to the container being loaded aboard vessel. Failure to provide such information could result in several compromises, as follows:

- Failure to adhere to the requirements of the SOLAS, IMDG and FAL regimes laid down by the IMO;
- The nullification of the Cargo Insurance policy under the provisions of the Maritime Insurance Act 1906.

The nullification of the Insurance Policy would thus also compromise and prejudice the General Average principle concerning both the safety of the vessel and the insurance of cargoes and their consequent indemnity if it were found that:

1) Neither the exporter nor the importer had properly insured the consignment in question;

2) Neither the insurance company nor the underwriters were made aware of the true nature of the consignment under the principle of *Uberrimae Fidei* (Utmost Good Faith);

3) Neither the Shipowners nor the Shipbrokers nor the Master of the Vessel were correctly informed of the true nature of the consignment;

4) The consignment (or the container in which it was placed) was not correctly stowed in accordance with IMO Regulations.

There is therefore the need for a fully transparent system of the transmission of cargo information to the carrier in the multimodal system long before the container or trailer is loaded aboard vessel. The nature of the international Supply Chain demands that information pertaining to cargoes is passed down the line from Supplier to Customer in order to ensure the smooth and efficient despatch and delivery of the consignment, and that all authorities and parties within the Supply Chain, especially from a transportation and national control perspective, are fully informed as to the nature and risk of the consignment in question. Even where no international frontier controls are involved, such as within the European Union, there is still a significant need for such flows of information, especially where mixed forms of transport are involved, such as road and sea, either from a Roll-On/Roll-Off perspective or a Short Sea Container perspective. The demands of the Short-Sea Marine Motorway require that integrated information flows pertaining to the maritime carriage of goods exist long before the vessel is loaded and sails, as the timescales involved between one part of Europe and another, especially on Baltic Sea or North Sea routes, are minimal. These flows start at the point of the Exporter or Seller, and progress through the freight agents, the Road Trucking Companies and Shipping Lines and the Port Authorities, as well as any Customs Authorities, to the Importer or Buyer. Such information flows should show the full extent of the consignment as well as the risks involved in handling and transporting it between the Seller and the Buyer.

The timely and efficient arrival of the consignment at the Buyer's premises should be reflected in the ability of all relevant parties and authorities to show that they were all party to the same accurate information pertaining to not only the method of transport involved in the movement, but also pertaining to the nature of the cargo itself. Any failure in the flow of information could result in at best a delay in the delivery of the consignment to the customer's premises, or at worst the destruction of the consignment and the potential loss of a marine vessel as a result in a severe accident occurring while the vessel was at sea, owing to a problem occurring with the consignment itself. This problem could, in turn, attract the attention of not only the Marine Accidents Investigation Board (MAIB) but also those responsible for maintaining the integrity of and compliance with the regulations of the SOLAS Convention, especially in cases where failure to report the true nature of the consignment insofar as its hazardous or dangerous nature was concerned by the exporter or the freight agent resulted in a catastrophe occurring at sea and the safety of the vessel carrying the cargo being compromised or prejudiced. The International Maritime Organisation (IMO) is seeking to address the problem of container security in the context of global security initiatives, but this initiative is designed more to fit into the present ISPS (International Ship and Port Security) framework, and does not necessarily address the transparency of cargoes inside a container, especially in the case of consolidated loads, where the information contained on a Bill of Lading or a Cargo Manifest may be less than explanatory or accurate.

THE VESSEL PERSPECTIVE

The state-of-the-art marine freighter or passenger liner bears little relationship to its forebears in terms of the technology of its control systems. Gone are the telegraphs between bridge and engine room, and equally gone are the conventional wheelhouses with their huge steering wheels. Everything is controlled today by complex on-board computer systems, from steering and navigation to engine control and position monitoring. Even the marine propulsion systems have changed, from the combinations of conventional stern-mounted screws linked to huge marine engines and bow-thrust mechanisms, to azymuth propulsion systems, where the propulsion systems can revolve through 360 degrees and is connected to smaller, more efficient diesel engines by an adjustable link mechanism, and which eliminates the need for a conventional rudder steering mechanism. The one main link with more traditional times is the vast array of Admiralty Charts ranged across the available desk space, although even this is giving way to a large extent to the ECDIS computerised charts. Today's control systems rely heavily on a mixture of GPS, VTS, AIS and conventional radar systems. From port of departure to port of destination, the vessel monitoring process from a navigation point of view revolves around the following systems:

- Leaving Port – **VTS/AIS**;

- Open Sea – **AIS/GPS**;

- Entering Port Approaches – **AIS/VTS**;

- Port Arrival – **VTS**.

The VTS systems allow for the close monitoring of vessels within port approaches and port areas themselves by the port authority, while AIS allows for the monitoring of vessels by any party concerned throughout their voyage, and indeed while the vessel is in port, as long as the AIS transponder is switched on. The drawbacks with any of these systems are that they identify the ship, but not its crew nor its cargo or complement of passengers, as well as the problem concerning the security of the information provided, especially in the case of AIS. However, the AIS system is still subject to a slight delay between the time the transponder emits the signal and the time this registers on the system and thus registers the ship's position.

All this may appear effective insofar as it exists, but it does not tell the full story. There are considerable gaps in the whole process, mainly because of the issue of the accuracy of vessels and cargo reporting, and these gaps are the issues of the greatest importance, owing to the risks posed by unreported cargo and other security considerations. Other risks also prevail, in particular the lack of monitoring of vessels outside the remit of the VTS and AIS systems, which could have an adverse effect on the security and safety of vessels covered by these systems. Despite the evident technological tools available to the ship's master and his crew, the view from the bridge may still be obscured by many external factors beyond his control.

The synopsis of procedures concerning the voyage of a cargo vessel may loosely be categorised as follows:

- The Ship's Agent and the Freight Forwarders verify specific documentation (e.g. Dangerous Goods Notes etc.) to ensure compliance with IMO requirements;

- The cargoes destined for loading aboard vessel are declared to Customs by electronic input;

- Customs clearance is given for the consignments to be loaded aboard vessel;

- The Ship is loaded at Port with the cargoes (e.g. containers);

- Bills of Lading are issued for all cargoes loaded aboard vessel, and the cargo information is also entered on the Cargo Manifest;

- A Copy of the Ship's Manifest is given to the Ship's Master by the Ship's Agent (the Port Agent) and a further copy of the Manifest is also submitted to Customs;

- The Ship's Master notifies the Port and the Customs Authority that all cargoes are loaded aboard vessel;

- The ship is given clearance to sail;

- The Master maintains contact with the Port VTS concerning the ship's movement out of the port, through the Channel and into the open sea;

- The ship maintains electronic contact with other vessels and land through the use of the AIS system.

The ship sails across the ocean to its destination. Upon the approach to the port of destination, the following action is undertaken:

- The Vessel's Agent notifies the Port of destination of the arrival of the vessel;

- The ship notifies the Port of destination 24 hours in advance with details of the ship, its crew and any hazardous or dangerous cargoes aboard vessel in accordance with the IMDG Code, and its intention to dock;

- The ship enters national territorial limits and notifies the port of details of its crew, its stores, and any other information required by the national authorities,

- The ship maintains contact with the port through the VTS system from the time it enters the port approaches, and proceeds to enter the port;

- A copy of the cargo manifest is submitted by the Port Agent to the Port Authority and the Customs Authority prior to the ship's arrival at port;

- The ship's master submits a FAL Declaration to Customs of all details of crew and stores on board;

- The ship's master gives a detailed report to the Port Authority complying with the regulations set down by the ISPS Code.

Although details of cargo reporting may have been covered earlier in this section of the study, they still have an overall bearing upon the safety and wellbeing of both the vessel and its crew. It should be noted that the ship's master can only report details of the cargo if he is fully aware of that cargo aboard vessel according to the cargo manifest. In many cases, the cargo may only be known by its groupage description, i.e. a generic description of the consolidated cargo in a LCL container load, and not by details of each individual consignment within that consolidated cargo. This absence of information may not yield vital information, such as the hazardous nature of an individual cargo, or whether such a cargo was [in]correctly stowed aboard vessel. It is this lack of information which may mask a much greater risk to the ship, its crew, and its location depending upon the location of other vessels close by, e.g. within the confines of port approaches, or where adverse weather conditions such as fog may be prevalent. It is this anomaly which may prejudice or compromise the safety and security of not only the ship and its crew, but also the safety of the surrounding environment including the port itself. There is a further risk prevalent if the exact nature of the crew is not fully known, concerning their professional competence to crew the vessel or even their nationality or even their motives for being aboard vessel at the time of the voyage.

A major problem arises where the Buyer (i.e. the Importer) arranges groupage shipments and has the cargo consolidated at a point in the country of departure under an Ex Works (EXW) basis. Given that the buyer initiated the transport of the various consignments, the Shipping Line will still issue both a Master Bill of Lading for the LCL groupage shipment as well as a set of House Bills of Lading, but may not necessarily issue the House Bills to the Buyer unless specifically requested. Thus, the exporter may never receive a copy of the House Bills of Lading relating to their consignment since they did not arrange the shipment. Nor will the exporter receive a copy of the Export Customs Declaration for that consignment, assuming that an individual Export Declaration is physically raised by the Freight Forwarder, which may not be the case in the event of a consolidated consignment. In many cases, this does not happen. There is thus no audit trail available to the exporter to show that their particular consignment was shipped. Furthermore, where a groupage consignment simply shows "Freight of All Kinds (FAK)" or a generic description such as "Cosmetic Products" or "Automotive Equipment", there is no specific means of verifying the individual consignments grouped within the container in question, as there may be the risk that no specific House Bills of Lading were raised for each individual consignment as far as the exporter is concerned. Furthermore, this lack of detailed information will also reflect on the Cargo Manifest issued to the Ship's Master and to Customs at the point of export.

The problem is compounded by the fact that the forwarding agent notifies the Port Agents about the cargo once the shipment has been arranged for loading aboard vessel. The freight forwarder is responsible for sending full details of the cargo to the Port Agent for the latter to incorporate the details of the consignment and the container in which it is loaded on the cargo manifest. The Port Agents are responsible for dealing with all affairs relating to the vessel while it is berthed at port, including the loading and unloading of the vessel, and the liability for conservancy and port handling charges. It is thus the responsibility of the Port Agent to ensure that the ship's master is made aware of all cargoes loaded aboard vessel, and that all hazardous or dangerous cargoes are notified in advance to the master of the vessel in order to ensure compliance with port regulations, SOLAS regulations and the general regulations concerning the correct stowage of all cargoes aboard vessel. If a freight forwarder does not submit the correct information concerning cargoes, especially those of a groupage or consolidated nature, to the Port Agent, the freight forwarder could be made liable for any accident or damage which could occur as a result of the failure to inform the Port Agents or the Ship's Master or even the Port itself of the nature of the cargo being loaded aboard vessel. In reality, the responsibility for correctly divulging information pertaining to the cargo lies with the exporter. If the exporter does not inform the freight forwarder of the true nature of the consignment, the rest of the chain of reporting is severely prejudiced, including the ramifications for insurance of the cargo in question.

In short, the neither the ship's master nor the shipping line nor the port authority may be entirely knowledgeable about the crew of the vessel or its cargo. Although the ISPS Code goes a long way to tightening up security measures aboard vessel as well as providing information about the crew, it only covers that which is known or is divulged in the company's interests. In the case of the ISPS Code, there are, however, likely to be cases where although the crew's nationality may be known, other information about each crew member may not be known because of the withholding of personal information by certain crew members for personal or other reasons. Furthermore, there is no internationally-binding code obliging the exporter or the freight agent to correctly declare all freight being loaded into a container, and in this way the cargo considerations are completely divorced from the issues of the nature of the vessel's crew. Even the recently-introduced ISO 28000 and 28001 standards allow the trader to compile and implement their own set of checklists and procedures concerning cargo security, and do not dictate the exact details of such procedures. The underlying principle is still one of *Uberrimae Fidei*. Thus, in an age of information technology and access to information, the data held by the Shipping Line pertinent to the cargo on any of its vessels may only be as accurate as the organisation inputting that information to the Shipping Line, such as a freight agent. With large-scale cargo consolidations, the risk of inaccuracy and increased risk on this basis is greatly increased. A ship will not report in to either a seaport or a control centre overlooking a narrow strait concerning the nature of its cargo if it is not aware of any hazardous or dangerous cargo on board, especially since the 24-hour reporting mechanism in place at many ports, especially those in the UK, is still voluntary and is not fully mandatory. The ship is entirely at the mercy of the shipping line's agents and the freight agents responsible for shipping cargo consignments. This level of uncertainty only adds to the risk of accidents or catastrophes occurring as a result of marine accidents, and thus severely compromises marine safety for the vessel, its crew and other cargoes aboard the vessel.

THE SHORE PERSPECTIVE

The aspect of maritime reporting is naturally important from the perspective onboard vessel. However, from the port perspective, there are many issues which beset port and landward activity which need to be addressed on a long-term basis, mainly as a result of recent maritime legislation which affects worldwide maritime activities.

The EU Directives covering the overall process of Vessel Monitoring and Tracking have meant that more sea lanes must be covered by some form of VTS system. The waters around southern

Scandinavia are being increasingly brought under some form of VTS activity, with the most recent being the Storebaelt (Great Belt) within Danish territorial limits. The process is presently underway to fully develop a VTS system to cover the Öresund, between Denmark and Sweden. And yet, there are still many sea areas, including much of the coastal waters surrounding the UK, which are not yet covered by an interactive VTS system similar to that at the Strait of Dover. Only the AIS system is being actively used around all UK waters, and even this is only effective if the vessels have their AIS transponders switched on. There are various AIS websites for public use, and these are in some ways the only way in which many organisations can monitor maritime activity around the UK coast. However, there is no fully-integrated VTS system for the whole of the UK, and every port manages its own affairs concerning vessel control activity. Indeed, there are still major ports in the UK which are not yet equipped with a VTS system, inferring that they have little, if any, monitoring or control facility over inward and outward vessel movements, despite the incidence of marine accidents close to their domains. Ports do not divulge information to other ports for a variety of reasons, and there is therefore no way of knowing a vessel's circumstances without being located at the port of arrival or departure. In short, the UK system of vessel control is severely fragmented, with information concerning a vessel's movements restricted to the authorities located at the vessel's port of arrival, unless it is passing through the Strait of Dover, in which case, that information is also known to the MCA's CNIS operations. Other than this, only the vessel's agents will retain information concerning particular vessels, their cargoes and their movements, and they will only convey that information to the port of destination.

Such information concerning the vessel's cargo is also becoming less manageable because of the increasing sizes of vessels. The latest vessels entering service with shipping lines such as Maersk, CMA CGM, China shipping and COSCO are well in excess of 100,000grt and can carry some 10000+ TEUs (Twenty-Foot Equivalent Units). The increasing number of containers carried aboard vessel inevitably results in a greater difficulty in managing such information as the compilation and transmission cargo manifests, as well as the problems associated with the loading and unloading of containers at any port visited. This additional burden of loading and unloading will also result in increased pressure on the ports to mange their infrastructural facilities, which inevitably leads to increased congestion of land-based traffic entering and exiting the ports.

Another area of concern stems from the fact that, in the UK, the Maritime & Coastguard Agency (MCA) has already rationalised its structure to the point that it no longer maintains the number of Coastguard stations around the UK coastline that it once did. Many of the MCA operations are not even controlled from coast-based stations, but are managed from inland-based centres. Even MCA operations concerning the North Channel, the Firth of Clyde and the Scottish West Coast are controlled from one building based at Gourock, on the upper reaches of the Firth of Clyde, far removed form such sea areas. It is assumed that in the event of a maritime emergency or incident, all operations can be controlled from this one centre. It has been confirmed by the MCA Office on the Clyde that it does not even use a VTS system for these areas, but relies on the AIS systems and information available. This approach is hardly contributing to compliance with the VTMS Directives issued by the EU Commission.

It is appreciated that legislation is designed to formalise and direct activities in a variety of sectors, but there are occasions where such legislation has led to increasing burdens upon those activities leading to questions being asked concerning the efficiency of those operations. The ISPS Code has been introduced by the IMO, and is being implemented by all ports worldwide. However, the smaller the port, the more difficult it is to incorporate the Code's requirements within an already-stretched scope of resources. Larger ports find it less difficult to comply with the regulations, as they already have a security-based system within which to operate. Small ports have to find the resources to incorporate such changes to their operating structures, and this inevitably leads to greater expenditure and other strains on such resources, as well as the burden of added levels of bureaucracy required to administrate such changes and activities. Add to this any port-based activities associated with the impact of the IMDG Code on HAZMAT movements and VTS requirements, and the system moves closer to overload. Additional burdens may now be placed on the system by the introduction of ISO 28000 and ISO 28001 standards, and this will inevitably stretch already-limited resources yet further.

In summary, the main Codes, Regulations and Standards which a Port must adhere to include the following:

- VTS (Seaward);
- AIS (Seaward);
- ISPS (Landward and Seaward);
- IMDG (Landward and Seaward);
- SOLAS (Seaward);
- FAL (Landward);
- ISO 28000/28001 (Landward).

Other issues, such as Port State Controls and the presence of both MCA and Customs are also prime issues in port management, as these controls refer equally to both vessel and cargo security. The Port Authorities are now so enmeshed in such regulations that they appear to need to spend more time complying with such regulations than in actually managing maritime activities. However, despite such regulations and controls, it is often the case that the Port's Harbourmaster is the last point of contact concerning the arrival of a vessel, as the shipping agents will already have arranged berthing formalities with the Port Authorities in advance, and the vessel does not necessarily report its arrival until it passes through the breakwaters and enters port, thus negating in part the whole rationale behind the reason for many of the regulations concerning vessel movements and port controls. However, the existence of VTS regimes in most major ports automatically identifies a vessel as it approaches the waters under the port's jurisdiction, and therefore it must declare itself to the port authority under such circumstances as it enters such controls. It must, therefore, state its identification details to the port authorities in advance of arrival at its berth. The only vessels which will have prior arrangements to account for such controls are those operated by authorised regular operators such as ferry companies, which run most short-sea routes on a daily basis.

The question must ultimately be asked as to whether the smaller ports will be able to maintain their operations for much longer in the light of the implementation of such regulations and the inevitable costs associated with such changes. As the threat of terrorism and the general concerns over maritime security increase, so too does the requirement for increasing levels of security at the ports. This inevitably costs time, effort and money, and many of the smaller ports are finding it difficult to keep up with the necessary changes imposed as a result of such requirements, especially as in general they do not receive financial aid from nation al authorities for the implementation of such changes. Even the larger ports are required to adopt more stringent measure with regard to both port, vessel and cargo security, especially under the requirements of the ISPS Code, and this is creating an atmosphere of radical change within the port environment, from both a landward and a seaward perspective, as well as an increasing level of bureaucracy associated with such changes.

THE ROLE OF THE SHIPPING AGENCY

Much of the mechanism relating to the reporting of the vessel and its cargo revolves around the role of the ship's agent. The agent represents the shipping line in most ports, and deals with all aspects of the ship's entry into port and the time it spends at the berth, as laytime for unloading, loading and maintenance. The agent is also responsible for communication with the Port Authority concerning the berthing of the vessel, the stevedoring arrangements for unloading and loading activities, the provision of ship's stores and the administration of and documentation for all such activities. It is also the duty of the agency to inform the harbourmaster of the arrival and departure of all vessels they represent, and in so doing, inform the harbourmaster and hence the port of all hazardous cargoes or problems with the vessel. The submission of this information depends upon how much information the master of the vessel holds concerning the cargo. Normally, the cargo manifest and the mate's receipt will give this information, but in cases of consolidations, the information pertaining to a cargo may be less than detailed or at worst inaccurate. The larger the vessel, the greater is its cargo capacity. The greater the amount of cargo carried, the greater the amount of documentary information required pertaining to that cargo. With the arrival of 10,000+ TEU container vessels of tonnages of 150,000grt plus, the greater the risk that this documentary information is less accurate or detailed on the grounds of the sheer volume of information required for the ship's manifest. And with this risk, there is a greater probability of a risk of danger owing to the lack of awareness on the part of both the ship's master and the agent of all hazardous or dangerous cargoes, or any other items potentially deemed as being prejudicial to the safety of the vessel, its crew or the port itself. Indeed, it is becoming evident that certain ports in Europe, including the UK, may not be able to handle such vessels, such is their size as well as the quantity of their containerised cargo.

It is the responsibility of the agent at the port of loading to ensure that the correct information is given to the vessel's master concerning the cargo being loaded aboard vessel, as the cargo manifest containing such information must agree with both the Bills of Lading and the Mate's Receipt, which is duly stamped and signed by the Master or the Mate. If the information should be lacking in any way, then it is the direct responsibility of the agent at the port of loading to shoulder any liability resulting from loss or damage in the event of an accident or a disaster befalling the vessel during the voyage or on arrival at the port of destination. In this respect, a great degree of professional responsibility is required on the part of the agent, along with a considerable knowledge of the rules and procedures involved in vessel management. In many cases, larger agency companies have offices in a variety of port locations, and deal with a wide range of vessel and freight-related activities, ranging from chartering through port and liner agency to freight forwarding and Customs clearance.

ISO 28000 / ISO 28001 AND SIX SIGMA

As well as initiatives introduced by organisations such as the IMO and the World Customs Organisation (WCO), the International Standards Organisation (ISO) has endeavoured to introduce a series of international standards implementing the individual Codes such as ISPS requiring all worldwide Port Authorities and Shipping Lines to implement ISO standards in order to maximise their security potential. The ISO 28000 initiative has been introduced to apply a security standard to the International Supply Chain, by implementing a set of procedures and checklists for all exporters and importers when shipping consignments of goods overseas. The standard requires each exporter to ensure that all consignments being exported are subjected to a series of checks prior to the goods being packed and containerised for security purposes, based on a security risk assessment, and in the form of a security management system. The purpose of the implementation of such a set of procedures is to anticipate any potential risk and reduce or eliminate it at the point of the goods being despatched from the exporter's premises. The drawback in the system is that it refers to the actual goods themselves, and the ability of the exporter to control the shipment. It does not necessarily relate to the documentation accompanying the consignment.

One of the main points of ISO 28000 is the Security Management System. It states the following:

- An organisation must establish, document, implement, maintain and continually improve an effective security management system for identifying security risks and controlling and mitigating their consequences;

- An organisation must define the scope of its security management system;

- Where an organisation outsources any processes affecting conformity with these requirements (including Ex Works shipments), the organisation must ensure that these processes are controlled, and that the necessary controls and responsibilities of such outsourced are identified within the security management system;

Under the Ex Works (EXW) principle this may be a vague area, as the exporter bears no responsibility for the actual shipment. However, within the Security Management System there are 5 main action elements, which are:

- Policy;
- Security Risk Assessment and Planning;
- Implementation and Operation;
- Checking and Corrective Action;
- Management Review.

This implies that a constant self-corrective action plan should be drawn up by the organisation and adhered to at all times, suggesting more responsibility being placed on the organisation for ensuring that it does have control over all its shipments, both inward and outward. In itself, this is a worthy solution, and it can be used effectively. However, the wheel has once again been re-invented, as the whole process defined above bears a similar relationship to that of the Six Sigma process.

The Six Sigma process can be defined as:

- Define;
- Measure;
- Analyse Data;
- Implement Changes;
- Control the Process.

Or DMAIC, for short. In reality, the organisation content to work within the 3-4 Sigma scale will encounter a problem level of between 25% and 40% or errors requiring addressing in a process. Working towards a Six Sigma level will reduce this to below 0.01% of errors in the system.

The actual table used to define the Sigma Level (Process Capability) of any organisation is based on the level of defects per million opportunities, i.e. each transaction. It seeks to control the level of allowable defects (if any defective operation can ever be seen to be allowable, as most organisations will seek to reduce their defect acceptance level to zero wherever possible).

SIGMA LEVEL (Process Capability)	Defects per Million Opportunities
2	308,537
3	66,807
4	6210
5	233
6	3.4

Probability of defects of different Sigma Levels

Although this system is primarily used in production processes to increase quality levels, it can also be used in the service sector equally effectively, especially in terms of the enhancement of security within the supply and logistics chain.

The use of such controls within the Six Sigma process can include:

- The number of correct reports issued in advance of the arrival of all vessels in port per month, compared with the number of actual reports submitted;

- The number of correct reports issued in advance of the arrival of all vessels in port per month, compared with the number of actual arrival of vessels;

- The number of correct cargo reports issued per manifest, compared with the number or actual entries on the manifest.

The analysis of such data will yield the number of successes against the number of actual reports, and will enable the authorities concerned to tighten up their procedures to ensure that all vessels arriving at any port must adhere to the reporting requirements set out at very least by EC Directive 2002/59/EC. It already appears that in many cases, the harbourmaster may not know about all movements of vessels into and out of the port prior to those involved with berthing the vessel and handling its cargo. According to EC Directive 2002/59/EC, the purpose of the exercise is for the vessel to actively submit an advance report to the port of arrival giving all its essential details, including cargo, prior to its arrival. This information must therefore be submitted by the vessel to the harbourmaster as well as to the port VTS operators in advance of its arrival, as well as by the vessel's agents at the port, a situation which does not happen with the required frequency.

This means that any organisation maintaining control over the security of its shipments will ensure that it will rarely, if ever, encounter problems relating to those shipments, as it will seek to ensure that all information relating to shipment documentation is correctly completed and recorded, and that it has full access to such information and documentation. This effectively rules out the present principle of Ex Works (EXW), and pushes it more towards Free Carrier (FCA) or further along the INCOTERMS chain.

It should be pointed out that the Six Sigma process works on the basis of Six Sigma (6 Standard Deviations) from the average calculated as the mathematical mean of any process, and that the closer an analysis comes to Six Sigma, the closer the process comes to perfection, as a Six Sigma measurement allows for virtually zero imperfections in a system. Indeed, the Six Sigma approach may work better than the ISO 28000 approach for a security management system.

ISO 28001 refers to Customs controls and how containers are packed and loaded aboard vessel. It refers not only to the consignment in terms of physical checks made prior to export, but that the cargo manifest refers to and agrees with the consignments within the container. Again, the information may not be sufficient enough to satisfy all requirements, in that agents still apply generic terms to consolidations, rather than necessarily recording all exact details of each consignment within the container. Only with the CT-PAT initiative has some attempt been made to itemise in detail all consignments entering the United States and Canada from overseas by maritime means. However, the same rules have yet to be applied to other countries, especially the European Union. The adoption by the WCO of a standard UCR (Unique Consignment Reference) for all imported and exported consignments is only part of the solution. In many cases, the UCR may only refer to a consolidated load, and does not necessarily refer to all consignments within that consolidation. There is still the risk that the information provided on either the Cargo Manifest or the Bill of Lading may bear little relation to the cargo actually loaded into the container and aboard vessel, and this may still emanate from the fact that the party arranging the shipment made the decision to consolidate every cargo loaded aboard the container, and simply instructed the agent to provide a basic set of information, rather than exact details of every load therein. This arrangement of the shipment also depends upon the Term of Delivery (the INCOTERM) used, and thus is open to considerable interpretation and discretion on the part of either buyer or seller.

The other main reason for Customs involvement is the move away from the examination of consignments at the port, and towards self-regulation by the trader. The Authorised Economic Operator (AEO) initiative is partially designed for this purpose. Any trader wishing to be approved by Customs for such status, namely a privileged fast-track form of clearance of consignments through Customs, will have to ensure strict compliance with a series of regulatory requirements partly based on the ISO 28001 initiative, and aimed at ensuring greater degrees of security and compliance in terms of information supplied by the trader to the Customs authority through electronic means. The electronic form of declaration has taken over from the traditional approach to examinations and clearance internationally, and in turn Customs frontier resources have been reduced, especially with regard to Port controls. In the UK, it is expected that the AEO status is to be initiated in 2007, and to be fully achieved some time beyond 2010.

Although ISO 28000 and ISO 28001 go a long way in highlighting risk in the Supply Chain and attempting to address and reduce this risk, they do not answer all the questions. The increasing size of container vessels and hence the increased amounts of cargo carried inevitably mean that more information for these cargoes is required, especially on an electronic basis, and hence there is a higher risk that such information may not be sufficiently scrutinised in detail to ensure that all cargoes are properly screened prior to entry into another country and cleared through border controls. The emphasis is to move the container through the port as quickly as possible to the trader's premises, with the minimisation of delays for examination on the way. Inevitably, there is the risk of corner cutting, and the fact that computers do not always make the correct decision. In this way, the risk of some information passing through the net is increased, and hence the risk of accidents occurring or threats of terrorist attack by exploiting any loopholes in the system, especially where the master of the vessel may still be unaware of the nature of all the cargoes aboard vessel because of omissions by the agents inputting the original information for each cargo at the time of loading aboard vessel.

THE SHORT SEA SECTOR AND THE 'MARINE MOTORWAY'

The issues raised to date have largely concerned deep-sea traffic on a global basis, and in general refer to containerised movements. However, a further area requiring scrutiny concerns the short sea sector, especially shipping movements within the Nordring (North Sea and Baltic) vicinity and the Mediterranean area. Both are major maritime areas in terms of their importance, and both are used by a mixture of container, bulk cargo and Ro-Ro (Roll-On, Roll-Off) trailer and passenger vessel movements. The container and bulk cargo operations are similar in many ways to the deep sea operations, as such movements are not necessarily frequent between the ports in the region, and refer to specific cargo loads. This said, the feeder services linking the North Sea ports with the deep-sea vessel movements out of the larger container ports are conducted on a very regular basis, with most feeder services out of Rotterdam, Antwerp and Felixstowe to the smaller ports operating on a weekly or twice-weekly basis at very least, as are those in the Mediterranean region from ports such as Genoa. The primary regular sailings in the North Sea and Baltic region, however, concern Ro-Ro ferry operations, with sailings several times a day in many cases, and on a daily basis in others. These services are conducted by Ferry Companies classified as Authorised Regular Operators, which are authorised by the maritime authorities in the countries where they operate to avoid the normal reporting requirements on the grounds that their ferries will be expected in port on a regular scheduled basis. These regular sailings are commonly referred to as the 'Marine Motorway' because of their frequency coupled with the fact that they carry large numbers of road vehicles, a facility often seen as a marine extension to the extensive road network throughout Europe. There are indeed many operators who believe that a ferry service is simply an extension of a roadway out to sea. It is often forgotten that a specific regime exists for the carriage of cargoes by such means of transport over and above that which exists for road haulage. This same principle of the marine motorway also applies to the container feeder services operating in the North Sea area as well, since their services operate several times per week between ports.

However, an absence of a reporting requirement does not absolve such operators from ensuring that information pertaining to their cargoes is correct and accurate. There is still the need for the master of a feeder vessel or a Ro-Ro Ferry to be absolutely certain as to the nature of the cargoes aboard vessel. In the case of feeder services, this requirement is an extension of the reporting and documentary requirement for the deep-sea element of the operation, as the cargoes aboard the feeder vessel will doubtless be trans-shipped at the intermediate port to a larger vessel for shipment to elsewhere in the world, or vice versa. The rules and problem issues applying to the transport of hazardous and consolidated cargoes therefore apply as much to feeder vessels as they do to their larger counterparts.

In the case of Ro-Ro traffic, however, the rules pertaining to cargo documentation are more vague and less well-controlled. Within the European short-sea regime, there are more simplified rules concerning the issue of shipping documentation than for deep-sea traffic, as there is no requirement for Bills of Lading. The cargoes carried are generally transported by road trailer, which is loaded aboard vessel as a unit, with or without its haulage tractor unit. The trailer will have been loaded at an inland point, and will be driven to the port of loading where it is driven aboard vessel. Upon the arrival of the vessel at the port of destination, e.g. Europoort Rotterdam, it will be driven off the ferry and on to its final destination elsewhere on the European continent. This integrated journey, including the ferry sailing, is covered by one single document, the Consignment Note (CMR). Although the ferry sailing is included as part of the movement, it is not necessarily specified on the document, although a separate note may be issued to the carrier for the maritime sector of the journey as evidence of contract of carriage by the ferry operator. Where the road carrier is an integrated part of the combined movement including the ferry operation, such as DFDS, then the maritime sector of the journey is an automatically-assumed part of the overall operation.

The CMR Consignment Note is raised by the carrier according to the instructions of the trader arranging the shipment. This document may cover a single trailer load, or it may cover a consolidated trailer shipment. Depending upon who arranges the shipment according to the relevant INCOTERM, the information provided on the CMR will be detailed or otherwise. In the case of consolidations, it is often the case where the information contained on the Master Consignment Note covering the whole consolidation is very vague and generic. For such intra-European movements, it is generally the case that only two INCOTERMS are used, i.e. EXW (Ex Works) or DDP (Delivered Duty Paid).

Where the consolidated shipment is arranged by the buyer on an Ex Works (EXW) basis, the information on the CMR may well be very limited and generic, and may not accurately reflect the details of all the individual consignments loaded into the trailer. In the case of the movement of hazardous goods by trailer, this lack of information could prove in itself dangerous, as the risk of accidents aboard vessel is heightened by the very fact that the documentary information pertaining to such cargoes is lacking, and could compromise the safety of the lives of the crew and passengers aboard vessel, as well as the integrity of other cargoes carried on the same vessel. Where the carriage of a consignment is arranged by the seller on a Delivered Duty Paid (DDP) basis, the risks of this omission of information are decreased, as the seller may well ensure that greater attention is paid to the correct recording of essential information on the CMR, as they require some form of proof of shipment.

The terms EXW and DDP are the most common terms used for road transport, as they reflect a direct integrated movement, and they are often referred to as "Freight Collect" and "Freight Prepaid" respectively, given the inference of the party responsible for the arrangement and payment of carriage of the consignment. Two comparative diagrams of this arrangement can be seen as follows:

1) Delivered Duty Paid

2) Ex Works

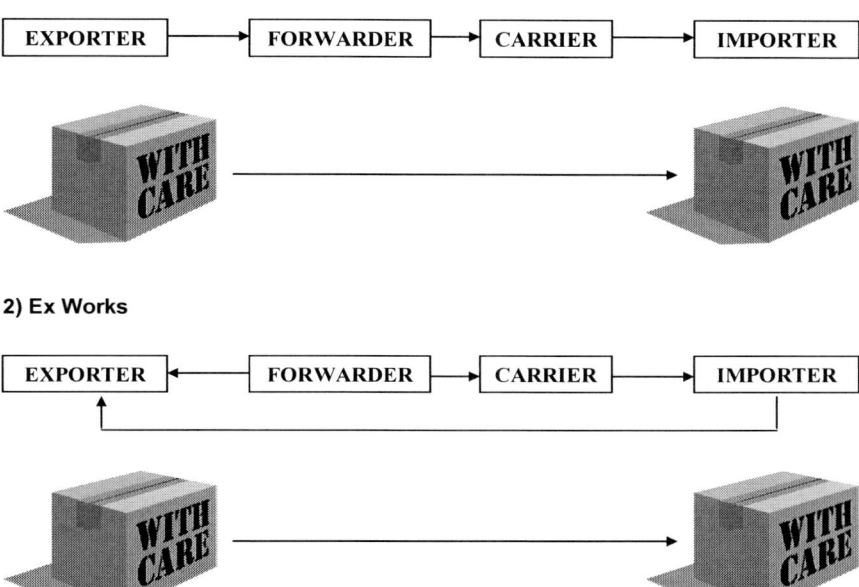

Note how, in the first diagram, the exporter arranges the shipment and ensures control over that shipment. In the second diagram, however, the exporter has absolutely no control over the shipment, as the buyer arranges everything, including the documentation. Under the terms of Ex Works, the buyer is not legally bound to send any proof of shipment, including the CMR, to the seller. Under maritime rules, this arrangement gives little control by the seller over how the consignment is being shipped by maritime means, and means that the maritime carrier is entirely at the mercy of the arrangement between the buyer, the freight forwarder and the carrier. If the buyer arranges the consolidation and gives little information to the forwarder concerning the nature of each cargo included in the consolidation, then the forwarder will in turn give little information to the carrier (and hence the shipping line) concerning the consolidation, hence the elevation of the risk with regard to the maritime shipment.

In this way, there are increased risks concerning the safety of the ferry and its complement, especially under the SOLAS Convention. Many cargoes are carried by ferries without the full knowledge of the master as to their nature, as the vessel's cargo manifest will not contain full information concerning these cargoes. In this respect, the risks to short-sea maritime safety are as great as those concerning deep-sea shipments and require addressing in terms of marine reporting in the same way as those pertaining to deep-sea operations. The simplification of regulations concerning short-sea shipments have in some ways prejudiced and compromised reporting requirements in terms of safety and compliance with international trade controls even more than the requirements for deep-sea traffic, with the result that in many cases, short-sea traffic may be seen as a greater risk than its deep-sea counterpart.

PERCEIVED ANOMALIES

In assessing the principle of marine reporting, several anomalies arise which require addressing in the maritime sector. These include:

- Requirements of the national maritime authority;
- The reporting of the vessel to the port of destination;
- The reporting of the vessel in restricted international waterways;
- The details included in the report;
- Shared responsibility between the owners of the vessel and the agents.

REQUIREMENTS OF THE NATIONAL MARITIME AUTHORITY

Each national maritime authority has its own national or supranational marine reporting requirements, as in the case of the European Union. Those requirements are based on the legislation passed by the national government, or, in the case of the EU, Directives issued by the Commission in Brussels. In the case of the EU Vessel Reporting and Monitoring Directives, each member state takes its own action based on its interpretation of the Directive. In the case of Denmark, a VTS system already exists covering the Storebaelt, the Strait passing though Danish national territory, but a system has yet to be implemented in the Öresund, the Strait separating Denmark and Sweden. Conversely, a mandatory Vessel Reporting System covering the Strait of Dover is jointly operated by the UK and French authorities, whereas there is no system whatsoever covering the North Channel, the Strait separating Scotland and Northern Ireland. All shipping movements through the North Channel are monitored at a distance by the AIS system used by UK Coastguards, and even this does not physically control or monitor vessel movements. It merely shows the vessel movements through the Channel on a computer screen at a considerable distance from the Strait, in the Coastguard building at the other end of the Firth of Clyde. This situation is detailed in a case study at the end of the text.

THE REPORTING OF THE VESSEL TO THE PORT OF DESTINATION

Unless the vessel's owners have their own representation at a port, it is normal practice for the vessel's agents at the port to report the arrival of the vessel to the Port Authority, although this practice is not necessarily carried out within the requirements set out in EC Directive 2002/59. This report will give details of the vessel, some general details of its cargo, and the berth, dock or wharf required for the purposes of unloading and loading. To this extent, some general details of the cargo are included, especially as the cargo manifest for the vessel must be submitted to the customs authority for the purposes of cargo examination by Customs should the need arise. However, with the increase in size of container vessels, the complexity and size of the cargo manifest has also increased. Besides which, although the 24-hour reporting rule applies for all vessels entering port (or at least an inbound report once the vessel has left its port of departure, assuming a voyage of less than 24 hours), the agent does not always report the arrival of the vessel to the harbourmaster, even in the case of the vessel carrying dangerous or hazardous (HAZMAT) cargoes. It is to be expected that as part of any reporting mechanism, the ISPS rules at Security Level 1 pertaining to the security arrangements for the vessel itself are obeyed when the vessel enters port. The rules pertain to the security plan of the vessel and those responsible for the vessel's security. It is often the case that the harbourmaster only receives information concerning the vessel's arrival via the port authority once the agent has already notified the port authority. In theory, however, the port harbourmaster will have a list of vessels expected to arrive at the port some time before their actual arrival, as the agent will have made arrangements for the docking of the vessel some time in advance of the vessel's arrival, usually some weeks. It is the express duty of the agent to complete a Declaration (The Agent's Declaration) to the port prior to the vessel's arrival, giving all relevant details of the vessel concerned. However, this declaration assumes all known facts are correct; it does not account for any sudden change in the vessel's condition or circumstances, such as accidents aboard vessel, problems with the vessel itself or its cargo.

In brief, therefore, it is the responsibility of the ship's agent to declare the vessel's arrival to the port authority well in advance of that arrival, and to ensure that all information about the vessel and its crew and cargo is known to the port and other authorities accordingly. However, the normal 24-hour reporting rule is not often obeyed, implying that certain information may not be transmitted to the port authorities in the acceptable manner. There are many instances where the harbourmaster is the last point in the chain of contact to know of the vessel's impending arrival at port. The port authority itself will however already be well aware of the vessel's arrival, having been informed by the vessel's agent well in advance of the vessel's arrival.

THE REPORTING OF THE VESSEL IN RESTRICTED INTERNATIONAL WATERWAYS

When a vessel is entering restricted international waterways such as the Strait of Dover, the Öresund or the Storebaelt, it is the duty of the master of the vessel to notify the international authorities of each country bordering the strait in question concerning the vessel's passage through the Strait. In this case, it is not the task of the vessel's agent to do this, as the vessel may not be calling at a port near the Strait in question. It is the direct responsibility of the master of the vessel to carry out this task. However, such reporting may not always be undertaken, as the use of AIS may simply pick up the vessel on radar and monitor it through the strait in question. Only where a mandatory vessel reporting system exists will the master be obliged to report the vessel's presence and intentions as part of its sailing plan, especially where the vessel may be carrying hazardous or dangerous cargoes. In this respect, a more proactive control regime such as VTS (Vessel Traffic Systems) facilitates a greater control over the vessel in question by allowing the constant monitoring of and contact with the vessel while it remains within the domain and scope of the control system. The drawback of the VTS regime is that it does not take account of details of vessel's cargo or its crew. As with the AIS system, it simply identifies the vessel and its registration details. Because of the VHF Radio Channel frequencies available for contact between the vessel and the monitoring authority, contact with the vessel's master may be maintained by radio link. However, the purpose of the VTS system is to monitor and track the vessel's movement. Although the VTS operator may issue guidance to the master of the vessel for the purposes of navigation through a channel within a restricted waterway, the system used does not actively intercept that vessel for security purposes, nor does it request details on the contents of the vessel. The information provided will refer to the identification of the vessel and its destination. In this respect, there is a distinct difference in the responsibility for the identification of the vessel depending upon whether the vessel is passing through a strait of international water or whether it is calling at a port in the area. It is this distinction which determines which party, i.e. the vessel or its agents, should declare the vessel's presence to the authorities.

THE DETAILS INCLUDED IN THE REPORT

The reports for the arrival of a vessel at port or its passage through a restricted international waterway differ radically in their content and detail. Details of the vessel's cargo, however general, are required for the vessel's arrival at a port, whereas these are not required at present for the purposes of a vessel's passage through a restricted international waterway. A report for a vessel passing through a strait deals solely with the identification of the vessel, whereas this information is increased to include general details of the vessel's cargo when it arrives at a port, partly as the vessel is entering national Customs territory when it arrives at the port and is therefore required to declare all items it carries, including details of the crew, passengers, stores and cargoes, according to the international IMO FAL regulations. Cargo reports are usually of a more detailed nature, given that the Cargo Manifest should give full details of all cargoes carried aboard the vessel. This document is also supported by the Mate's Receipt, which is the document showing that the master of the vessel is certain of all the cargoes carried by that vessel. This set of documents should also be supported by all Bills of Lading relating to the cargoes aboard vessel, although in cases of consolidations, FAK (Freight of all Kinds) or "Said to Contain", this is often not the case. To this extent, cargo manifests and other reports may be scant in the details they provide, which does not give rise to adequate security of cargo or even the safety or security of the vessel itself. Even in an age of increasing tonnages of cargo vessels, there is still the need for detailed reports of the cargo of any vessel, and this detail should be known by any relevant authority whether a vessel is passing through a strait or entering a port. In this way, such details can be passed between the authorities concerned in order to allow for the full transparency of any maritime reporting regime.

SHARED RESPONSIBILITY BETWEEN THE OWNERS OF THE VESSEL AND THE AGENTS

Ultimately, the owner of the vessel is responsible for the safety, security, upkeep and well-being of the vessel at all times, although it devolves a certain degree of that responsibility to the agents when the vessel enters port. However, the owners of the vessel equally devolve the responsibility of the reporting of the vessel to different parties depending upon the circumstances of the vessel at a particular point in its voyage. The sailing plans are the responsibility of the master and the crew, as well as any charter-parties using the services of that vessel. The reporting mechanisms required for sailing through restricted international waters are the responsibility of the master of the vessel, while the responsibility for declaring the vessel's arrival at a port are devolved to the ship's agent at the port in question. In this respect, the vessel's owner takes little responsibility for the vessel's activities, other than those basic legal responsibilities required of the owner. The rest is split between the vessel's master, the agents and perhaps the vessel's charterer.

There is a requirement, therefore, for a degree of collective responsibility relating to all parties involved, concerning who should accept responsibility for what function. It is unfortunate that the use of electronics for the purpose of vessel monitoring does not allow for in-depth scrutiny of information relating to both the vessel and its contents. Various rules pertaining to the responsibility for various degrees of reporting functions are often overlooked in the interests of expediency, and often do not account for the complete situation concerning the presence of a vessel in a specific location, especially in an international strait or on the approach to a port. If information is not required or specifically requested, it will not be divulged. A major area of anomaly concerns how much information should be divulged by the operators of a vessel, the vessel's agents or the vessel itself. The net result is that between all these considerations, there is no standardisation in the detail or the amount of information available to the maritime authorities from any vessel. It is ultimately this anomaly which needs to be addressed, in order to achieve a complete control over not only a vessel's movements but also what it carries, for overall security purposes.

There are therefore several anomalies in the present marine reporting structure which can at any time give rise to breakdowns in communication between any vessel and the national authorities. Many of the anomalies refer to the level of perceived basic or essential information required by each of the authorities against the actual information available, as well as the incompatibility of various existing systems with each other, but the main area of concern is to what extent maritime security is being prejudiced by the lack of essential information pertaining to not only the vessel itself and its sailing intentions, but also the cargo it carries and the lack of accurate information pertaining to that cargo. If such details, such as cargo or passengers, are not adequately reported, then safety or security issues could be severely compromised. In an age of insecurity and uncertainty, such failure to fully report any information relating to the vessel or its cargo engenders an increasing level of risk, which may in turn compromise the level of national security for any nation concerned.

IMPLICATIONS OF THE *ERICA*, *PRESTIGE* AND *HYUNDAI FORTUNE* DISASTERS

In 2002, the Tanker *Prestige* split apart during a fierce storm off the North-West Spanish Coast and her cargo of crude oil was lost into the sea. A similar fate befell the tanker *Erika* off the French Coast in 1999, in ways similar to the loss of the tanker *Amoco Cadiz* off the French Coast in 1978. The SafeSeaNet system was implemented by the European maritime authorities to endeavour to avoid the repetition of such disasters. The notion of the system is to maintain an information base on all commercial vessels and the risks they pose to the maritime environment. However, the basis for the SafeSeaNet initiative was the risk posed primarily by vessels designed to carry bulk hazardous cargoes especially carriers of crude oil and chemicals, and thus the regime was designed around the dissemination of information concerning the nature and state of these vessels. The SafeSeaNet initiative has been partly responsible for ensuring the reduction in illegal spillages of oil as a result of tank cleaning at sea, along with other legislation passed over the past few years. However, there was no provision made for the mandatory reporting of such vessels when approaching national territorial waters other than the customary 24-hour reporting rule when the vessel approaches its port of destination, and the VTS systems presently in operation are only designed to provide an information-based system as well as monitoring the progress of any vessel within the scope of the VTS system. There is, as such, no proper reporting system in operation requiring a vessel to report into the national authorities on its approach to national territorial waters, other than the US and Canadian 96-hour reporting regimes in operation.

The case of the container vessel *Hyundai Fortune* reinforces the need to establish a regime requiring the master of a commercial vessel to be fully aware of all his cargoes, especially in the case of container vessels, and to be able to report this information in advance of entering national territorial waters. On March 21 2006, a fire broke out aboard the 5000 TEU container vessel "Hyundai Fortune" while sailing through the Gulf of Aden, on her way to the Suez Canal and the European Ports. Just after mid-day, an explosion ripped through the lower cargo area and hull of the vessel and aft of the accommodation area, sending between 60 and 90 containers falling into the ocean. The explosion caused a massive blaze which spread through the stern of the vessel, including the accommodation area in the vessel's superstructure. As a result of the fire, secondary explosions occurred in seven containers above deck, which, it was discovered later, were full of fireworks. This fact was not known to the vessel's master at the time of the disaster, but was only discovered later as a result of extensive investigations into the vessel's cargo. It was also ascertained that as many as one third of the vessel's complement of containers were damaged by the inferno. Every container aft of the accommodation area was either incinerated or lost at sea. It has been conjectured that the latter, larger explosions which crippled the vessel were caused by the detonation of the fireworks as a result of the heat resulting from the initial blaze.

The main element of the issue concerns the knowledge of the cargo by the master of the vessel. It would appear that the containers holding the fireworks were all in close proximity to each other. Under the rules of stowage aboard vessel, any containers known to contain hazardous or dangerous cargoes must not be stowed together in a place close to the management of the ship or its accommodation area. They must be stowed well apart from each other, away from the areas of accommodation, and their presence must be known and understood by the vessel's master, as in accordance with the SOLAS regulations it is the master who must ensure that all steps are taken to reduce the risk of spillage or destruction or the risk of threat to other cargoes or even the vessel itself, while the cargo is in transit. In the case of the need to report the vessel's impending arrival at a port or even the vessel's presence in limited waterways such as the Strait of Dover or the Storebaelt, the risk of disaster is increased where the master of the vessel is not aware of certain cargoes aboard vessel, especially those of a hazardous or dangerous nature. If such a disaster had occurred in areas of water more limited than the Gulf of Aden, such as the Strait of Dover, the results would have been even more catastrophic, especially as there would have been no specific report issued to the UK or French maritime authorities concerning the hazardous nature of the cargoes aboard vessel. Previous incidents in the Strait of Dover have reflected similar circumstances, where a collision occurred between two vessels, and the resulting fire aboard one of the vessels resulted in the release of toxic vapours. One of the contributory factors of this fire was that certain containers of hazardous chemicals had been stowed in the forward area of one of the vessels, and these containers were damaged in the collision. The possibility of absence of knowledge of these cargoes by the master of one of the vessels may have contributed to a lack of information reported to HM Coastguards at Dover, coupled with a failure by one of the vessels to adhere to its correct separation lane.

Vessel reporting must be based on the risk posed by the vessel and its cargo to the maritime environment and the region which it is approaching. The higher the risk, the greater the need for a robust mandatory vessel reporting system imposed by either a national or a supranational government. A simple dissemination of existing known information concerning a vessel or its whereabouts is insufficient. There is the need for commercial vessels to physically report into a national authority prior to entering national territorial waters and state its sailing plan, its cargo and its intended port of destination. In this way, decisions can be taken earlier concerning how to handle, monitor and control the vessel's movements prior to its entry into port, as well as making adequate provision for its safe arrival at port and security concerning the unloading or discharge of its cargo. Although provisions are presently made for the arrival of the vessel at port by the shipping agents, these provisions are made upon the level of knowledge available concerning the cargo of the vessel, and do not necessarily account for the actual details of the cargo which may not always be known by all parties concerned, details which may compromise the safety and security of the vessel and its cargo, as exemplified by the disaster on board the container ship *Hyundai Fortune* in March 2006.

CHAPTER SEVEN

MARINE ACCIDENTS AND THEIR AFTERMATH

This chapter could have been entitled "A Chapter of Accidents", given how regularly maritime history is punctuated by accidents and disasters. The effectiveness of marine reporting can be seen in how quickly disasters involving vessels are reported to the national authorities, and how such reports are duly dealt with. In some cases, there is no time to report a problem, as the vessel quickly sinks, and in such cases even extensive investigations do not necessarily ascertain the truth concerning the catastrophe. The present legislation concerning the carriage of hazardous and dangerous cargoes, and the need for the monitoring of vessels carrying such cargoes was enacted by the European Union was implemented as a result of the sinking of the tankers Erika and Prestige, and accounts of the disasters involving both these vessels is included in this chapter.

In the early part of 2008 alone, two vessels came to grief off UK waters, namely the ferry *Riverdance* and the freighter *Ice Prince*. These, however, are relatively minor affairs compared with the serious accidents of the past number of years involving container vessels, bulk carriers and tankers. It is predominantly the disasters involving tankers which have caught the headlines, with much of international maritime policy decisions having been taken as a result of such disasters. However, these disasters, especially those involving the tankers Erika and Prestige, have led to serious soul-searching with regard to the impact of marine disasters involving pollution on the coastal environment, as well as the safety of traffic on the high seas. Add to these other disasters involving container vessels such as the *Hyundai Fortune* and the *MSC Napoli*, and the whole issue of marine reporting and maritime safety becomes a much more major issue. Even historic disasters in the 1960s and 1970s involving vessels such as the *Torrey Canyon*, *Berge Istra*, *Berge Vanga* and *Derbyshire* have aroused deep concerns in the maritime sector with regard to vessel safety, and to what extent measures were available to monitor the movements of such vessels prior to their loss.

TANKERS

The tanker *Torrey Canyon* was the first of the big supertankers capable of carrying a cargo of 120,000 tons of crude oil, and was wrecked off the western coast of Cornwall in 1967, causing an environmental disaster. When originally built in the United States in 1959, she had a capacity of 60,000 tons dwt, but she was enlarged in Japan to 120,000 tons deadweight capacity. At the time of the accident, she was owned by Barracuda Tanker Corporation, a subsidiary of Union Oil Company of California, but chartered to British Petroleum (BP). She was 974.4 feet (297.0 m) long, 125.4 feet (38.2 m) beam and 68.7 feet (20.9 m) draught.

She left the Kuwait National Petroleum Company refinery at Mina al-Ahmadi, on her final voyage on 19 February 1967, with full cargo of crude oil, reaching the Canary Islands by 14 March. From there her planned route was up the European coast to the oil port of Milford Haven.

On 18 March 1967, owing to a navigational error, the *Torrey Canyon* struck Pollard's Rock in the Seven Stones reef between the Cornish mainland and the Scilly Isles.

This was the first major oil spill resulting from a maritime disaster. A reasonably adequate outline of how to deal with a coastal oil spill had been issued to local authorities some years previously, but had apparently been forgotten or overlooked, and it was therefore widely reported that no plans had been prepared beforehand to deal with such an incident. The tanker had to be prepared to deliver its cargo to anywhere in the world, and so it only had small-scale charts. She also used LORAN (Long Range Navigation) radio navigation system, but not the more accurate Decca Navigator system. When the risk of collision with a fishing fleet became obvious, there was some confusion between the Master and the helmsman (who was actually the cook and had little experience) as to whether she was in manual or automatic steering mode; by the time this was resolved, it was too late, as she grounded on the Seven Stones reef. Unsuccessful attempts were made to float the ship off the reef, and during these attempts, one member of the Dutch salvage team was killed. The ship broke apart after being stranded on the reef for several days, and was eventually bombed by aircraft from the Royal Navy and RAF several days later, in attempt to break her up further. Attempts to use foam booms to contain the oil were also of limited success due to their fragility in high seas.

Some 50 miles (80 km) of French and 120 miles (190 km) of Cornish coast were contaminated by the oil which spilled from her tanks. Around 15,000 sea birds were killed, along with huge numbers of marine organisms, before the 270 square miles (700 sq km) of oil slick dispersed, although a significant amount of damage was also caused by the heavy use of so-called detergents to break up the slick. These detergents were the first-generation variants of products originally formulated to clean surfaces in ships' engine-rooms, with no concern over the toxicity of their components, and many observers believed that they were officially referred to as "detergents", rather than the more accurate description of "solvent-emulsifiers", to encourage a comparison with the much more benign domestic cleaning products. Some 42 vessels sprayed over 10,000 tons of these dispersants on to the floating oil, and they were also deployed against oil washed up on the surrounding beaches.

Claims were made by the British and French Governments against the owners of the vessel and the subsequent settlement was the largest ever in marine history for an oil claim. The British Government was only able to serve its writ against the owners by arresting the *Torrey Canyon*'s sistership, the *Lake Palourde*, when she put in for minor provisions at Singapore, four months after the oil spill. The French Government, alerted to the presence of the *Lake Palourde*, pursued the ship with motor boats, but were unable to board and serve their writ.

The disaster led to many changes in international regulations, for example the Civil Liability Convention (CLC) of 1969, which imposed strict liability on ship owners without the need to prove negligence, and the 1973 International Convention for the Prevention of Pollution from Ships, later modified by the Protocol of 1978 (MARPOL 73/78), signed 17 February 1973.

On 24 January 1976, the grounding of the VLCC (Very Large Crude Carrier) Olympic Bravery, fortunately empty, caused a spill of 1,200 tonnes of bunker fuel. On 16 October the same year, a third incident occurred with the shipwrecking of the tanker Boehlen off the shore of the island of Sein, which led to a spill of 7,000 tonnes of its cargo of heavy Venezuelan crude.

On the morning of 16 March 1978, the oil tanker *Amoco Cadiz* (109700 grt), en route from the Persian Gulf to Rotterdam with 227,000 tonnes of crude oil, encountered stormy conditions with winds gusting up to 130 km/h. At around 09:45am, a heavy wave hit the ship's rudder and it was found that she was no longer responding to the helm. This was due to the shearing of Whitworth thread studs in the Hastie four ram steering gear, built under licence in Spain, causing a loss of hydraulic fluid. Attempts to repair the damage were made but proved unsuccessful. While the message "no longer manoeuvrable" and asking other vessels to stand by was transmitted at 10:20am, no call for tug assistance was issued until 11:20am. At this time, the captain of the *Amoco Cadiz* requested the assistance of a tug boat. The German tug *Pacific* responded and contacted the *Amoco Cadiz* at 11:28am, offering assistance under a Lloyd's Open Form. It arrived on the scene at 12:20pm, but because of the stormy sea as well as delays apparently caused by the captain of the tanker, a tow line was not in place until 2pm and broke off at 4:15pm. A second, larger, tug boat, the *Seefalke*, was by this time already making its way to assist the *Amoco Cadiz*. Several attempts were made to establish another tow line and the *Amoco Cadiz* dropped its anchor trying to halt its drift. Finally a successful tow line was in place at 8:55pm. The mass of the tanker was however too much to control and the small tug only succeeded in slowing down the drift of the tanker. As the weather conditions deteriorated, with winds reaching force 8, with gusts of up to 9 to 10, the tanker drifted to within 5 miles of the coast. The heavy seas and size of ship made the tug boats useless and the *Amoco Cadiz* was subsequently driven by the heavy seas onto the reef of Men Goulven rocks, near the small port of Portsall. At 9:04pm, the *Amoco Cadiz* hit the bottom for the first time, flooding its engines. It grounded again at 9:39pm, this time ripping the hull and starting the oil spill. It was only at 23.18pm when the captain of the *Amoco Cadiz* finally sent out an SOS distress message requesting immediate assistance. The crew of the stricken vessel was rescued by helicopters of the French Navy at midnight, except the captain and one officer who remained on board until 5am the next morning. At 10am, March 17, the supertanker broke in two, releasing its entire cargo of 1.6 million barrels (219797 tons) of crude oil. Because of the ongoing storm, it broke again on March 28 and the wreck was later completely destroyed by depth charges from the French Navy.

Many of the internal tanks were broken in the accident and the first oil slicks quickly reached the coast. A 12-mile long slick and heavy pools of oil were spread on to 45 miles of the French shoreline by northwesterly winds. Within two weeks, the entire cargo had spilled out into the sea and, dragged by the winds and currents, polluted some 360 km (225 miles) of French coastline, from Brest to St. Brieuc in Brittany. Prevailing westerly winds during the following month spread the oil approximately 100 miles east along the coast. This was the largest oil spill caused by a tanker grounding ever registered in the world. The consequences of this accident were significant, and it caused the French Government to revise its oil marine pollution response plan (the Polmar Plan, similar to the IMO's MARPOL regulations, where the French Navy is responsible for all offshore anti-pollution operations), to acquire marine pollution equipment stocks (Polmar stocks), to impose vessel traffic lanes in the Channel and to create a marine reporting system. The French Government, along with the local communities affected, prosecuted the Amoco company in the United States. After 14 years of complex proceedings, they eventually obtained 1,257 million francs (€190 million), less than half of the claimed amount.

The *Amoco Cadiz* disaster was by no means the last oil spill to hit Brittany. On 28 April 1979, the bulk carrier *Gino*, loaded with heavy Boscan fuel (higher density than water), sank off Ushant (Ouessant) Island after a collision. On 7 March 1980, the Madagascan oil tanker *Tanio* spilt in two during a storm off Batz Island, and her stern sank with 6,000 tonnes of heavy fuel. On 31 January 1988, one of the tanks of the Italian oil tanker *Amazzone* lost 2,100 tonnes of crude oil in a storm off Penmarc'h. This series of oil spills led to a desire to change the course of such events in Brittany, and to see the polluters pay for the damage they had caused.

The *Exxon Valdez* was an oil tanker owned by the former Exxon Corporation. It gained widespread infamy after an oil spill on 24 March 1989, in which the tanker, bound for Washington, USA, hit the Bligh Reef in Prince William Sound, and spilled an estimated 10.8 million US gallons of crude oil. This has been recorded as one of the largest spills in U.S. history and one of its largest ecological disasters.

The vessel had an all steel construction, and was built by the national Steel and Shipbuilding Company in San Diego. A relatively new tanker at the time of the spill, it was delivered to Exxon in December 1986. The tanker was 300 m long, 50 m wide, and 27 m in depth (987 ft by 166 ft by 88 ft), weighing 30,000 tons empty and powered by a 31,650 shp (23.60 MW) diesel engine. The ship could transport a maximum of 1.48 million barrels (200,000 tons) of crude oil at a sustained speed of 16.25 knots (30 km/h) and was employed to transport crude oil from the Alveska consortium's pipeline terminal in Valdez, Alaska, to the lower 48 states of the United States. The vessel was carrying about 1.26 million barrels, or about 53 million US gallons, of crude oil at the time it ran aground.

The oil tanker *Exxon Valdez* departed the Valdez oil terminal in Alaska at 9:12 pm on 23 March 1989 with 53 million U.S. gallons of crude oil bound for Washington. A harbour pilot guided the ship through the Valdez Narrows before departing the ship and returning control to the ship's master. The ship manoeuvred out of the shipping lane to avoid icebergs. Following the manoeuvre and sometime after 11 pm, the captain departed the wheel house and was in his stateroom at the time of the accident. He left the third officer in charge of the wheel house and an able seaman at the helm with instructions to return to the shipping lane at a prearranged point. *Exxon Valdez* failed to return to the shipping lanes and struck Bligh Reef at approximately 12:04 am on 24 March 1989.

Beginning three days after the vessel grounded, a storm pushed large quantities of fresh oil onto the rocky shores of many of the beaches in the Knight Island chain.

According to official reports, the ship carried 53.094,510 million U.S.gallons of oil, of which 10.8 million U.S.gallons (9.0 million imp gal/41 million Litres) were spilled into the Prince William Sound.

The first cleanup response was through the use of a dispersant, a surfactant and solvent mixture. A private company applied dispersant on 24 March with a helicopter and dispersant bucket. Because there was not enough wave action to mix the dispersant with the oil in the water, the use of the dispersant was discontinued. One trial burn was also conducted during the early stages of the spill, in a region of the spill isolated from the rest by a fire-resistant boom. The test was relatively successful, reducing 113,400 litres of oil to 1134 litres of removable residue, but because of unfavourable weather conditions no additional burning was attempted in this cleanup effort. Mechanical cleanup was started shortly afterwards using booms and skimmers, but the skimmers were not readily available during the first 24 hours following the spill, and thick oil had a propensity to clog the equipment.

Exxon was widely criticised for its slow response to cleaning up the disaster, and it was claimed that the Valdez community felt betrayed by Exxon's inadequate response to the crisis. Working with the US Coast Guard, which officially led the response, Exxon mounted a cleanup effort that exceeded in cost, scope and thoroughness any previous oil spill cleanup. More than 11,000 Alaska residents, along with some Exxon employees, worked throughout the region to try to restore the environment.

The cause of the incident was investigated by the National Transportation Safety Board, which identified the four following factors as contributing to the grounding of the vessel:

- The third mate failed to properly manoeuvre and navigate the vessel, possibly due to fatigue and excessive workload;

- The master failed to provide navigation watch, possibly due to impairment under the influence of alcohol;

- Exxon Shipping Company failed to supervise the master and provide a rested and sufficient crew for the *Exxon Valdez*;

- The US Coast Guard failed to provide an effective vessel traffic system.

The Board made a number of recommendations, such as changes to the work patterns of Exxon crew in order to address the causes of the accident.

After the spill, the *Exxon Valdez* was towed to San Diego, California, arriving on 10 July 1989, and repairs began onboard on 30 June 1989. Approximately 1,600 tons of steel were removed and replaced in the month of July 1989, totalling $30 million of repairs to the tanker. After its repairs, the *Exxon Valdez* was renamed the *Sea River Mediterranean*, later shortened to *S/R Mediterranean*, then to simply Mediterranean, and sailed under the Marshall Island flag. It was still sailing as of August 2007, and is currently owned by SeaRiver Maritime, a wholly owned subsidiary of ExxonMobil. Although the Exxon corporation tried to return the ship to its Cuba fleet, it was prohibited by law from entering Prince William Sound again. A schedule was also set for the gradual phase in of a double-hull design for all future oil tankers, providing an additional layer between the oil tanks and the ocean. While a double hull would likely not have prevented the Valdez disaster, a Coast Guard study estimated that it would have cut the amount of oil spilled by 60 percent.

On 12 December 1999, the Maltese-registered tanker *Erika* broke in two off the coast of Brittany, France, whilst carrying approximately 30,000 tons of heavy fuel oil. Some 19,800 tons were spilled. The sunken bow section contained 6400 tons of cargo and the stern a further 4700 tons. The bow section sank within 24 hours, and the stern section sank on December 13 while under tow. It is estimated that when the *Erika* broke up, 10,000 tons of the cargo was in the bow section, 10,000 tons in the stern section, and that 10,000 tons were spilled. The Erika broke up in storms 70 kilometres from the French coast spilling 10,000 of the 30,000 tons of heavy fuel oil it was carrying. This was found to be equal to the total amount of oil spilled worldwide in 1998. The economic consequences of the incident were soon experienced across the region, with a drop in the income from tourism, loss of income from fishing and a ban on the trade of sea products including oysters and crabs. The disaster triggered new EU legislation concerning the transportation of cargoes by sea, especially hazardous and dangerous cargoes such as petroleum, and this legislation is highlighted in the overall text.

The *Erika*, built in 1975, was one of eight sister ships built in the 1970s in Japan. They were at the cheaper end of the market, quite safe but light on steel, given claims that she was carrying some 10% less weight in terms of her steel structure than many other tankers of a similar size. Apart from the *Erika*, three of the other sisters had also suffered major structural damage, possibly because of their light construction. Despite the troubled reputation of her sisters, the *Erika* was allowed to carry on working with only minimum maintenance.

Corrosion problems had been apparent on the *Erika* since at least 1994, with, according to US Coast Guard records, details readily available to port state control authorities and potential charterers. In addition, and contrary to SOLAS regulations, there were numerous deficiencies in her firefighting and inert gas systems, pointing to a potential explosion risk on the tanker which broke up off the French coast last month. The newspaper "Lloyd's List" reported that severe corrosion had been discovered by chance just weeks before the incident. However, no immediate remedial action had been taken. These revelations added to the growing concern in France that the subsequent spill of heavy crude oil would not have occurred had notice been taken of substantial clear signals that there were problems with the 37,283 dwt ship. According to publicly-available US Coast Guard records obtained by Lloyd's List, *Erika* had been inspected in a variety of US ports on several occasions since 1994.

Her certificate of financial responsibility, a document legally required by tankers wishing to trade in US waters, had expired in March 1999, and had not been renewed as of the end of November that year. In an inspection July 1994, holes were discovered on parts of the main deck, indicating that signs of corrosion were already in place more than five years ago. It was also found that there were holes in both the portside and starboard inert gas system risers, which are critical items of safety equipment. Firefighting equipment was also in bad condition.

Many of the vessel's problems had simply been patched up, rather than being properly repaired. In a further inspection in 1997, the US Coast Guard ordered that no cargo operations requiring the use of inert gas systems should be conducted until permanent repairs had been undertaken. Pinhole leaks remained in several pipe systems, contrary to Safety of Life at Sea convention regulations. There was yet more evidence of corrosion, with the ship's watertight doors not sealing properly. *Erika* switched from Bureau Veritas to Registro Italiano Navale in 1998, which authorized her to continue operations despite the French society's order for a full inspection.

On 8 December 1999, the 37000 ton tanker *Erika* left Dunkerque, in northern France, and sailed down the Channel bound for Livorno, Italy, with a cargo of 20,000 tons of heavy fuel oil. Erika was an old vessel reaching the end of her life, and because of her age she was considered a "bargain basement charter" working for half the price of a safe modern tanker. She was never to make her final destination. As the vessel entered the Bay of Biscay, she ran into a heavy storm. Oil tankers are built to withstand such conditions but the *Erika* encountered difficulties. The storm worsened and by mid afternoon on 11 December, she started to list to starboard by 10-12 degrees. In mountainous seas, the ship's hull was cracking and water was being taken on board. In the hours that followed, her captain slowly lost control of her, and the vessel began to disintegrate. The next morning the *Erika* broke in two and started to sink. Thousands of tons of oil, approximately half of her load, leaked from her cargo tanks. As a huge blanket of oil drifted towards the coastline of Brittany and the television images of the first oil-stricken birds were transmitted around the world, the inquest began into one of the tanker industry's worst disasters. The resulting pollution devastated 400 km (250 miles) of coastline and within weeks had killed or maimed 300,000 sea birds.

After the sinking, the French investigators set about trying to trace the owner of the *Erika*. But progress was hampered because of a complex world of nominal companies and commercial uncertainties, seen by the investigators as unacceptable and against the public interest. The audit trail led through seven different countries, with responsibility for the disaster being levelled at a variety of organizations and companies who had some part to play in the operation of the tanker. Fifteen individuals and corporations were eventually sent for trial for her sinking, including her charterers, the Italian owner of the vessel, his manager and the captain of the vessel. On 16 January 2008, Total SA, Giuseppe Savarese (the shipowner), Antonio Pollara (the handler) and RINA (the expert company) were sentenced to pay indemnities of €192 million (US$280 million), plus individual penalties. The official French investigators now believe that the cause of the break-up lies with repairs carried out to the ballast tanks less than two years before she sank. These repairs had been surveyed and passed by the Italian Authority RINA, the Registro Italiano Navale e Aeronautica, based in Genova, Italy.

The investigations into the *Erika* disaster undertaken by the French government and the Maltese maritime authority concluded that age, corrosion, insufficient maintenance and inadequate surveys were all strong contributing factors to the structural failure of the ship. There was a widespread agreement that the *Erika* disaster and other the recent accidents involving oil tankers indicated a need for additional international measures to eradicate substandard vessels, particularly substandard oil tankers, given the catastrophic impact such ships may have on the marine environment in the case of an accident.

In November 2002, the tanker *Prestige* split in two and sank off the North West Coast of Spain. It contained 70,000 metric tons of oil and almost doubled the damage caused by the US tanker *Exxon Valdez* off the coast of Alaska. The *Prestige* was a Greek-operated single-hulled oil tanker, officially registered in the Bahamas, but with a Liberian-registered corporation as the owner. The ship had a deadweight tonnage of approximately 81,000 tons, a measurement that put it at the lower end of the "Aframax" class of tankers, smaller than most carriers of crude oil but larger than most carriers of refined products. It was classified by the American Bureau of Shipping and insured by the London Steamship Owners' Mutual Insurance Association, a shipowners' mutual known as the London Club.

On 13 November 2002, while the *Prestige* was carrying a 77,000-ton cargo of two different grades of heavy fuel oil, one of its twelve tanks burst during a storm off Galicia, in northwestern Spain. Fearing that the ship would sink, the captain called for help from Spanish rescue authorities, hoping that the vessel would be brought into harbour. However, pressure from local authorities forced the captain to steer the ship away from the coast and head northwest. Reportedly after pressure from the French government, the vessel was once again forced to change its course and head southwards into Portuguese waters in order to avoid endangering France's southern coast, especially considering the disaster which had befallen the tanker Erika just under three years previously. Fearing for its own shore, the Portuguese authorities promptly ordered its navy to intercept the ailing vessel and prevent it from approaching further.

With the French, Spanish and Portuguese governments refusing to allow the ship to dock in their ports, the integrity of the single hulled oil tanker was deteriorating quickly and soon the storm took its toll when it was reported that a huge 40-foot section of the starboard hull had broken off, releasing a substantial amount of oil.

At around 8:00 AM on 19 November, the ship split in half, and sank completely that same afternoon releasing over 20 million gallons of oil into the sea. The oil tanker was reported to be about 250 kilometres (some 150 miles) from the Spanish coast at that time, which, although outside the Spanish territorial sea, was still inside the 200-mile EEZ. An earlier oil slick had already reached the coast. The Greek captain of the *Prestige* was taken into custody, accused of not co-operating with salvage crews and of harming the environment. After the sinking, the wreck continued leaking oil. It leaked approximately 125 tons of oil per day, which polluted the sea bed and contaminated the coastline, especially along the territory of Galicia. The affected area is not only a very important ecological region, supporting coral reefs and many species of sharks and birds, but it also supports the fishing industry which is vital to the regional economy. The heavy coastal pollution forced the region's government to suspend offshore fishing for six months. For several months after the disaster, multiple oil slicks reached the coast of Spain and

Southern France, and oil has continued to cause environmental havoc along the affected coasts. Some 4,000 Scottish seabirds died following the disaster. These are puffins which flew south to breed in areas off Spain where the oil slicks continued to spread along the northern coastline.

Initially, the Spanish government thought just 17,000 tons of oil had been lost, and that the remaining 60,000 tons would freeze and not leak from the sunken tanker. In early 2003, it announced that half of the oil had been lost. That figure has now risen to about 63,000 tons according to some sources. In total, 20 million gallons, amounting to 77,000 tons of fuel oil were spilled off Spain's north-west coast, with the severest damage being suffered along the coast of Galicia. In the two years following the sinking, engineers used robots to seal cracks in the tanker's hull, now 4000 metres below the sea surface, and slowed the leakage to a trickle of 20 litres a day. By 2004, engineers had removed the 13,000 cu m of oil remaining in the tanker by drilling of small holes in the wreck, using remotely operated submersibles like the one that originally explored the wreck of the liner *Titanic*. The oil was then pumped into large aluminium shuttles, especially manufactured for this salvage operation, which were then floated to the surface. The original plan to fill large bags with the oil proved to be too problematic and slow. After the oil removal was completed, a slurry rich in microbiological agents was pumped into the hold to speed up the breakdown of any remaining oil. The original total estimated cost of the operation was over €100 million, which ultimately rose to €2.5 billion for the cost of the clean-up to the Galician coast alone, compared with a cost of US$3 billion for the clean-up on the Alaskan coast following the grounding of the US tanker *Exxon Valdez*.

A report by the Galicia-based Barrie de la Maza Economic Institute criticised the Spanish government's handling of the catastrophe. The government was criticized for its decision to tow the ailing wreck out to sea, where it split in two, rather than into a port, thus, to a certain extent, by-passing its obligations under both the Territorial Sea Convention and the UNCLOS, and to this extent, it has been argued that the Spanish government's refusal to allow the ship to take refuge in a sheltered port was a major contributing factor to the scale of the disaster. However, the condition of the tanker was already ascertained before the disaster, and it was reported as being substandard at one of the ports it visited before Spain. Indeed, investigators into the disaster learned that prior to the spill the Prestige had set sail from St. Petersburg, Russia, without being properly inspected. The *Prestige* had been inspected several times, including by the U.S. Coast Guard, which cleared it to sail. In 1991, the vessel sailed to China to have cracks in its hull welded. Rescue operators who attempted to salvage the Prestige before it sank believed that the cracks concerned might have been responsible for the leak, and that the ship split in two along the line of one or more of those welds. It travelled to the Atlantic Ocean via the shallow and vulnerable Baltic Sea. Complaints made be a previous captain about numerous structural deficiencies within the ship were rejected, and the captain later resigned in protest.

Blame, however unfounded, was apportioned to the following parties:

- Latvia – where the ship was loaded with its fuel;

- The UK – the ship was apparently heading for Gibraltar and the British authorities refused it permission to land;

- Spain and Portugal – for not allowing the ship to dock and for sending out warships; and

- The Swiss-based Russian trading company that owned the tanker.

Many vessel owners and operators avoid inspections, fines, and urgently-needed repairs by sailing the vessels under a flag of convenience and avoiding harbours with tough inspection systems. The *Prestige*, for example, was registered in the Bahamas by a company that was incorporated in Liberia, but the ship was managed by a separate company with offices in Greece. It was chartered by a Russian company registered in Switzerland, but the heavy fuel oil that it was carrying from Latvia to Singapore belonged to a British company. The captain was Greek, and his crew were Filipino. The governments of Spain and Portugal may also have contributed in a significant way to the magnitude of the disaster. The tanker sprang a leak when it hit a floating cargo container, in either Spanish or Portuguese waters. When the *Prestige* attempted to sail into a safe harbour to find shelter from stormy winds and high waves and to have the oil pumped off, it was turned away by both Portuguese and Spanish warships, as both governments feared the harmful effects of the tanker's cargo would have on the fishing and tourism industries in the region. It took a Spanish tug 14 hours to hook a line to the *Prestige*, which was allowed to drift within five miles of the Spanish coast, leaking oil all the way. The tug then pulled it out to sea and directly into high waves that eventually broke the ship in two.

Since the disaster, oil tankers similar to the *Prestige* have been directed away from the French and Spanish coastlines. The European Commissioner for Transport at the time, the Spaniard Loyola de Palado, encouraged the policy of a ban of single-hulled tankers. This proposal was followed up with a decision taken some time later, to have all single-hulled tankers phased out by the US and most other countries by 2012. The sinking of the *Erika* off the coast of France in December 1999 led to a new, accelerated phase-out schedule for single-hull tankers, including the revision of regulation 13G (regulation 20 in the revised Annex I which entered into force on 1 January 2007) of MARPOL 73/78, and the *Prestige* incident of November 2002 led to further calls for amendments to the phase-out schedule for single hull tankers.

In March 2006, new oil slicks were detected near the wreck of the *Prestige* which investigators found to match the type of oil the Prestige carried. A study released December 2006 led by José Luis De Pablos, a physicist at Madrid's Centre for Energy and Environmental Research, concluded that between 16,000 and 23,000 tons of oil remained in the wreck, as opposed to the 700 to 1300 tons claimed by the Spanish government. It was also concluded that bioremediation of the remaining oil failed, and that bacteria corroding the hull could produce a rupture and quickly release much of the remaining oil and create another catastrophic spill.

Since 1 January 1996, Governments have been able to propose to the IMO the introduction of mandatory ship reporting systems in areas where there are special environmental or navigational concerns, although this did not prevent the disaster involving the tanker *Prestige*. Mandatory reporting systems require ships to report in to shore authorities when they reach a designated routeing system and give the ship's name, cargo and other information. This enables the ship to be identified on radar and its course plotted throughout the system.

In December 2000, the IMO adopted mandatory requirements for the carriage of Automatic Identification Systems (AIS), capable of providing information about the ship to other ships and to coastal authorities automatically. The regulation in SOLAS Chapter V (Safety of Navigation) requires AIS equipment to be fitted and used aboard all ships of 300 gross tonnage and upwards engaged on international voyages, cargo ships of 500 gross tonnage and upwards not engaged on international voyages, and passenger ships irrespective of size built on or after 1 July 2002.

Existing tankers (those constructed before 1 July 2002), have had to fit and use AIS equipment not later than the first survey for safety equipment on or after 1 July 2003.

BULK CARRIERS

The MS *Berge Istra* was a ship owned by Norwegian shipping company Sig. Bergesen d.y. and registered in Liberia, an ore-bulk-oil (OBO) carrier of 227,550 metric tonnes deadweight (DWT), built at the Uljanik shipyard, in the port city of Pula in Croatia, in 1972. She was en route from Tubarão in Brazil to Japan in December 1975 with a cargo of iron ore when contact was lost with the vessel in the Pacific Ocean near the island of Mindanao, Philippines, on 30 December 1975. After one week, on 7 January 1976, the ship was reported missing, but the ensuing search operation yielded no results and was called off on January 10 of that year. 30 people lost their lives. There were two survivors, Spanish citizens Imeldo Barreto Leon and Epifanio Lopez, who were picked up from a life raft on 20 January 1976, following several days adrift, by Japanese fishermen. It later transpired that the cause was probably inadequate clearing of the holds of inflammable gasses before loading a full cargo of iron ore in Japan. There was an explosion causing a hull rupture and she had sunk like a stone. At Lloyds of London they rang the Lutine Bell.

To this day, thirty years later, the shipping company maintains secrecy with regards to the cause of the accident. The most prominent theory holds that the cause could have been explosions caused by oil residue in the cargo compartments that were filled with iron ore. MS *Berge Istra* was, like its sister ship MS *Berge Vanga* which disappeared under similar circumstances four years later, an OBO carrier, i.e. a ship which could transport both oil and iron ore.

The MS *Berge Vanga* was also an ore-bulk-oil (OBO) carrier of 227,912 deadweight metric tonnes (DWT). The ship was, like the *Berge Istra*, owned by Norwegian shipping company Sig. Bergesen d.y. and registered in Liberia, and she too was built at the port city of Pula, Croatia in 1974.

The ship was on route from Brazil to Japan, loaded with iron ore, when contact was lost with the vessel in the South Atlantic in November 1979. The ship vanished and the ensuing search operation yielded no results. 40 people lost their lives. Some debris resembling parts from the tanker was located, but no survivors were ever found. Even now, very little is known about the disaster, and the investigation after the accident was held behind closed doors. The principal theory holds that the cause could have been explosions caused by oil residue in the cargo compartments. MS *Berge Vanga* was, like its sister ship MS *Berge Istra*, which disappeared under similar circumstances four years earlier, a ship which could transport both oil and iron ore. After these two disappearances no more combination ships such as this were built, and oil was never again transported alongside ore in the same vessel.

The Bibby Line, a long-standing Liverpool-based shipping company, entered into a consortium with several other shipping lines including Furness Withy in the 1960s, called the Seabridge consortium, operating several vessels, all bulk carriers. It agreed to contribute several of them, the *English Bridge* (76012 grt), built in 1973 by Swan Hunter at Haverton Hill, Teesside, the vessels *Pacific Bridge* (44795 grt), built in 1967, and the *Atlantic Bridge*, later renamed *Dorsetshire* (44842 grt), built in 1968, and the *Liverpool Bridge*. The *Pacific Bridge* had a less than happy career, after she had been sold to overseas owners. In 1990, following loading of iron ore at Saldanha Bay, South Africa, a hatch collapsed into one of her holds, disabling her, and she was duly wrecked off the South African Coast in early July of that year, following the refusal of two South African Ports to accommodate her following the mishap. The *English Bridge* was later renamed *Worcestershire*, and remained in the fleet until 1979, when she was sold off. In November 1986, as the *Kowloon Bridge*, she was sailing across the Atlantic Ocean from Canada to the Hunterston terminal, on the Scottish Clyde Coast, when the crew reported cracks in her hull just forward of the superstructure (Frame 65). She successfully reached Bantry Bay, in South-West Ireland, and the decision was made to continue to Scotland. However, not far into the voyage, she lost her rudder, and shortly before midnight on 23 November, the crew were lifted off the stricken vessel by RAF helicopter. The following day, she was blown ashore on the Stags, Eire, and before assistance could arrive, she broke her back and was completely wrecked.

In 1976, Bibby Line purchased the largest vessel ever owned by the company, the *Liverpool Bridge* (91655 grt), an ore-bulk-oil (OBO) carrier which was built by Swan Hunter at Haverton Hill, Teesside, and delivered to Bibby Tankers Ltd for charter to the Seabridge consortium. She was laid up in Norway during the global recession of the late 1970s, but resumed operations with Bibby Line in early 1980. On 11 July 1980, she sailed from Sept-Iles (Seven Islands), in the St. Lawrence estuary, Canada, bound for Kawasaki, Japan, with a full 165,000 ton load of concentrated iron ore pellets. She berthed at Cape Town, South Africa, on 6 August. Five weeks later, on 9th September, she reported her position as 25.19N, 133.11E, 230 miles south-east of the Japanese island of Okinawa. Six hours after reporting her position, her master reported at 09:30 local time, that she was hove to in a severe storm (Typhoon "Orchid"), and adding that she would be late in arriving at port. She was never seen or heard from again, and disappeared without trace with the loss of all 42 crew members and 2 officers' wives during the typhoon. On 24th October, an empty lifeboat, which appeared to have been torn from its davits, was spotted by the Japanese vessel *Taiej Maru* 700 miles away in the Luzon Strait, off the Philippines. The *Derbyshire* had become the largest British built and owned vessel to be lost at sea, in some ways equating with the disasters which had befallen the Norwegian-owned OBO vessels *Berge Istra* and *Berge Vanga* only a short while before. The subsequent enquiry blamed the loss of the vessel on the typhoon, but the families of the victims and their Trade Union believed that a design fault in the vessel had caused it to break in half before an SOS could be sent out, especially in view of the fact that a smaller vessel, the *Alrai*, formerly the *Athelmonarch*, had survived the typhoon. They based their belief on that fact that cracks had been found in Frame 65, just for'ard of the superstructure, on five other similar bulk carriers built by Swan Hunter, and they cited the fate of the ill-fated *Kowloon Bridge*, formerly the *English Bridge/Worcestershire*, which had broken its back after drifting ashore in Eire, albeit some six years after the *Derbyshire* disaster. If it could be proven that the *Derbyshire* was lost due to a design flaw, rather than an 'Act of God' or *force majeure*, then a claim for compensation, estimated at £60,000,000, could be lodged. In October 1987, a second enquiry declined to examine the design fault theses, as there was no evidence relating to the disaster, and there were no survivors to testify as to what had happened. On 23rd January 1989, following a House of Lords decision, the Wreck Commissioner issued a statement saying that the loss was unexplained and that there was no specific reason for the loss.

However, the families of the victims and the maritime trade unions were still not satisfied with the result, and in 1994, the International Transport Workers Federation financed an expedition which eventually found the wreck lying some 2.5 miles deep, 400 miles east of Okinawa. The Department of Transport appointed Lord Donaldson, an eminent Law Lord, to review the new development, and he concluded that a detailed underwater survey of the wreck would cost approximately £2,000,000. Jointly funded by Britain and the EU, the survey was conducted in two phases between 1997 and 1998 during which 153,774 still photographs and some 200 hours of high-definition film were taken. By pasting together the individual photographs, it was possible to produce, as a single picture, large expanses of the wreck in clear black-and-white images. With the new evidence now available and in view of certain allegations made against the ill-fated vessel's crew, the Deputy Prime Minister, John Prescott, ordered, in December 1998, a full re-opening of the formal enquiry in the High Court. The hearing commenced on 5th April 2000, and continued for 54 days during which time the evidence was fully examined.

It was concluded by Mr. Justice Colman that, from the condition of the wreckage and the data derived from the model tests carried out back in the UK, the initiating cause of the loss was the destruction of some or all of the ventilators and air pipes located on the foredeck by sustained green water (ocean waves) loading over many hours by crashing over the vessel's bows in the course of 8th and 9th September, the height of the storm. Water was therefore able to enter the bosun's store, machinery spaces and probably the ballast tanks in substantial quantities, and possibly to a minor extent, the vessel's fuel tanks (bunkers). The *Derbyshire* then developed a downward trim by the bow which, although imperceptible from the bridge, had the effect, as the bow settled lower and lower in the water, of accentuating green water loading on the hatch cover of No. 1 hold as the sea conditions became even more severe over the course of that day. By about 17:00 in the late afternoon, those conditions had deteriorated so severely that there was likely to have been green water loading in excess of the collapse strength of No. 1 hatch cover, the hatch closest to the bow. Once the hatch cover gave way under the sheer weight and volume of the water, the water would enter No.1 hatch, very rapidly filling the large ullage (empty) space above the cargo and thereby causing the ship to go still further down by another 3.7 metres, even considering the fact that she was riding low in the water considering her deadweight cargo. It was estimated that the filling of No. 1 hold with water could have taken as little as 5 minutes or as much as 16.5 minutes. This flooding in turn caused the green water loading progressively on No. 2 hatch cover and rapidly to increase until it exceeded the collapse strength of that hatch cover, at which point No. 2 hatch collapsed and water then entered No. 2 hold. No. 3 hatch suffered the same fate. According to the hearing, at that point, the *Derbyshire* was irretrievably lost, probably minutes later. It is probably the sheer weight of water entering the holds which sheered the hull in at least two places, separating the bow from the main section of the hull, and then separating the superstructure and the stern of the vessel from the rest of the hull, as well as shattering the vessel as discovered from the photographs taken of the wreck lying on the seabed. The empty lifeboat from the vessel was examined and found to have been wrenched with such violent force from its davits as to suggest to what extent the vessel's destruction had been so rapid. The crew had stood no chance whatsoever, and no blame was attached to them for the loss of the ship. She was effectively destroyed by a series of rogue giant waves, the force of which she was not designed to withstand.

CONTAINER VESSELS

The container vessel *Hyundai Fortune* was a conventional container vessel, completed by Hyundai Heavy Industries in 1996, displacing 64054 grt with a length of 274.2 feet (83.6m) and a draught of 24.2 feet (7.4m). She had an operational speed of 25.6 knots and a container capacity of 5551 TEU (Twenty-Foot Equivalent Units), and was registered in Panama. She was owned by the shipping company Hyundai Merchant Marine, and operated between the Far East and Europe. Up to 2006, her career had been uneventful, and she had hitherto suffered no major mishaps. In March 2006, she was en route from ports in China and Singapore to Europe on a regular route, when just after mid-day on 21 March 2006, in the Gulf of Aden, 60 miles to the south of the coast of Yemen, she suffered a huge engine room explosion, as she headed towards the Red Sea and the Suez Canal. Between 60 and 90 containers were hurled into the sea, and the fire rapidly became a massive blaze which spread upwards to the container stacks, and right through the stern of the vessel, including the accommodation quarters of the vessel and the container stacks immediately forward of the superstructure and accommodation area. Further violent explosions and an inferno erupted as a result, caused by the ignition of seven containers full of fireworks, which had all been stowed together at the stern of the vessel, close to the accommodation area of the vessel. Photographs taken by aircraft which arrived on the scene showed that a large part of the hull had been blown out below deck and above the waterline on the port side of the vessel.

Efforts to contain the inferno failed, with the result that all 27 crew of the vessel were forced to abandon ship. They were rescued by the Dutch naval destroyer *HNLMS De Zeven Provincien* (The Seven Provinces). This naval vessel was involved in maritime security operations in the area as part of the joint-forces Operation Enduring Freedom. One sailor from the stricken container ship was evacuated to the French aircraft carrier *Charles de Gaulle* with severe injuries. Two days later, firefighting tugs arrived on the scene, but even considering the assistance now available to fight the blaze, the vessel continued to burn for several more days, such was the intensity of the fire. General Average was declared by the insurers, and it would appear that at least one-third of the containers aboard vessel were damaged by the blaze. Every container aft of the superstructure was either incinerated or lost at sea. Most of the containers forward of the superstructure remained intact, although following the loss of power of the vessel following the initial explosion in the engine room, any cargo in the refrigerated containers would have quickly perished. The combined cost of the vessel and its lost cargo eventually amounted to over US$3 million, with the net result that the vessel was sold for scrap, such was the extent of the damage it had suffered. The hull was towed to Salalah, in Oman, and the undamaged containers were offloaded for transport to Europe on other vessels. The hull was then left at the port awaiting a decision to send it for scrap.

Theories concerning the cause of the explosion varied. Possibilities concerning a violent reaction of the chemical calcium hypochlorite were proposed, as explosions aboard vessels such as *Hanjin Pennsylvania*, *CMA Djakarta*, *Aconcagua*, *Sea Land Mariner* and *DG Harmony* were suspected to have been caused by similar circumstances. The investigators of the disaster also considered that volatile cargo, specifically, the seven containers of fireworks, may have detonated due to heat, triggering the larger explosion which crippled the ship. It became clear that the containers full of pyrotechnics should never have been stowed so close to the accommodation quarters of the vessel, especially at the vessel's stern, where vital propulsion and steering equipment on board the vessel would be vulnerable to any explosion or fire. It became evident that there was a possibility that the shippers of the fireworks had not notified the agents or the carrier of the full or true nature of the consignments. As a result, in every possibility, the containers loaded with the fireworks were loaded by the port handlers without any prior knowledge of what the cargoes were. To this extent, the fault and the ultimate responsibility could be seen to lie with the shippers, who in legal terms could be held liable for contributing in some way to the disaster, owing to a failure to correctly report the nature of the cargo to the shipping agents under the duty of care placed upon them by the basic insurance principle of *Uberrimae Fidei* (In utmost good faith). Because of this oversight, the carrier itself would in all probability have been unaware of the nature of the hazards of having seven containers loaded with fireworks stowed so closely to the accommodation quarters of the vessel, a policy which is normally prohibited under the SOLAS (Safety of Lives at Sea) Convention. In any case, as a result of the disaster, Hyundai Merchant Marine placed an immediate moratorium on all shipments of fireworks by their vessels. With other shipping lines also refusing to carry potentially unstable cargoes, container insurers started to express concern that shippers would misdeclare the contents of containers in order to have their cargoes shipped, thus compromising the safety of both vessels and crews.

The container vessel *MSC Napoli* (53409 grt) was a container vessel with more of a history than the *Hyundai Fortune*. She had a length of 275.66 metres (904 ft) and a draught of 13.8 metres (45 feet), and was launched in 1991 from the Samsung Heavy Industries shipyard at Koje, and had a capacity of 4734 TEU, with a crew of 31. In 2001, while she was operated by the French shipping company CMA CGM under the name *CMA CGM Normandie*, she was en route from Port Kelang, Malaysia, to Jakarta in Indonesia, when she ran aground on a reef in the Singapore Strait and remained aground for several weeks. She was duly repaired at the Hyundai-Vinashin Shipyard in Vietnam, which included the welding of more than 3,000 tonnes of metal onto the hull to reinforce her structure. She was later transferred to the Nedlloyd fleet and renamed *Nedlloyd Normandie*, before being transferred yet again to the fleet of Mediterranean Shipping

Company (MSC), and placed under the UK flag, this time being renamed *MSC Napoli*. It was under this guise that she sailed from Belgium bound for Portugal in mid-January 2007. On 18 January 2007, she encountered storm force conditions while sailing through the western part of the Channel, with severe gale force winds and huge waves. She sustained structural damage, with a huge crack appearing on one side of her hull and the engine room becoming flooded. By this time, she was some 50 miles (80 km) off the coast of the Lizard, Cornwall.

The crew of the vessel sent out a distress call, and soon after the order was given by the captain to abandon ship. Several hours later, all 26 crew from the vessels were rescued by helicopters from the Royal Navy Fleet Air Arm, and were airlifted to the Royal Navy station at Culdrose, Cornwall. The following day, 19 January, the vessel was taken under tow by the salvage tugs *Abeille Bourbon* and *Abeille Liberté*, based in France. It was decided to tow the vessel to Portland Harbour, 140 miles away and considered to be the nearest safe port, although it was claimed by others that the vessel could have been accommodated in Falmouth Bay, which lay much closer to her location. Because of the forecast of strong winds, as well as an increase in the list of the stricken vessel, the decision was made to take refuge in the relatively-sheltered confines of Lyme Bay, overlooked by the Dorset/Devon coastline. Because of the vessel's deteriorating condition, doubts were raised as to its ability to withstand the sea conditions on the way to Portland, and the decision was taken by the Secretary of State's Representative in Maritime Salvage and Intervention (SOSREP), who was leading the salvage response team of the Maritime & Coastguard Agency (MCA), to deliberately beach the *MSC Napoli* in Lyme Bay, one mile off Branscombe Beach, near the coastal town of Sidmouth and also Britain's first natural World Heritage site, the so-called "Jurassic Coast", known for its large deposits of fossils. This location was chosen because it was claimed that there was a greater chance of minimising the impact of environmental damage caused by potential spillage of oil and any waste, and enabling salvage work to remove the vessel and her cargo to take place. 103 of her containers fell into the sea, and oil spilt some five miles to the north-east, affecting some sea-birds, although an anti-pollution vessel proceeded to the scene to disperse the oil. Of the 41,773 tonnes of cargo on board the vessel, it was claimed that 1684 tonnes were of products classified as dangerous by the IMO. However, the main issue which led to calls for tighter security was the invasion of people on to Branscombe Beach, where several containers from the stricken vessel had been washed ashore. Despite warnings from the police concerning the illegal removal of goods washed ashore, many people descended to the beach and commenced their own "clean-up" activity, removing any items deemed valuable, including several BMW motorcycles, empty wine casks, perfume and automotive parts. Eventually, the situation became so chaotic that the police were forced to use powers under the Merchant Shipping Act 1995, which had not been used for over 100 years, to force people to return goods which they had "salvaged" without informing the authorities. After some time, the oil was removed form the vessel, and the flotsam was cleaned up from the beach, although by this time, other items from the vessel were being washed up along the UK's south coast all the way to the Isle of Wight, such were the sea currents in the area. Eventually, the MCA invoked powers under the Merchant Shipping Act 1995 concerning goods seemingly collected as treasure trove from wrecks. As the vessel was lying in UK internal waters, it had become the responsibility of the UK national authorities concerning its disposal and its contents, and this also inferred that responsibility for the wreck and its contents lay with not only the MCA but also HM Revenue & Customs, given their control over goods entering the country, despite the fact that there was no Customs representation close to the vessel's location. However, to avoid any further pillaging, the local Constabulary erected fences around the beach as well as road blocks on local roads to prevent public access to the area.

On 9 July 2007, the *MSC Napoli* was refloated, but was immediately re-beached as a 3-metre gash was discovered in her hull. The decision was made to break her into sections *in situ*, and this was achieved over three attempts using explosives, the final detonation attempt on 20 July 2007 proving fully successful, when the sections of the vessel were finally split apart. In August 2007, the bow section of the vessel was taken to the Harland & Wolff yard at Belfast for disposal and recycling. Before it was able to enter the yard, HM Coastguard placed a 500-metre exclusion zone around the section while it was secured in Belfast Lough, preventing public access to the wreck. The stern section remained at Branscombe, where work commenced in May 2008 to break the section up, a task that was expected to last five months. The cost of the whole salvage operation was estimated to be in the region of some £50 million. The Marine Accident Investigation Branch (MAIB) of the MCA duly conducted an investigation into the disaster, and a report was published at the end of April 2008. Today, nothing remains of the vessel, and she is simply yet another piece of data in the long list of accidents to have befallen vessels at sea.

CHAPTER EIGHT

PRACTICAL SOLUTIONS

SUMMARY AND APPRAISAL

It can be seen that a variety of separate individual Marine Reporting Systems exist at present, both in the UK and elsewhere in the world. These systems have evolved over several years, and have come into being for a variety of reasons, mainly by necessity rather than by choice. These systems may overlap, but equally may not cover every aspect of maritime safety or security. Indeed, the overlapping of the systems involved may create more bureaucracy than is actually necessary, and which may cause more problems than solve them. Maritime activity, like other forms of transport, is punctuated by accidents, and these accidents have often precipitated the need to implement legislation or regulations to avoid or reduce the risk of such accidents occurring in the future. However, as the average size of commercial ships increases, so does the risk of a major catastrophe occurring as a result of a marine accident. However rigorous the regulations pertaining to the control of maritime activities, accidents or incidents still occur, and these may result in a varying degree of loss of life or harmful effects to the marine environment depending upon the severity of the incident. To this extent, the scope of present Marine Reporting systems extends to a variety of functions. These can be summarised as follows:

- Reporting Marine Accidents and Incidents;

- Compliance with the SOLAS-based Regulations laid down by the IMO;

- The use of VTS systems as required by the VTMS Directives;

- The use of AIS as a general monitoring system;

- Traffic Separation Schemes (TSS), where appropriate;

- General Ship and Port Security as dictated by the ISPS Code;

- Navigational Security;

- Crew Reporting;

- Passenger Reporting;

- Customs Cargo Reporting and Security.

The present set of Marine Reporting requirements may affect various elements of the maritime process, but they do not necessarily overlap, nor can they be used in conjunction with each other for the common good of the overall maintenance of maritime security with respect to both vessel and complement, be it passenger or cargo. As has been shown, different reporting regimes exist for different sectors and purposes, but there is no standardised or harmonised reporting system which may be collectively accessed by all pertinent authorities, be it regulatory or otherwise. The VTS systems allow for the reporting of vessels but not their cargoes, and the AIS initiative similarly allows for the monitoring of the movement of vessels but, like VTS, does not take into account their cargoes. The European Marine Reporting System (EMRS), including the SafeSeaNet initiative developed by the European Maritime Safety Association (EMSA), goes some way to address some of the issues at stake, namely the issues of the reporting of hazardous or dangerous cargoes prior to the vessel's arrival at port, but even this falls short of a fully-integrated all-embracing system given the following:

- The passage of vessels through limited waters, rather than simply arrivals at port;

- The relationship of SafeSeaNet solely with the HAZMAT Directive, and hence its emphasis on the reporting of hazardous or dangerous cargoes;

- A lack of total transparency concerning documentary information pertaining to the carriage of cargoes by sea;

- The transition from manual documentation to electronic information facilities;

- The ability and willingness of all relevant EU Member States to fully participate in and contribute to such a venture.

Thus, a port authority will not automatically gain access to cargo information pertaining to Customs controls or other security issues, unless the cargo is of a hazardous or dangerous nature and is reported as a specific cargo either individually or as part of a consolidated load, and requires specialist handling at the port. Equally, the agent handling the vessel may not know the exact nature of the cargo aboard the vessel, or even the state of the vessel itself, unless prior warning has been given by the vessel's master. In this respect, certain activities such as the 24-hour reporting rule pertaining to hazardous or dangerous cargoes do not change; they simply become more complex under the EMRS initiative and the future Consolidated European Reporting System (CERS). Similarly, a Customs Authority may not gain access to details about a specific vessel and its cargo unless it specifically targets such a vessel through either intelligence, the use of the AIS, or by consulting with a Port Authority or the relevant Shipping Company. And, above all, HM Coastguard has little power to board vessels other than for reasons of seaworthiness or a potential danger to other shipping in the vicinity.

In short, the present reporting systems refer to the movement of vessels, and not their contents, other than known hazardous cargoes and waste products on board vessel. The EC Directives

2000/59 and 2002/59 require all vessels exceeding 300grt to report prior to any entry into port or an anchoring area, all hazardous goods, cargoes and vessel-generated waste at least 24 hours prior to arrival, and to this extent the SafeSeaNet (SSN) system was developed. However, in the case of consolidated cargoes, this information may not be known by the vessel's master, and in some cases, there may be a reluctance on the part of the master of the vessel to report all necessary information to the port or harbour authority, or even the national maritime authority. In general, the reporting systems available are limited in their nature, and do not cover all aspects of maritime information reporting. Even the new CERS system, when it is eventually fully implemented, is not designed to take into account all aspects of the cargoes of vessels and even the destination of these vessels.

Furthermore, the coastguard or national maritime authority may not wish to know every detail about a vessel passing through an international or national strait of water to a destination beyond that country, unless it has specific reason to do so, for security or safety reasons. Many of the vessels transiting the Storebaelt or the Öresund are not calling at either Danish or Swedish ports, but are passing from the Baltic Sea to the North Sea en route for another destination outside the Danish or Swedish controls. The same is true of the Channel between Dover and Calais. Most vessels passing through the Strait of Dover will be heading either westwards bound for the Atlantic Ocean, or eastwards bound for a North Sea port such as Antwerp, Rotterdam or Bremerhaven. In the case of the Strait of Dover, a mandatory traffic separation scheme exists, as does a mandatory vessel reporting system. In the cases of the Öresund and the Storebaelt, this is not so. These two straits rely on a VTS regime to simply monitor the passage of vessels through the straits, regardless of their destination or their cargoes.

The main issue with AIS and VTS systems is that they act as *monitoring* instruments, rather than *control* instruments. The monitoring of a vessel and its course simply allows a shore-based authority to watch a vessel either visually, on radar or on electronic graphics, and not intervene in the event of deviation or incident. With VTS, communication may be maintained with the vessel in order to issue navigational instructions or to ascertain the vessel's intended course, but it does not exercise controls over the vessel concerning all the information pertaining to both the vessel and its cargo. The extended use of VTS to cover passage through Straits such as the Öresund, between Denmark and Sweden, or the Storebaelt, within Danish territorial waters, simply monitors the vessel's progress, but does not empower the Danish or Swedish Authorities to require that the vessels transiting these stretches of water report into the Authorities of either country prior to accessing these waters, with details of both the vessel and its cargo. In this respect, both AIS and VTS display significant shortcomings, as they do not exercise control over the vessel's movements and intentions.

As the size of container ships increases towards the 10,000 TEU level, so the quantity of cargo carried per vessel increases, and consequently so does the risk of the inability to fully report all cargoes carried on such vessels. The ability of CUSCAR to deal with cargo manifests for such vessels may be lessened, and there is equally a significant risk that certain cargoes of a hazardous or high-security nature on board such vessels may go unreported until they are unloaded at their destination. This risk is heightened owing to vague descriptions of consolidated cargoes on

Ocean Bills of Lading such as *"Said to Contain…"* and *"Freight of all Kinds"* (FAK), phrases already prohibited from use by the United States and Canada under the CT-PAT initiative, and which have also been banned from use as a result of the implementation of the Entry Summary Declaration (ENS) system, which is similar to the US AMS (Advanced Manifest) system, by the European Union on 1 January 2011, as a result of Regulation 1875/2006 concerning the implementation of the Community Customs Code. Some of this risk is diminished by the information contained in manifests pertaining to FCLs (Full Container Loads), where the information on the container manifest refers specifically to the precise load carried within that specific container, as opposed to Consolidation LCLs (Less-than-Full Container Loads), where more general, abbreviated information is contained in the manifest and hence the Master (Groupage) Bill of Lading. The larger the ship, the greater the quantity of cargo carried, and hence the greater the risk of information not being conveyed to the national Authorities owing to the sheer volume and complexity of information held in the form of cargo manifests. In this respect, there is the risk of the compromise of maritime security measures on the grounds of the sheer quantity of cargo information carried on board ship or pertinent to the vessel and its cargo, and this may, to a certain extent, fly in the face of the IMO ISPS regime. Even given the complexity of such information availability, there is still the need for the Ship's Master to complete the IMO FAL forms for Customs purposes and file them with the national Customs Authority when the incoming vessel arrives at port. These forms are separate from the cargo manifest, and refer to the vessel's crew and ship's stores, as well as any passengers aboard (although the complexity of the information available in the case of cruise liners requires a more in-depth set of information being required in such cases).

However, the parallel declaration functions of both the ISPS Code and the FAL Forms, both sanctioned and implemented by the IMO, give some picture as to the nature and status of the vessel and its crew at the time of entering port. The information required to be submitted to the port under the ISPS Code details the identity and security level of the vessel concerned, whereas the IMO FAL Forms detail the declarations concerning the crew and personal contents carried aboard the vessel which are to be submitted to the Customs Authority at the time of berthing of the vessel. Although such procedures are carried out on a manual basis, they do give some measure of reporting security. However, there is no reason why such reporting requirements could be integrated or harmonised, as well as being presented and submitted in electronic format, for the purposes of supplying information to both the Port Authority and the Customs Authority simultaneously. Indeed, if such procedures were to be made electronic, then the same information could be submitted in its entirety from the vessel to both the Port and Customs Authorities simultaneously prior to the vessel's arrival in Port, ideally at the point it entered the 3-Mile Limit. Given the present electronic capabilities of reporting systems, it is equally simple enough to imagine that the vessel's cargo could be reported in the same way, for the purposes of both Port Security and the Customs Authorities. Given equally that this manner of advanced reporting to the port authority is mandatory for all vessels carrying hazardous or dangerous cargoes, then it would be a logical progression to extend such reporting mechanisms to all cargoes carried by inbound vessels. Adding to this the dimension already set as precedent by the US and Canadian Authorities as stated above, namely that the Terms "Said to Contain…" or "Freight of all Kinds (FAK)" cannot be used for the purposes of inward cargo reporting to the authorities, then it would also be mandatory for all groupage consolidated cargoes to be described in some detail within the vessel's Cargo Manifest, including Tariff Commodity Codes, Quantities and Values, to both the Customs Authority and the Port Authority in advance of the vessel's arrival by electronic means. This would then imply that all reports submitted to the national authorities could be made in advance of the vessel's arrival on an electronic basis, and could thus be more easily integrated in a standard reporting procedure.

At present, therefore, the following vessel reporting regimes exist every time a vessel enters port:

- 24-hour Advance Reporting;
- SafeSeaNet;
- VTS;
- ISPS;
- IMO FAL;
- CUSCAR;
- IMDG HAZMAT (where necessary);
- Consolidated European Vessel Reporting (CERS).

Each of these regimes is totally independent of each other (other than the relationship between the CUSCAR and electronic FAL regimes), and they are managed and governed by different authorities. Add to these the reporting requirements under the VTM Directive, especially the use of AIS, along with the EMRS initiative, and the reporting system becomes not just more complex and indeed bureaucratic, but borders on the unwieldy and unmanageable.

The reporting mechanisms can also be grouped into two main categories with regard to the actual requirements for reporting:

- Vessel Operational Reporting (Identity and Position), comprising AIS and VTS;
- Port Reporting (Cargo Management, Security, Inward and Outward Navigation).

The operational aspect of reporting concerns the movements of the vessel with relation to other vessels, especially in international waters, and its identity. The port aspect of reporting concerns the relationship of the vessel (and what it contains) with the port, and its ability to satisfy national territorial control requirements.

The 24-Hour Reporting rule applies as much to basic formalities as it does to the specifics of actual national security, which it also addresses. However, it does safeguard the port of arrival to a certain extent against the risk of hazards or accidents in the event of an unanticipated incident concerning a vessel's arrival in port. The exception to the rule concerns the activities of authorised regular operators, who can overcome the 24-hour rule by a regular input of information concerning their regular sailings, especially on the short-sea routes within or around EU territorial waters. This said, it would appear that for the purposes of national security in terms of Immigration and Customs controls, as well as safeguards against perceived threats, there is little or no provision for an all-embracing or fully-integrated system of marine reporting. This does not, however, say that the need for such a regime does not exist and that any threat to the Realm has receded. In an era of greater threats to national security through international terrorism, there is a greater need than ever for an integrated, all-inclusive, reporting system which enables a whole range of national authorities to gain vital information from a centrally-accessed marine reporting information system. This is especially required for Customs controls, where it has been shown by evidence of the reduction in national resources that it is no longer possible for the national Customs Authorities in much of the EU to provide adequate controls at the ports themselves or even on the water, as used to be the case. When it comes to the point that the national Customs Authority requests the port to provide information concerning irregularities concerning imported and exported cargoes, and that certain Coastguard authorities distance themselves from issues of national maritime controls and policing, then it is evident that there is a significant vacuum in the regime of national maritime controls which requires filling. Given also that each port keeps information individual to its own requirements, and does not divulge such information to other ports in the country, there would appear to be no standardisation or commonality of information available for the benefit and well-being of the security of the national interest. The view held by Port Authorities is that they already comply with existing legislation and maritime directives – why should they be required to invest further time, effort and resources in applying further measures of security. Although such privacy and protection of information may be justifiable according to the constraints laid down by Data Protection Legislation, it does not prove beneficial to those parties or authorities throughout the UK or the EU requiring information which could affect the process of collective national or international security. In the event of the threat of terrorist acts, the excuses of Data Protection or reluctance to invest in greater degrees of maritime security cannot and will not be used as a defence. Even the combined efforts of GPS, VTS and AIS cannot prevent a catastrophe from occurring if the vessel is under the control of those seeking to wreak havoc in either busy shipping lanes, the approaches to a major seaport, or production platforms in the Continental Shelf. Such monitoring methods merely facilitate the position of spectators in a vast arena of destruction and catastrophe.

The progression of the various initiatives concerning Marine Reporting and Monitoring of Shipping Movements as part of or alongside the various IMO Directives has resulted in the following anomalies:

- Little synergy or interrelationship (loosely described as "joined-up communication") between each method of maritime reporting regime, with a large amount of information available in each sector which is not or cannot be transmitted to or transferred to other reporting mechanisms for various reasons;

- Marine Reporting Mechanisms are extremely specific in their nature, and refer to Shipping Movements between one Port and another, thus involving the relevant specific authorities of only those Ports party to such movements;

- The Marine Reporting Mechanisms presently in place are limited in scope and do not necessarily allow for the involvement of national authorities or the application of national territorial controls in their nature;

- Marine Controls appear to be driven by self-governance, self-maintenance and self-application by the Shipping Industry, and have omitted the inclusion of national authorities in their implementation and application, other than checks maintained on the seaworthiness and safety of the vessels themselves by Inspectors employed by such Authorities as required by Directives and national statutory legislation;

- The monitoring of Shipping Movements is restricted to simply *monitoring* of the movement of vessels in a limited fashion in specific maritime regions, and allows for neither surveillance nor control by national authorities (except in the case of the CNIS facility at the Strait of Dover, where action may be taken by the Coastguard Authority against vessels contravening the TSS);

- Scant provision exists for control measures on the part of EU national maritime authorities to combat either the threats of international terrorism or catastrophes caused by negligence or wilful acts at sea, whether or not such acts may be committed inside or outwith the scope of national territorial limits;

- National Authorities empowered to monitor coastwise activities have few powers of monitoring or control, and have been rationalised to such a degree that their ability to control or monitor specific stretches of coastline has been severely compromised.

It is appreciated that the world has entered the electronic and technological age, and thus relies heavily on the dissemination of information by electronic rather than documentary means, as well as a reduction in manpower associated with a variety of functions owing to the transfer of information sources to computerised means, but it must also be appreciated that there is still a need for specific controls concerning the defence of the nation and the maintenance of both maritime defences and maritime security in several ways. These ways are at present governed by computerised systems in parts of the country considered remote from the areas they are supposed to cover, and in so doing have drastically reduced the manpower so vital in ensuring that marine activities are correctly monitored and controlled as part of an efficient marine control strategy. To this extent, it is believed that such reductions in coastwise controls may have severely compromised the ability of those responsible for guarding the coastline to adequately perform the tasks required as part of a national maritime defence strategy.

As observed in the previous sections, it may be ascertained that the knowledge of the Ship's Master of his Cargo depends very much upon the information presented to him by both the Freight Forwarders and the Ship's Agents. Indeed, the Freight Forwarder is only as good as the information submitted by Exporter or Importer depending upon who is responsible for the carriage of freight on the vessel, which is ultimately subject to the correct use of the INCOTERMS. Failure to define the correct INCOTERM means failure to define who is responsible for the shipment, and hence who is responsible for the correct delivery of information pertaining to the cargo to the Freight Forwarder. Ship's Agents and Brokers deal with the vessels themselves as well as the submission of Cargo Manifests; Freight Forwarders are responsible for the booking of cargoes aboard such vessels. Exporters and Importers are responsible to the Freight Forwarders for the necessary provision of information relating to the cargo to be carried by the Shipping Line. Both parties are also responsible to the Shipping Line to ensure that all relevant information is passed to the Ship's Crew to ensure a safe voyage, as well as to Insurance Brokers and the relevant Port and Customs Authorities. There is thus a significant inter-relationship between all parties to ensure proper communication between all concerned and ensure that the cargo has been correctly declared. Failure to provide such information could result in disaster or at best the risk of an accident or mishap on board the vessel. Hence the need for a more rigorous and tightly-disciplined reporting system to ensure that all such parties comply with all necessary regulations and requirements pertaining to the safe carriage of cargoes by maritime vessels.

TOWARDS AN INTEGRATED REPORTING SYSTEM

It is recognised that the UNCLOS does not impose a standard requirement for marine reporting, and leaves this to national interests. The primary function of UNCLOS was to consolidate and classify the overall International Law pertaining to the Sea, and the various responsibilities of each nation in upholding the Rule of Law pertaining to such matters, as well as the defence and protection of its own national maritime territorial limits. Equally, the function of the International Maritime Organisation (IMO) has to a large extent revolved around issues posed by the SOLAS (Safety of Lives at Sea) Convention, and this function upholds, promotes and maintains the security and safety of vessels and their crews. Any initiative of Marine Reporting has evolved over the years in answer to either marine disasters or security requirements, and consequentially has, as a result, evolved in a somewhat piecemeal manner, rather than by process of managed or ordered integration. Although the IMO is an international organisation, it does not impose legislation (other than Safety Conventions) upon national governments, and inevitably it is the responsibility of each national government to impose its own national legislation concerning maritime safety, security and management, in accordance with the rules laid down by the UNCLOS. Hence the worldwide disparities and variances in Marine Reporting mechanisms between each country, although in general each country with international maritime interests maintains similar practices concerning the reporting of dangerous or hazardous goods as required by the various IMO Conventions. However, such reporting mechanisms do not generally relate to overall maritime security issues concerning the overall reporting of vessels (other than the IMO ISPS Code required to be used by all ports) and their cargoes when entering national territorial waters, and this function is left to the responsibility of national governments depending upon their perception of security risks.

The time has come, therefore, for the whole issue of Marine Reporting to require review, re-assessment, overhaul, update and consolidation, especially for the purposes of addressing the issues detailed above, as well as considering the vast array of reporting systems presently in operation in a seemingly dysfunctional manner. At present, a whole series of different forms of Marine Reporting exists, but deals with a variety of forms of reporting and thus separates out which party benefits from each reporting measure, as well as stretching the administrative resources of several ports to the limit. Systems presently in existence include:

- 24 Hour Advance Reporting of ocean vessels prior to arrival at port;
- VTS Regimes;
- ISPS;
- IMO FAL Declarations;
- Customs Cargo Reporting (CUSCAR);
- CNIS Reporting (Channel TSS);
- Dangerous/Hazardous Goods Reporting;
- Automatic Identification System (AIS);
- Marine Accident and Incident Reporting.

In turn, these systems can be sub-categorised depending upon their application to either vessel reporting and monitoring in relation to other vessels or reporting systems relating to entering or leaving port for the purposes of cargo or passenger handling.

These categories can be simplified as:

TRAFFIC MONITORING

- GPS;
- VTS;
- AIS;

- CNIS Reporting (Channel Activities);
- Marine Accident & Incident Reporting.

PORT REPORTING

- 24-hour Advance Reporting;
- ISPS;
- IMO FAL Reporting;
- Customs Cargo Reporting (CUSCAR);
- HAZMAT Reporting;
- CERS Reporting.

The traffic monitoring systems are more pertinent to vessels moving within channels or sailing into and out of ports. However, the information presently available to each vessel with relation to other vessels within the vicinity relates to the vessel itself, rather than its cargo. The need is therefore to expand this information base to include the nature of the cargo aboard vessel as well as information concerning the vessel itself.

The port information systems relate more to the loading and unloading of cargoes themselves, as well as information concerning the vessel's crew, which pertain to the vessel's laytime in port. Hence the need to address issues of security and controls while the vessel is in port. At present, information concerning these issues is based on individual reports being issued on behalf of the vessel, its crew and its cargo. Other than the ISPS and HAZMAT Reports which are destined for the Port Authority, the other reports pertain to cargo declarations to Customs and should thus be simplified and streamlined for the purpose of easy and efficient access to information by Customs, the Port Agents and Freight Forwarders.

On board vessel, technological advances have now resulted in more integrative information access, with the emphasis on electronic graphic displays rather than manual or paper-based information. This is exemplified in the use of the ECDIS electronic chart displays on bridge monitors rather than simply in the conventional Admiralty Chart paper format.

The rapid advance in technology has also resulted in ship-borne systems, especially in the navigational and control functions, being made more efficient and user-friendly. It has always been customary for each vessel to use the detailed Admiralty Charts for the UK Coastline and beyond in paper format, and to this day it is commonplace to find specific charts displayed somewhere on the bridge of commercial vessels. With the progression of time, however, electronics have taken over, and today, the paper charts are being supplanted by the **ECDIS** (Electronic Chart Display System) accessible on computer screens in the Bridge Control Room. These charts can be regularly updated, and can be downloaded onto the vessel's internal computer systems in a short time. Given the storage capacity of today's computer systems, a whole variety of electronic charts can be downloaded for all worldwide routes the vessel is likely to ply, and these can be accessed by the ship's master and navigation officers at the touch of a button. Given that the GPS systems also allow for accurate positioning, the ship's position with relation to any of the charts being used is also a vital instrument in the accurate navigation of the vessel.

Note that the references to specific Charts are still included in the overall ECDIS format, as these can be referred to on a specific basis, and apply to more specific and detailed maritime regions and coastlines. In reality, the actual ECDIS Chart as viewed on the bridge screen on board the vessel shows all the details found on a conventional paper-based chart, and can be used in conjunction with several other charts at the same time. To a large extent, the ECDIS Chart also resembles the electronic charts used by the VTS systems in most major ports, and to this extent, could be integrated with such VTS systems to provide an enhanced navigational reference system for both seaport and vessel alike. Although ECDIS overviews will be used on a more general basis, the Ship's Master can therefore access more detailed chart information, and can therefore maintain better control over navigation within more congested or restricted areas, in particular when entering or leaving port. At the touch of a button, information pertaining to the vessel's position, speed and course can be accessed by an Officer simply by using the vessel's onboard computer system without the need to refer to manual means, and this information can also be transferred to the vessel's control systems, thus allowing for automatic changes in the vessel's course and speed wherever necessary. The ECDIS Chart can also be accessed at the flick of a button on the bridge control systems, allowing for interface with not only other electronic charts but also other computer graphics concerning the ship management systems.

The difference between both charts is that where the specific ECDIS chart for a particular region shows the various channels, buoys and other hazards for the purpose of navigation, the AIS chart shows the position of all commercial ships and their direction of sailing in the region. The AIS charts are not in general used aboard vessels; the AIS system used on the vessel's bridge shows a database readout of the identification, position and direction of sailing of other ships in the proximity of the vessel using the readout. Thus, the ship's master will simply use the AIS system for reference purposes, and will not be able to identify the target vessel's position on a chart other than by the use of radar devices. If, however, the full graphic facility of AIS were to be installed on all commercial vessels, then this facility combined with the ECDIS display could be used more effectively for a variety of purposes to identify a vessel's position with relation to all the surrounding channels and other markings and hazards.

Owing to the effectiveness of the AIS system, the vessel has full access to information concerning not only its own position, but also the positions of other vessels in the vicinity relative to its own position in all kinds of weather conditions. It has been noted on various occasions, however, that in good weather conditions, the ship's master still prefers to identify a vessel by visual contact rather than by electronic means, suggesting that old and traditional habits die hard, and that there is no substitute for traditional tried and tested methods of navigation and positioning. Indeed, it has also been noted that despite the mandatory installation of the AIS system on board all commercial vessels over 300 grt, the information appears on the vessel's screen in database format, and is often not used owing to the activities of the vessel's crew on the bridge, and is in many cases seen as surplus to existing requirements. It is, however, widely admitted that the combined use of GPS, AIS, maritime radar and conventional navigational means give the ship's master a very accurate detail of his vessel's position at any one time, thus showing that the advances in onboard computer technology have greatly assisted the vessel's crew with their work alongside the traditional methods of navigation. The latest advance in the AIS regime is that it now takes into account the activities of small vessels such as fishing vessels and yachts, especially those vessels falling into the non-commercial category, where originally these vessels were not included. Given the latest stage, Stage B, of the AIS initiative, it is now possible for the skipper of any vessel to locate the presence of most other vessels in the maritime vicinity and ensure that collisions or other incidents are avoided.

ECDIS Charts can be downloaded from computer networks depending upon the regular routes plied by the vessel concerned. Regional regular sailings only require a small number of ECDIS charts pertinent to the limited areas covered, especially in the case of the Short Sea shipping networks, whereas deep sea networks, e.g. Transatlantic, Transpacific or Far East – Europe sailings require a larger number of ECDIS charts and hence a more powerful onboard computer to access each chart as required. Add to this the potential links with VTS as far as vessel reporting and monitoring for inward and outward movements to and from seaports, and the overall synergy starts to emerge, from the generic movements of vessels within international waters and hence under the scope of AIS, through the use of VTS monitoring where the vessel enters a channel approaching a port, right up to the point where that particular vessel enters the port itself and berths at the allocated quayside.

It is this envisaged combined scenario which would bear a similarity to the aviation principles of air traffic control, where the national air traffic control centre monitors an aircraft's flight path until it approaches the airport of destination, where control is passed from the national flight control centre to the local airport control centre for the purpose of guiding the aircraft through final approach to landing on the runway. In the same way that there is a necessity to co-ordinate the activities of national air traffic control alongside those of local airport control, the same requirement now exists for the control of maritime traffic into and out of all seaports, given not only the increasing sizes in commercial vessels but also the relative congestion in the case of many of the major international seaports throughout the European Community.

ECDIS, however, is not as widely used as its potential would suggest, and only the modern vessels are being equipped with such control systems. It is an automatic and standard practice for ocean-going commercial vessels presently under construction to be equipped with state-of-the-art navigational systems, as the cost of installation is absorbed in the overall cost of construction and fitting-out. However, this absorption of costs cannot be applied to the re-equipping of existing vessels at present in operation. There would be a considerable cost in updating the systems on vessels in use for some time for such electronic controls. Hence the need for the foreseeable future for the traditional Admiralty Charts in paper form, in both commercial and leisure craft, which are still seen as the standard means of navigation in both international and territorial waters. In this respect, it is unlikely that all vessels at present plying the high seas would be re-equipped in the foreseeable future with the ECDIS System, unless legislation is passed by national governments making such use mandatory. Nonetheless, the advantages of such systems are clearly evident, and make the task of navigating the high seas and territorial waters that much less onerous.

The IMO Sub-Committee on the Safety of Navigation (NAV) decided at its session in June 2005 that all high-speed marine craft should be fitted with and should use ECDIS on a mandatory basis. This would be achieved by making amendments to the International Code of Safety for High-Speed Craft 2000 (2000 HSC Code), which would then require ECDIS facilities to be fitted to all new craft and to all existing craft under a phase-in schedule with a proposed final implementation date of 2010. Furthermore, the Sub-Committee decided that there should be a Formal Safety Assessment (FSA) study on the use of ECDIS on ships other than high-speed craft and passenger ships prior to any discussion on a possible carriage requirement for other ships. In reality, all new commercial vessels are being equipped with the ECDIS system at the time of construction, although many deck officers still prefer to use the manual charts for convenience.

The systems thus available to the crew of a vessel for the purposes of navigation and onboard control and monitoring are as follows:

- AIS;
- VTS;
- GPS;
- ECDIS;
- Radar Systems;
- VTS / VHF Channels.

As seen on the above diagrams, there are certain similarities between the ECDIS computer displays and the graphic displays shown on the AIS internet system. The ECDIS system shows coastlines and channels, as well as obstacles such as sandbanks, reefs, wrecks and buoys, exactly as shown on paper-based charts. At present, AIS information concerning proximate vessels shows up as database information on the vessel's AIS screen, but does not appear as a geographic image on that screen in the way that an image appears on the AIS website.

Given the similarities between both ECDIS and AIS systems, it would appear possible that the ECDIS system could be combined with the AIS system to show a vessel's position relative to the channels she was located in, relative to the chart applicable to the locality. Further integration could be achieved by adding the graphic element of VTS to the ship's monitoring system. The previous illustrations show this similarity. The new generation of cruise liners and cargo vessels are being equipped with more integrated navigation and location systems which encompass the above technologies, as well as the GPS radar and navigations systems, but there remains the issue of ensuring that all relevant crew members are competent to use the new technology and do use it to its fullest extent.

To a degree, a certain element of this initiative has been achieved. It is already possible to use the AIS system to facilitate a vessel control regime, by way of electronic contact with the vessel. The VTS technology itself uses AIS formats to identify and monitor vessels entering port areas, although VTS itself generally refers to port-related traffic control, rather than the monitoring of vessels in open water. There are, however, instances where certain Coastguard Authorities are investing in VTS systems where maritime traffic density is relatively high, such as in the Southern North Sea areas. This initiative has resulted in part from the successful VTS system used in the Strait of Dover, although the VTS systems being implemented further up the UK's East Coast are not as complex as that used in the Channel area. However, the VTS systems being used do not necessarily contain provisions for the inclusion of ECDIS charts detailing Channel markings and other hazards.

Technology has, nevertheless, allowed for the development of VTS/AIS systems where such chart and control systems may now be integrated. A new electronic system has been developed in Canada which integrates both ECDIS and AIS systems by an organisation called ICanMarine (website www.icanmarine.com). The system, called "*Horizon*", uses both types of technology as well as integrating with VTS regimes to monitor and control vessel movements. The advantage of the Canadian system is that it can be used both on board vessels and in shore-based establishments, although at present it is only being used in North America.

There is thus the possibility of several steps to achieving some degree of integration in electronic, navigational and security-based reporting systems. These steps are detailed as follows:

- An integration of the AIS, ECDIS and VTS systems would be the **First Step** in detailing not only the navigational hazards in the area, but also other ships in the vicinity;

- The **Second Step** would be to add to the AIS system details of ships carrying dangerous or hazardous cargoes, specifically identifiable to individual vessels as well as to Coastguards, whose facilities should automatically be equipped with AIS and ECDIS to show the areas concerned and the maritime traffic in these areas;

- The **Third Step** would be to require all vessels to declare their cargoes for AIS and other Maritime Security purposes, thus enabling both Masters of other vessels and also the land-based maritime authorities to establish not only the nature of the vessels concerned but also the nature of their cargoes. This information would also be automatically available to all other ports in the area based on their use of AIS or any other future marine reporting system;

- The **Fourth Step** would be to use the EMRS as a basis for constructing a fully-integrated regime for EU purposes, allowing not just for the integrated reporting of hazardous cargoes, but in reality for all cargoes (as well as passengers and crew, where appropriate) to a Regional Co-Ordination Centre. This information could then be dispersed to any national authority requiring information of a maritime nature, including the following authorities:

- Admiralty;

- Coastguards;

- National Competent Maritime Authority;

- Customs;

- Shipowners;

- Shipbrokers and Shipping Agents;

- Freight Forwarders;

- Port Authorities;

- Police Authorities.

A fully-integrated reporting system which effectively allows all interested parties to derive information from a central database pertaining to their own needs is urgently required, and must be implemented with all interests in mind, be they Admiralty, Customs, Coastguards, Ports, Shipping Agents or Shipowners. The issue of cost prevails without doubt, especially concerning the responsibilities relating to the funding of such an initiative, but in the interests of the preservation of the national status quo, security must prevail over that of cost. Such a system must also take into account the issue of small craft, particularly pleasure and leisure craft such as cruisers and yachts, which are not presently covered by any Marine Reporting System or Regime, and are often crewed by people less qualified than most professional mariners. At present, these categories of small craft are not covered by any standard reporting requirements, but given the potential danger that they pose to the movement of commercial and military vessels, especially in areas such as the Channel and the Firth of Clyde, there is an immediate need to include these vessels as well in the overall scheme of activities. This need exists to ensure that no major incidents occur or that the movements of such vessels are being sufficiently regulated and monitored for security reasons.

Whether it is practical to extend the scope of AIS to include such types of craft or whether a more integrated, all-embracing Marine Reporting regime would be more appropriate in such cases is yet a matter of discussion. Even given the nature of commercial marine traffic movements, there is nevertheless a need for a more integrative Marine Reporting system covering not only the nature of vessels, their identification and their navigational movements, but also the nature of their cargoes and, in the case of ferries and cruise liners, passengers. This system should also be used to cover every port in the country, even throughout the European Union, enabling each port to allow its information concerning Ship Movements, Sailing Plans and Cargo details, however basic, to be accessed by other ports and authorities should the need arise, especially in the eventuality of unplanned or urgent diversions. However, such information should still be privy to only security-approved personnel, and therefore should be subject to electronic security measures such as passwords or other forms of screening, in order to uphold the provisions of the Data Protection Act.

The structure of such a reporting system should thus allow for the following information to be reported:

VESSEL:

- Identification of the Vessel (IMO Identification, Name of Vessel);
- Sailing Plan and ETA;
- Flag of the Vessel;
- Crew of the Vessel (ISPS/FAL);
- Size of the Vessel (Dimensions and Tonnage);
- Direction of the Vessel;
- Position of the Vessel;
- Port of Departure;
- Port of Destination;
- Declaration of Ship's Stores (Customs Purposes) – IMO FAL Requirements;
- Declaration of Crew and Passengers – IMO FAL Requirements.

CARGO:

- Contents of the Vessel (Passenger/Cargo);
- Nature of Cargo (Bulk/Container);
- Hazardous / Non-Hazardous;
- Container Numbers (where appropriate);
- Quantity of Cargo per Container / Bulk Cargo;
- Full Electronic Cargo Manifests compressed into ZIP format;
- Details of all consignments contained in each consolidated load, with the terms STC and FAK eliminated from use;
- Commodity Codes of all Cargoes transported (Container/Bulk);
- Cargo Values;
- Customs Status of Cargo (EU Free Circulation / non-EU uncleared)

Some of this information is already in existence as part of the AIS or the FAL Reporting systems, but requires expanding and integrating to include the other elements stated above, subject to the conditions allowed under the Data Protection Act. In the case of AIS, the information concerning the destination, route and identification of the vessel is known, while the FAL procedures deal with vessels berthing at port. The overall information database should also be integrated into existing IMO regimes in one electronic format, rather than the several in operation at present. Other information, in particular that pertaining to Customs status, is contained on Cargo Manifests reported as part of the CUSCAR (Customs Cargo) Reporting mechanism, but is only privy to the specific port of arrival rather than other ports elsewhere in the UK. Equally, such information is available to Shipping and Freight Agents, but is only used in full as far as the submission of Import Declarations to HM Revenue & Customs is concerned, and in its raw and basic format is insufficient to enable the Customs Authority to accurately judge the true status of each individual cargo on board ship. Given the expected increase in such information as a result of the increase in size of container ships, this information should be initially compressed, e.g. in ZIP format, but with the facility for the manifest to be downloaded and opened on the computer, and container numbers to be highlighted on the electronic system to enable the authority concerned to access and scrutinise specific information pertaining to the cargo contained in a specific container on board ship by accessing the specific container number on the manifest in either a random (e.g. 1 in 10) or specific manner. Such reporting should also apply to all Authorised Regular Shipping Services as well as other intra-EU and non-EU ships, given the diversity in Customs status of the cargoes carried by such ships. It should be noted that the Customs Authorities of all EU member States are presently engaged in assessing the issue of collective security concerning imports into the EU, and the maritime issue figures within this review. The US and Canadian models are being considered, although as yet there is still a wide gap between the structures on each side of the Atlantic. It should also be noted that, whereas marine reporting systems for export of cargoes and the departure of vessels exist in the EU, there is nowhere near the same extent of outward reporting in the case of the United States ports.

To this extent, the regimes covered by the ISPS and FAL systems could also be integrated, especially given their implementation by their common creators, the IMO. Given the perceived overlap to a certain extent between the FAL reporting system and the ISPS Code, there is value in considering the feasibility of combining and integrating the two regimes into one, thus creating a single, more comprehensive reporting mechanism concerning both vessel security and content issues. This would also reduce the administrative and bureaucratic burden undertaken at present by most ports concerning the arrival of commercial vessels.

The information provided in the integrated reporting system should thus be available to the following parties:

- Every EU Port Authority in the proximate area of the arrival of the vessel (e.g. East Coast UK);

- Port Health Authorities;

- All relevant and proximate EU Customs Authorities;

- Police Authorities (where appropriate);

- Admiralties of each pertinent EU Member State;

- Coastguards of all pertinent EU Countries;

- Shipbrokers and Shipping Agents;
- Freight Forwarders;
- Lloyd's List / Lloyd's of London.

It is proposed that the problem of creating such an integrated reporting system may be facilitated by either of three possible solutions:

1) The full integration of existing reporting systems;

2) The creation of a new uniform umbrella system incorporating the principles and structures of all existing systems;

3) The extensive standardisation and harmonisation of existing reporting mechanisms to provide overlap and synergy with each other, as well as reducing the amount of administration and bureaucracy.

1) THE FULL INTEGRATION OF EXISTING REPORTING SYSTEMS

The first scenario requires the total integration of existing individual marine reporting systems in existence throughout the European Union, which are at present governed by and pertain to national conditions and constraints. Even considering the policy of the EU towards integration of national policy within a pan-EU framework, the work required to integrate the reporting systems of each EU Member State, bearing in mind the different conditions under which they function, would be complex and time-consuming at very least.

2) THE CREATION OF A NEW UNIFORM UMBRELLA SYSTEM

The second scenario involves the creation of a new, security-based, Marine Reporting System to be used as standard throughout the European Union, in line with existing policies concerning the collective control over EU territory and initiatives concerning shipping movements between EU Member States. This scenario would also require the enhancement of Coastguard powers throughout the EU, with the creation of a pan-EU Coastguard Regime with the same powers as are bestowed upon the US and Canadian Coastguard Authorities. Such a System would then allow for the use of existing systems such as VTS and AIS, but within a more controllable and manageable regime capable of controlling the entire maritime network bounded by the 200-mile and 12-mile limits around the whole of the EU Coastline. This regime would automatically control all area of sea within these limits, including the Straits presently accounted for in existing reporting controls, such as the Strait of Dover, the Öresund and the Strait of Gibraltar. It would give the power to each national Coastguard authority to control its own national sector of territorial water to ensure strict compliance of all vessels sailing into and within such waters with national maritime controls. It would also ensure that vessels entering EU waters from elsewhere would be automatically subject to EU Reporting Controls, and that failure to submit such full reports would render the vessel liable to interception by a vessel from any of the EU Authorities.

3) THE EXTENSIVE STANDARDISATION AND HARMONISATION OF EXISTING REPORTING MECHANISMS

The third scenario would involve the harmonisation of each existing system with the other reporting systems in use, to provide synergy between all such reporting systems on an international and domestic basis, enabling the user to switch from one reporting system to another without requiring individual independent authorisation to use each system on an individual basis, thus also pooling the efforts of each national or supranational authority in ensuring the maintenance of the regime as a whole. This would also require each system to be readily available to all maritime users for the same purpose – the overall dissemination and transparency of maritime security information pertaining to both ships and their cargoes to all relevant authorities in the form of what would amount to a form of matrix-based structure.

4) A TWO-LEVEL REPORTING SYSTEM CONCERNING OPERATIONAL REPORTING AND ARRIVAL/DEPARTURE REPORTING

As discussed earlier in this section, there is the perception that present reporting systems can be grouped into two categories, namely *Operational*, concerning the vessel's movements, and *Arrival/Departure*, concerning the vessel's relationship with the port. The integration of ECDIS, VTS and AIS facilities would give a greater degree of control to Masters of vessels and shore-based controls alike, by providing a common set of electronic graphic controls for the purpose of both navigation and maritime traffic control. In the other category, the reporting regimes required for entry into port, i.e. FAL and ISPS, could also be integrated as a single reporting system, also covering the reporting of hazardous or dangerous goods. One category would therefore be of a more graphic nature, while the other would refer to the electronic management of documentary and record-keeping control for the purposes of control by national authorities for compliance purposes. While a vessel is within the scope of international waters, it is subject to operational reporting requirements; while it is entering or leaving the jurisdiction of national territorial controls, it is subject to a set of arrival and departure reporting requirements.

Given the political and security uncertainties of the world at present, the purpose of such an integrated system and the information held therein would be that it would apply to and would be accessible all EU Countries, regardless of whichever particular EU Country was the destination of the vessel in question. Thus a vessel deviating from its intended course as defined by its sailing plan could be tracked and monitored using other devices such as AIS, and if the vessel refused to submit proper reports, it could be intercepted and if necessary seized. The Royal Navy and Customs already hold powers to engage in such activities, but the ability of both organisations to maintain the presence of vessels around the UK coastline to carry out such preventive activities is somewhat limited due to the constraints dictated by finite resources. However, there would be also be the need to increase the powers held by the Maritime and Coastguard Agency to a level used by their counterparts in the United States and Canada, i.e. the powers of interception and, where necessary, arrest of vessels deemed to pose a threat or seen as providing insufficient satisfactory information to the Coastguard. In this respect, the EU Coastguard regime would also require the ability to track and monitor vessels throughout the entirety of the EU Coastline, such as presently happens with the CNIS at Dover. The foundations are already in place, such as CNIS and mandatory reporting for Vessels carrying Dangerous or Hazardous Goods – the need now exists for an extension of this to cover all commercial vessels, as well as small or pleasure craft equipped with modern navigational and technological equipment. In some cases, the added security risk pertaining to warships and submarines requires that commercial vessels make known their existence and position, in case of the risk of collision with a naval vessel or because of the security aspects pertaining to the presence of a naval vessel such as a nuclear submarine, especially in areas such as the Firth of Clyde or the Channel.

Furthermore, the present reporting system must be extended so that every port within a specific radius of a specific port of destination of any arriving vessel has common access to information presently reported to individual ports, and which is not accessible to any other ports on the same coastline or elsewhere in the UK. There are many cases where ships are diverted to other ports for reasons of safety, capacity or weather, and regardless of this, given the increasing awareness of the need for greater degrees of national security, the details of any vessel entering UK Territorial Waters and its cargo or passengers should be made available to all ports anywhere near the actual port of destination, as well as the Admiralty, Customs and Coastguard authorities proximate to the area. Furthermore, HM Coastguard should in any case be given more powers of coastal control and monitoring, including the boarding and arrest of vessels where appropriate, in a way similar to its counterparts in North America.

It is appreciated that the constraints of the Data Protection Legislation, along with the consideration of the interests of national security, do not allow for the automatic dissemination of information between many authorities and parties. However, in the interests of national security, the need for the sharing of information concerning possible breaches of national security becomes paramount, especially concerning the issue of maritime security. The prevalence of international terrorism and the perceived threat to national security have made it inevitable that a consolidation of marine reporting systems is not only necessary but also urgent. Without it, the threat posed to the security of not only shipping but also seaports becomes ever greater and more sinister. This said, the widespread and public access to and use of the AIS system does unfortunately allow for various organisations of a more dubious nature, e.g. terrorist groups or self-styled "environmentalist" organisations, to monitor, and on various occasions intercept, the movements of vessels subject to high security risk status, such as those carrying cargoes of a specifically dangerous nature, in particular nuclear-radioactive cargoes. Since May 2005, the online AIS facility has been structured in such a way that only organisations with the ability to pay for subscription to the facility can access "live" information pertaining to shipping movements, thus reducing the risk of unauthorised users gaining up-to-the-minute information pertaining to such movements, and thus reducing some of the security risk, especially the risk posed by the carriage of sensitive or dangerous cargoes. In the case of nuclear and radioactive cargoes, the IMO has created a specific set of conditions for the carriage of such cargoes, and only specific ships are equipped and cleared for such use under the INF conditions. Even so, as commercial vessels over the 300 grt threshold, they are obliged to carry and use the AIS facilities (as well as specific defensive facilities), and this may still render them vulnerable in terms of monitoring on the AIS website or by other ships using the AIS facility. In this case, the AIS system may be seen as less than totally secure, when one considers the need for secrecy and confidentiality surrounding the carriage of nuclear cargoes by sea. On the plus side, the AIS facility can enable such ships to be avoided by other maritime commercial traffic as well as be monitored by national authorities to ensure that they adhere to their arranged sailing plans.

The question of funding to facilitate such activities is always raised as a counter to the benefits of such ventures, and it is inevitable that private or commercial funding for the whole issue of the enhancement of Marine Reporting requirements would not be the ultimate answer. Government funding is vital in ensuring that the defence of the realm is maintained, and it is equally believed that any increase in maritime reporting and control activities undertaken by national authorities such as the MCA or even the Admiralty must be funded from Government sources. How high the cost would be depends largely upon the nature of any proposed development to the Marine Reporting and Control structure required, as well as the limitations of information technology involved in such a venture, depending upon the complexity of the integration or harmonisation concerned. It must be pointed out that in North America, considerable amounts of money have been invested in both the US and Canadian Maritime Control sectors, including the Coastguard Agencies of both Countries, but it should also be recognised that such expenditure can only be viewed as a vital necessity to national well-being rather than a luxury, considering the attacks and threats made by various parties against the United States over the past few years, and the potential of such threats to the UK as well, given its stance and importance in the world arena. Any additional funding required for the upgrading of individual Port facilities would possibly originate from revenue gained by such ports, as is already the case with the implementation of the new AIS systems worldwide, although it would be reasonable to imagine that public sector or governmental funding could be made available, given the input and contribution in such proposed reporting systems by several government departments.

However, such funding is a small price to pay compared with the cost of economic disaster resulting from acts of terrorism or even the cost associated with ecological and environmental disasters resulting from acts of maritime negligence as has been seen all too frequently over the past few years. Even something as common as an oil spillage from a VLCC Tanker results in massive amounts of money spent on cleaning up from the effects of widespread hydrocarbon pollution to the shoreline, let alone the intangible costs associated with the destruction of marine wildlife. And all because either the tanker ran aground for a variety of reasons, or a collision occurred at sea, or quite simply because the tanker was engaged in illegal tank-cleaning operations in sea areas where such activities are expressly forbidden, and polluted the marine environment. Even the activities of the North Sea Continental Shelf arouse questions from a variety of organisations, particularly those concerned with the environment, given the risk of disused platforms providing hazardous obstacles to shipping and causing harm to the environment.

In short, prevention is better than cure. In this case, the reference is to the prevention of marine accidents, incidents and disasters. Indeed, it is often not only the accident or disaster which is the problem, but also its aftermath and consequences, as shown by the environmental and ecological calamities caused by the wrecks of various oil tankers, let alone the economic consequences. The case of the large crude petroleum carriers is particularly concerning, since the nature of the bulk cargo carried by such vessels on the high seas is of itself a major cause for concern. The wreck of a hull is one thing; the spillage of a hazardous cargo is another, and as seen by the resulting insurance claims the results are far-reaching. A quick diagnosis and resolution of the problem is far more expedient than overlooking the problem and allowing it to fester and become significantly more compounded over a period of time. Ultimately, such oversight would cost the establishment dear, principally as a direct result of lapses in the maintenance of marine security, although other factors, such as negligence or mechanical breakdown, can contribute to a certain extent. Lessons learned as a result of both marine accidents, involving container vessels such as the *Hyundai Fortune* and the *MSC Napoli*, tankers such as the *Erika*, the *Amoco Cadiz* or the *Exxon Valdez*, and terrorist activities, such as the seizing of the Cruise Liner *Achille Lauro*, have shown the need to invest in more robust Marine Reporting systems in order to protect national and, in the case of the European Union, supranational interests. It could be argued that the US and Canadian models of maritime reporting and security may seem heavy-handed and over-protective, but in an era of worldwide political uncertainty and increased security consciousness, it is better to invest in a robust system which protects the national maritime interest and which tightens up all reporting mechanisms than to allow room for vulnerability caused by an assumption that existing systems cover all eventualities by electronic means without allowing for the anomalies and uncertainties caused by the human frame of mind. There are already a series of useful systems of various kinds concerning Marine Reporting, but they are either specific to the reporting requirement, such as SSN, ISPS, AIS or HAZMAT, or concern a specific location, such as the Traffic separation Scheme (TSS) imposed by the CNIS at the Dover Strait.

In conclusion, therefore, the necessity now exists to integrate all marine reporting systems in a standardised and harmonised form to cover all shipping movements around all UK/EU port and territorial sea locations for reasons of both expediency and security, and to expand these systems to include all aspects of cargo reporting as well as vessel reporting. This integration should, therefore, include all types of reporting mechanisms pertinent to both vessels and cargoes, and should take into account their arrival at or departure from all UK ports, as well as those vessels passing close to UK shores en route to other non-UK destinations. Given similar needs throughout the European Union, the same initiative should also be pursued throughout the EU as a whole. The legal and regulatory basis already exists for such an initiative, but the need now exists for action to be taken to implement such measures on the grounds of national, supranational and international security, as well as on the grounds of the prevailing need to harmonise data and information resources in the area of maritime security, thus satisfying the needs and requirements of all organisations involved in the maritime sector.

Ultimately, the subject boils down to one simple issue: if aircraft are required to report in to both national and local Air Traffic Controls prior to arrival at an airport, then maritime vessels should be required to report in to national and local maritime controls prior to arrival at port. The same set of control procedures should apply to maritime traffic as it does to air traffic.

In addition to the theoretical arguments submitted in support of an integrated Marine Reporting regime, three case studies have been compiled to illustrate the shortcomings in the present system, and ways to resolve some of the issues at stake. These are:

- The Storebaelt and the Öresund (Scandinavia – Denmark and Sweden);
- The North Channel (Scotland and Northern Ireland) and the Pentland Firth (North of Scotland);
- The Canadian Reporting Systems.

These case studies represent three entirely different approaches, but are related in the sense that they are both located within national territory, with the exception of the Öresund, which separates Denmark and Sweden. The first case study addresses an existing regime, albeit only implemented a short while ago, namely the Storebaelt VTS system, the second addresses an area where there is no system whatsoever – the North Channel, as well as a limited system in the Pentland Firth covering the ports of the Orkney Islands, while the third addresses a fully-integrative reporting regime covering Canadian territorial waters.

CHAPTER NINE

CASE STUDIES

CASE STUDY 1 – THE 1936 MONTREUX CONVENTION REGARDING THE REGIME OF THE TURKISH STRAITS

The **Montreux Convention** concerning the Regime of the Turkish Straits was a 1936 agreement that gave Turkey control over the Bosphorus Straits, the Sea of Marmara and the Dardanelles and regulates military activity in the region. Signed on 20 July 1936, it permitted Turkey to remilitarise the Straits and imposed new restrictions on the passage of warships and combatant vessels. It is still in force today, albeit with some amendments.

Geographically, Turkey straddles the boundary dividing Europe and Asia. Sitting astride the Dardanelles and the Bosporus, Turkey controls the warm-water naval access of Russia, the Ukraine, and the Commonwealth of Independent States (CIS). Control of the straits between the Black and the Mediterranean Seas has long been a matter of major interest to Russia, as well as other nations bordering the Black Sea. Historically, Russia has viewed such control as a major influential factor over its own sovereignty.

Turkey must still adhere to the principles of the international law and the UN Convention on the Law of the Sea of 1982, but this can cause problems as there are variances between the two Conventions.

The Bosphorus straits are considered international waterways and Turkey is prohibited from restricting their use in peacetime. Turkish maritime authorities can check ships for sanitary conditions and safety and can charge tolls, but cannot stop their passage. The terms international waters or transboundary waters apply where any of the following types of bodies of water (or their drainage basins) transcend international boundaries: oceans, large marine ecosystems, enclosed or semi-enclosed regional seas and estuaries, rivers, lakes, groundwater systems (aquifers), and wetlands [1]. Oceans and seas, waters outside national territorial control.

The Convention gives Turkey full control over the Straits and guarantees the free passage of civilian vessels in peacetime. It severely restricts the passage of non-Turkish military vessels and prohibits some types of warships, such as aircraft carriers, from passing through the Straits. The terms of the convention have been the source of controversy over the years, most notably concerning military access by the Russian naval fleet to the Mediterranean Sea.

Background and History

The convention was one of a series of agreements in the 19th and 20th centuries that sought to address the long-running "Straits Question" of who should control the strategically vital link between the Black Sea and the Mediterranean Sea. In 1923 the Treaty of Lausanne had demilitarised the Dardanelles and opened the Straits to unrestricted civilian and military traffic, under the supervision of the International Straits Commission of the League of Nations.

By the late 1930s, the strategic situation in the Mediterranean had significantly altered with the rise of the Fascist Party in Italy, which controlled the Greek-inhabited Dodecanese islands off the west coast of Turkey and had significantly militarised the region with the construction of fortifications on the islands of Rhodes, Leros and Kos. The Turks feared that Italy would seek to exploit access to the Straits to expand its power into the eastern Turkish region of Anatolia and the Black Sea region. There were also significant fears of rearmament in Bulgaria. Although Turkey was not permitted to refortify the Straits it nevertheless did so secretly.

In April 1935, the Turkish government despatched a lengthy diplomatic note to the signatories of the Treaty of Lausanne proposing a conference on the agreement of a new regime for the Straits and requested that the League of Nations authorise the reconstruction of the Dardanelles forts. In the note, Turkish foreign minister Tevfik Rüstü Aras explained that the international situation had changed greatly since 1923. At that time, Europe had been moving towards disarmament and an international guarantee to defend the Straits. The Abyssinian Crisis of 1934-1935, the denunciation by Germany of the 1919 Treaty of Versailles and international moves towards rearmament meant that "the only guarantee intended to guard against the total insecurity of the Straits has just disappeared in its turn." Indeed, Aras said, "the Powers most closely concerned are proclaiming the existence of a threat of general conflagration." The key weaknesses of the present regime were that the machinery for collective guarantees were too slow and ineffective, there was no contingency for a general threat of war and no provision for Turkey to defend itself. Turkey was therefore prepared

"to enter into negotiations with a view to arriving in the near future at the conclusion of agreements for regulations of the regime of the Straits under the conditions of security which are indespensable for the inviolability of Turkey's territory, in most liberal spirit, for the constant development of commercial navigation between the Mediterranean and the Black Sea."

The response to the note was generally favourable, and Australia, Bulgaria, France, Germany, Greece, Japan and the Soviet Union, Turkey, the United Kingdom and Yugoslavia agreed to attend negotiations at Montreux in Switzerland, which commenced on 22 June 1936. Two major powers were not represented: Italy, whose aggressively expansionist policies had prompted the conference in the first place, refused to attend and the United States declined even to send an observer.

The attending countries agreed to abolish the International Straits Commission and return the Straits zone (the Dardanelles, the Sea of Marmara, and Bosphorus) to Turkish military control. They allowed Turkey to remilitarize the straits, which had been prohibited under the 1923 Lausanne Convention as part of the peace treaty that finally formally ended the hostilities begun in 1914. The new Montreux Convention also modified the 1923 rules for the passage of vessels through these waters, and this Convention of 1936 [20 July 1936, 173 LNTS 213,219] was ratified by Turkey, Great Britain, France, the USSR, Bulgaria, Greece, Germany, Yugoslavia, and Japan (with reservations). While the United States is not a signatory to the Convention, it has historically always complied with its provision.

Turkey, the UK and the Soviet Union each put forward their own set of proposals, aimed chiefly at protecting their own interests. The British favoured the continuation of a relatively restrictive approach, while the Turks sought a more liberal regime that reasserted their own control over the Straits and the Soviets proposed a regime that would guarantee absolute freedom of passage. The British, supported by France, sought to exclude the Russian fleet from the Mediterranean Sea, where it might have threatened the vital shipping lanes to India, Egypt, and the Far East. In the end, the British conceded some of their requests while the Soviets succeeded in ensuring that the Black Sea countries - including the USSR - were given some exemptions from the military restrictions imposed on non-Black Sea nations. The agreement was ratified by all of the conference attendees with the exception of Australia and Germany, which had not been signatories to the Treaty of Lausanne, and with reservations by Japan, and came into force on 9 November 1936.

Britain's willingness to make concessions has been attributed to a desire to avoid Turkey being driven to ally itself with, or fall under the influence of, Hitler or Mussolini. It was thus the first in a series of steps by Britain and France to ensure that Turkey would either remain neutral or tilt towards the Western Allies in the event of any future conflict with the Axis.

TERMS AND CONSEQUENCES OF THE CONVENTION

The Convention consists of 29 Articles, four annexes and one protocol. Articles 2-7 consider the passage of merchant ships. Articles 8-22 consider the passage of war vessels. The key principle of freedom of passage and navigation is stated in articles 1 and 2. Article 1 provides that "The High Contracting Parties recognise and affirm the principle of freedom of passage and navigation by sea in the Straits". Article 2 states that "In time of peace, merchant vessels shall enjoy complete freedom of passage and navigation in the Straits, by day and by night, under any flag with any kind of cargo."

The International Straits Commission was abolished, authorising the full resumption of Turkish military control over the Straits and the refortification of the Dardanelles. Turkey was authorised to close the Straits to all foreign warships in wartime or when it was threatened by aggression; additionally, it was authorised to refuse transit from merchant ships belonging to countries at war with Turkey. A number of highly specific restrictions were imposed on what type of warships are allowed passage. Non-Turkish warships in the Straits must be under 15,000 tons. No more than nine non-Turkish warships, with a total aggregate tonnage of no more than 30,000 tons, may pass at any one time, and they are permitted to stay in the Black Sea for no longer than three weeks. The number of foreign warships permitted in the Straits at any one time is restricted to one. Black Sea states are given more leeway, being authorised to send capital ships of any tonnage through the Straits (but only one at a time and specifically excluding aircraft carriers). They are also allowed to send submarines through the Straits, with prior notice, as long as the vessels have been constructed, purchased or sent for repair outside the Black Sea. The less restrictive rules applicable to Black Sea states were agreed as, effectively, a concession to the Soviet Union, the only Black Sea state other than Turkey with any significant number of capital ships or submarines. The passage of civil aircraft between the Mediterranean and Black Seas is permitted, but only along routes authorised by the Turkish government.

The terms of the Convention were largely a reflection of the international situation in the mid-1930s. They largely served Turkish and Soviet interests, enabling Turkey to regain military control of the Straits and assuring Soviet dominance of the Black Sea.

Although the Convention restricted the Soviets' ability to send naval forces into the Mediterranean Sea, thereby satisfying British concerns about Soviet intrusion into what was considered a British sphere of influence - it also ensured that outside powers could not exploit the Straits to threaten the Soviet Union. This was to have significant repercussions during World War II when the Montreux regime prevented the Axis powers from sending naval forces through the Straits to attack the Soviet Union. The Axis powers were thus severely limited in naval capability in their Black Sea campaigns, relying principally on small vessels that had been transported overland by rail and canal networks. Auxiliary vessels and armed merchant ships occupied a grey area, however, and the transit of such vessels through the straits led to friction between the Allies and Turkey. Repeated protests from Moscow and London led to the Turkish government banning the movements of "suspicious" Axis ships with effect from June 1944 after a number of German auxiliary ships were permitted to transit the Straits.

DEVELOPMENT OF THE CONVENTION SINCE 1936

On 7 August 1946, following Turkish elections, the Soviet Union renewed its demands for a revision of the Montreux Convention governing access to the Black Sea, and Soviet naval activity in the region began. The Soviet Union demanded that Turkey's control of the strategic Dardanelles Strait, guaranteed by the Montreux Convention in 1936, be modified in Russia's favour. Among other things, the Soviets wanted joint rights with Turkey to use bases in the straits. On 10 August 1946, the Turkish Premier reaffirmed Turkey's intent to continue opposition to the Soviet demands. The United States objected to the Soviet demands, and President Truman approved plans to send a naval task force into the eastern Mediterranean. In the coming months, US and UK naval activity in region greatly increased, and on 18 October, Turkey rejected the Soviet demands. In the same time period, the Communist insurgency in Greece grew dramatically.

The Convention remains in force today, with amendments, though not without dispute. It was repeatedly challenged by the Soviet Union during World War II and the Cold War. As early as 1939, Stalin sought to reopen the Straits Question and proposed joint Turkish and Soviet control of the Straits, complaining that "a small state [i.e. Turkey] supported by Great Britain held a great state by the throat and gave it no outlet." After the Molotov-Ribbentrop Pact was signed by the Soviet Union and Nazi Germany, the Soviet Foreign Minister Vyacheslav Molotov informed his German counterparts that the USSR wished to take military control of the Straits and establish its own military base there. The Soviets returned to the issue in 1945 and 1946, demanding a revision of the Montreux Convention at a conference excluding most of the Montreux signatories, a permanent Soviet military presence and joint control of the Straits. This was firmly rejected by Turkey, despite an ongoing Soviet "strategy of tension". For several years after World War II, the Soviets exploited the restriction on the number of foreign warships by ensuring that one of theirs was always in the Straits, thus effectively blocking any nation other than Turkey from sending warships through the Straits. Soviet pressure eventually resulted in Turkey abandoning its policy of neutrality; in 1947 it became the recipient of US military and economic assistance under the Truman Doctrine of "containment" and joined NATO, along with Greece, in 1952.

The Montreux Convention was conceived in haste during the inter-war years. It had not been revised to keep pace with either technological or political changes. The definitions of the various classes of warships were taken verbatim from the London Naval Treaty of 25 March 1936 (the so-called Second London Naval Treaty). Though the USSR was not a party to this Treaty, the countries which drew up the London Naval Treaty represented the leading naval powers of the era. They, and not the Soviets, excluded aircraft carriers from the category of capital ships. Annex II of the Convention defines aircraft carriers as "surface vessels of war, whatever their displacement, designed or adapted primarily for the purpose of carrying and operating aircraft at sea. The fitting of a landing-on or flying-off deck on any vessel of war, provided such vessel has not been designed or adapted primarily for the purpose of carrying and operating aircraft at sea, shall not cause any vessel so fitted to be classified in the category of aircraft-carrier." Aircraft carriers are a separate category defined as "surface vessels of war, whatever their displacement, designed or adapted primarily for the purpose of carrying and operating aircraft at sea". The Soviet Union proposed the general principle that the straits be closed to aircraft carriers. This was a significant departure from the Lausanne Convention, which had allowed their passage.

Russian aircraft carriers in the Black Sea were first seen as "aircraft transports" in the Imperial Russian Navy during the First World War. Often converted passenger liners, these ships would carry a number of seaplanes that would be hoisted overboard for launch and then recovered back onto the ship after they had returned and landed. On 6 February 1916 two such seaplane tenders launched a 10-aircraft attack on the Turkish Black Sea port of Zonguldak. Later in 1916 the Imperial Naval Air service attacked the Bulgarian seaport of Varna in the same manner. These seaplane tenders did not long survive the Revolution.

The Soviet Union and its successor, the Russian Federation, have repeatedly sought to evade the ban on aircraft carriers passing through the Straits by designating large aircraft-carrying warships as "heavy aircraft-carrying cruisers", although Western nations regard such ships as aircraft carriers. In 1976, the USSR sent the aircraft carrier *Kiev* through the Straits. The episode was repeated in 1991 when the Russian aircraft carrier *Admiral Kuznetsov* transited the straits.

By the 1960s entire classes of ships and weapons moving about on the world's oceans today were unheard of in 1936 and thus were unaccounted for in the Straits regime. The Soviets developed several unique types, combining the attributes of an aircraft carrier with the awesome power of a missile cruiser. The weapons and sensors aboard these ships contributed as much to their capabilities as did their aircraft.

The two *Moskva* class ships were introduced in 1967 and were homeported in the Black Sea. They deployed to the Mediterranean, the Atlantic and the Indian Ocean. They were designated as "aviation cruisers" at least in part to avoid problems with the 1936 Montreux Convention, which prohibited passage of "aircraft carriers" through the Dardanelles. Many Western analysts concurred with an anti-submarine definition of the ships' purpose.

In 1976 and again in 1979, Turkey allowed Soviet aircraft carriers to transit the Bosphorus and Dardanelles Straits in violation of the 1936 Montreux Convention. Some NATO states voiced strong opposition to these moves, since the Soviet carriers posed a significant threat to the US Sixth Fleet and NATO forces. But others argued that over the years the Montreux Convention had been amended de facto to provide for the transit of Soviet Kiev-class aircraft carriers. Turkey, which was solely responsible for the day-to-day interpretation of the convention, had challenged neither the Soviet classification of these ships nor their transit rights. No other signatory raised any formal objection, and since the United States was not a signatory to the Convention, the US Government had no standing in the matter.

The original designation for the Kiev class was Large Antisubmarine Cruiser (*Bolshoi Protolovadochnyi Kreizer*). The *Kiev*, launched in 1975, carried a complement of 12-13 Yak-38 STOL aircraft and 14-17 Kamov Ka-25 helicopters and was designed to locate and destroy US ballistic missile-carrying submarines. When the *Kiev* transited the straits in July 1976 under this designation, there were accusations in the West that Turkey itself was violating the convention by going along with this subterfuge.

The passage of US warships through the Straits also raised controversy, as the convention forbids the transit of non-Black Sea nations' warships with guns of a calibre larger than eight inches (203 mm). In the 1960s, the US sent warships carrying 305 mm calibre ASROC missiles through the Straits, prompting Soviet protests. The Turkish government rejected the Soviet complaints, pointing out that guided missiles were not guns and that such weapons had not even existed at the time of the Convention's signature so were not restricted by the Convention.

Capital ships of the Black Sea powers may transit the straits provided that they do so in accordance with the Convention. The Black Sea powers (the Soviet Union, Bulgaria, and Romania) have two additional options, one involving submarines and the other permitting their "capital ships" with a tonnage greater than 10,000 to transit the straits.

The Convention applies specific limits with regard to individual and aggregate tonnage and numbers. These limitations effectively preclude the transit of capital ships and submarines of non-Black Sea powers through the Straits, unless exempted under Article 17. Article 17 of the Convention permits a naval force of any tonnage or composition to pay a courtesy visit of limited duration to a port in the straits, at the invitation of the Turkish Government. In such instances, the tonnage and numbers limitations of the Convention do not apply. Warships of non-Black Sea powers may not remain in the Black Sea longer than 21 days.

In April 1982, the Convention was amended to allow Turkey to close the Straits at its discretion in peacetime as well as during wartime.

The United Nations Convention on the Law of the Sea (LOS Convention), which entered into force in November 1994, has prompted calls for the Montreux Convention to be revised and adapted to make it compatible with the LOS Convention's regime governing straits used for international navigation. However, Turkey's long-standing refusal to sign the LOS Convention has meant that Montreux remains in force without further amendments.

The safety of vessels passing through the Bosphorus has become a major concern in recent years as the overall volume of traffic has increased greatly since the Convention was signed, namely from 4,500 in 1934 to 49,304 by 1998. As well as obvious environmental concerns, the Straits bisect the city of Istanbul with over 11 million people living on its shores; maritime incidents in the Straits therefore pose a considerable risk to public safety. The Convention does not, however, make any provision for the regulation of shipping for the purposes of safety and environmental protection. In January 1994 the Turkish government adopted new "Maritime Traffic Regulations for the Turkish Straits and the Marmara Region". This introduced a new regulatory regime "in order to ensure the safety of navigation, life and property and to protect the environment in the region" but without violating the Montreux principle of free passage. The new regulations provoked some controversy when Russia, Greece, Cyprus, Romania, Ukraine and Bulgaria raised objections. However, they were approved by the International Maritime Organisation (IMO) on the grounds that they were not intended to prejudice "the rights of any ship using the Straits under international law". The regulations were revised in November 1998 to address Russian concerns.

On August 27 2008, Russia said all countries should comply with the Montreux Convention and called for full implementation of the agreement restricting the movement of non-Turkish military shipping in Turkey's straits. Russia's Ambassador to Ankara's remarks came after the United States demanded to use straits to send two hospital ships carrying aid to Georgia in an apparent move that would violate the Convention. Turkey did not allow the passage of another two United States naval vessels, which exceeded the weight limit defined in the convention, instead allowing three lighter warships to pass through its straits.

THE ESSENCE OF THE 1936 CONVENTION

Merchant shipping of any flag and with any cargo has freedom of transit in the straits during peacetime and during wartime whenever Turkey is not engaged in belligerent activities. Turkey may, however, require merchant ships to stop at a station upon entering the straits for the purposes of sanitary and health control. During wartime when Turkey is a belligerent, merchant shipping of countries not at war with Turkey has freedom of transit of the straits so long as those countries maintain their obligation of neutrality (e.g. not to provide support to another belligerent). Turkey may require such ships to commence transiting the straits during daylight hours.

During peacetime, light surface vessels [defined as warships displacing more than 100 tons but not above 10,000 tons] of all powers may transit the straits after giving prior notice to Turkey as required by the Convention. Turkey may waive the notification requirement if the warships were transiting for the purpose of providing humanitarian assistance. The choice of "light surface vessels" as the largest warship allowed through the straits effectively kept the new German "pocket battleships" out of the Black Sea -- a primary goal of the Soviet negotiators.

The 1936 Convention comprises 29 Articles, four annexes and one protocol. Articles 2-7 consider the passage of merchant ships. Articles 8-22 consider the passage of war vessels. The key principle of freedom of passage and navigation is stated in articles 1 and 2. Article 1 provides that "The High Contracting Parties recognise and affirm the principle of freedom of passage and navigation by sea in the Straits". Article 2 states that "In time of peace, merchant vessels shall enjoy complete freedom of passage and navigation in the Straits, by day and by night, under any flag with any kind of cargo."

According to Article 2 of the Montreux Convention, merchant vessels were guaranteed complete freedom of transit and navigation. This has not been superseded by the 1982 Law of the Sea Convention, whose Article 36(c) provides that its transit passage articles do not affect "the legal regime in straits in which passage is regulated in whole or part by long-standing international conventions in force specifically relating to such straits." In the 1990s Turkey imposed new navigation rules for the Straits as part of its continuing effort to "sell" the Baku-Ceyhan export pipeline. Under these new rules Turkey can demand more advance notice for the passage of a vessel through the Straits. Turkey can also stop any vessel on legal grounds and can require more ships to use local pilots and Turkey can raise transit fees by a factor of five.

The Turkish Straits and the Montreux Convention, which once served primarily to protect the Soviet Union from superior hostile fleets, now also appear to have limited what would otherwise be a major Russian advantage: proximity of a large fleet and its bases to a major theatre of crisis and potential war. In this respect the Montreux Convention was a potential problem for the Soviets since 1964, when they began maintaining a permanent naval presence in the Mediterranean. However, it is also an excellent example of how a single sovereign State can control a waterway which is used for the purposes of international passage, while enjoying total national control over that waterway.

CASE STUDY 2 – SCANDINAVIAN WATERS: THE STOREBAELT AND ÖRESUND

Shipping passing from the Skagerrak to the Baltic Sea and vice versa must use one of two waterways to make this journey. The two waterways are the Storebaelt, to the west, and the Öresund, to the east. The Storebaelt lies entirely within Danish waters, whereas the Öresund (The Sound) is a narrow strait of water separating Denmark from Sweden, and to this extent is a limited international waterway covered by the same rules of the UNCLOS as the Strait of Dover.

Map of Denmark, showing the Storebaelt (Denmark) and Öresund (Denmark/Sweden) Straits

THE STOREBAELT (GREAT BELT)

The Storebaelt is the Strait of water separating the Danish islands of Fyn and Sjaelland, and lies entirely within Danish territorial waters. The islands are linked by two bridges carrying the roadway across Danish territory, which in turn are linked to each other by the island Sprogø. A railway link also crosses the Strait at the same point, but uses a tunnel in place of the larger suspension bridge, which only carries the road. The larger of the two bridges is a suspension bridge, to the east of the Strait, beneath which passes all shipping up and down the Strait.

Because of the channel's width restrictions, a VTS system is in force requiring all vessels passing through the Strait to report in to the Danish Maritime Authorities, and to adhere to a Traffic Separation System regime similar to that of the Strait of Dover. The Vessel Traffic System is called the "Great Belt System" (GBT), and is based on and operated in accordance with the provisions of the IMO Resolution on Guidelines for Vessel traffic Services. It is recommended that vessels also carry a pilot through the Strait, in accordance with local regulations. The reporting system is mandatory, and requires all vessels passing through the Strait to report into the Danish Authorities at the points designated by the VTS system, to the north and south ends of the strait. Categories of vessels required to participate in the vessel reporting system are:

a) All vessels with a gross tonnage equal to or exceeding 50grt; and
b) All vessels with an air draught of 15 metres or more.

These vessels must report in to the Storebaelt (Great Belt) Traffic System when entering the designated VTS area, and must maintain contact with the authorities until they leave the VTS area. Once through the Strait, they proceed into international waters at each end of it, and hence out of the control zone.

The full geographical extent of the VTS regime ranges from the northern edge of the Storebaelt, to a point linking the islands of Langeland and Omø, at the south end of the Strait. All shipping traffic must follow a route designated by the Danish Maritime Authorities, and must make itself known to the authorities the moment it enters the Strait.

The Storebaelt waterway is defined for vessel traffic control purposes, as far as VTS is concerned, with a designated T-Route, which is the defined route required by the maritime authorities for all shipping through the Strait to follow. It should be noted that all shipping is directed through the Østerrenden, i.e. the Eastern Channel, beneath the Østerrenden Suspension Bridge, which carries the main east-west road across the Strait.. This bridge allows the maximum clearance available to shipping through the Strait, although the height of the bridge span above the water level still imposes certain restrictions upon shipping through the Strait. There is therefore the VTS requirement for each vessel to state its air draft so as to ensure sufficient capacity for the vessel's clearance beneath the bridge, as well as all other information required by the authorities operating the VTS system, such as tonnage, length, beam and draught, as well as the vessel's identification details.

The more general reporting system covering Danish waters as a whole is known as SHIPPOS, the Ship Positioning system, and chiefly concerns vessels carrying hazardous cargoes, especially oil carriers, gas carriers, chemical carriers and carriers of radioactive cargoes. In the light of these vessel movements, the prime purposes of the SHIPPOS reporting system are as follows:

- To inform shipping about the movements of large vessels, so that smaller vessels can take into account the limited manoeuvrability of those larger vessels and in order to avoid the risk of larger ships encountering one another in areas difficult to pass;

- To inform ships about navigational hazards en route and deviations from normal conditions of current, water level, and wave height;

- To facilitate the early and effective pollution combating action by the authorities in case of a marine accident;

- To notify the authorities immediately about any deficiency or obstruction in the Strait which could affect the safe navigation of vessels and which could affect the marine and coastal environment, and about the observation by vessels of pollution in the vicinity.

The AIS traffic movements can be reflected against the VTS routes shown on the first of the two maps. Note the restricted width of the Channel used beneath the Østbro (Eastern Bridge) spanning the Østerrenden part of the Strait. The VTS and AIS systems simply allow for the monitored movements of maritime traffic through the Strait.

Where the first image shows the designated routes of shipping through the Strait, the second diagram shows a snapshot of the actual shipping movements themselves as reported through the AIS system. It can be noted that the actual movements bear a significantly close resemblance to the routeings as shown on the first image, in line with the requirements of the VTS system as used in the Strait.

The vessels use VHF Channel 11, and must transmit and report the following details:

- Vessel's Name and Call Sign;

- Position;

- Course (N or S-bound);

- Speed;

- Pilot embarked;

- Vessel's route (Østerrenden [East] Channel, Northbound or Southbound;

- Defects and Deficiencies; and

- Dead weight tonnage and air draft.

In the light of a collision between two vessels sailing in opposite directions in the Strait in 2005, one of which subsequently sank, there is reason to review this regime to include cargo details and vessel details in such reports, in effect implementing a mandatory vessel reporting system. Oil pollution from the sunken vessel, the "Vertigo", could have proven a challenge to the environmental controls imposed by the Danish Government. Given the mandatory Vessel Reporting System controls exerted by Coastguards over the Strait of Dover over vessels sailing in either direction, especially those vessels carrying hazardous cargoes, the same regime should apply for all vessels passing through the Storebaelt, especially as many of those vessels will not be calling at a Danish Port.

The reporting system as it stands is limited, and does not take into account all aspects of vessel movements and information concerning those vessels. It refers more to the actual movement of the vessel and its basic identification details, but does not necessarily request information concerning the destination of a specific vessel nor its cargo, unless the cargo is of a hazardous nature, in which case the European requirements concerning vessel reporting regimes should apply.

THE ÖRESUND

The Öresund has already been highlighted previously in this study because of its narrowness, particularly at its northern end, and because, unlike the Strait of Dover, it has no Maritime Reporting mechanism in place as yet, other than the recent tender in 2006 for the implementation of a Vessel Traffic Monitoring System (VTS) along similar lines to that operated in the Storebaelt. Laws passed in the 19th Century allow shipping passing through the Strait to onward destinations to maintain international status and thus enjoy the status of innocent passage. However, in the present-day circumstances of the increasing need for global security, especially in the maritime sector, the right of innocent passage does not infer that there is no need for the vessels concerned to pass through a narrow international Strait without some degree of notification to the national authorities on each side of the Strait the nature of both the vessel and its cargo, especially in cases where the cargo is of a hazardous nature.

At present, the main procedure applying to the Öresund Strait is the need for every vessel passing through the Sound to take on board a pilot at either end depending upon its direction of sailing. The EC Directives 2000/59 and 2002/59 imposed a regime relating to the reporting of hazardous cargoes by the master of a vessel entering port or anchorage, which has resulted, in the Swedish case, in an information-processing system known as the FartygsRapporteringsSystemet – FRS (Vessel Reporting System) to which information concerning each vessel is reported. However, in the case of vessels passing through the Strait bound for destinations elsewhere, the pilot is not required to ask the Ship's Master the nature of the cargo on board the vessel unless the nature of the vessel is already evident, such as a Crude or Chemical Carrier, where the cargo will automatically be classed as hazardous. In other cases, such as carriers of general or containerised cargoes, this evidence will not be obvious to either the pilot or the Danish and Swedish Maritime Authorities.

The Öresund Bridge, carrying road and rail links between København and Malmö, already poses a hazard to ships sailing northwards through the Sound, whereas ships sailing southwards pass through the Sound over the open stretch of water under which passes the Öresund Tunnel taking the railway and motorway out of Kastrup, in the area of Amager and the Drogden Channel on the Danish side of the Sound, to the island of Pebbarholm and onto the bridge. The Sound at this point is still narrower than the Strait of Dover, and thus requires constant monitoring. To this extent, the need for a mandatory Vessel Reporting System is vital, in order to control shipping through the Sound for several reasons:

- Maritime Security;

- Hazardous or Dangerous Cargo Shipments;

- Pilotage Controls;

- Statistical Monitoring for governmental and commercial maritime requirements;

- International Security.

Although the volume of traffic between the North Sea and the Baltic Sea may be nowhere near as great as through the Strait of Dover, the conditions of passage are the same in the Öresund, given the narrowness of the Sound, along with the channels and obstacles within the Sound itself, such as the Danish islands of Saltholm and Pebbarholm at the south end and the Swedish island of Ven further north in the Sound. Varying weather conditions also can give rise for increased vigilance by ships' crews, along with the size of many vessels transiting the Sound such as bulk carriers, cargo ferries and the large Passenger Cruise liners and ferries. The Port of København (Copenhagen} is host to a large number of such vessels, and many will sail through both ends of the Strait as part of their voyages. Add to this the transversal sailings of the ferries across the Sound on the Helsingør/Helsingborg route and the routes from Southern Sweden (Skåne) to Poland and Germany, and also Skåne and København to the Danish Island of Bornholm. These sailings combined with the transit sailings through the Sound provide an immediate need for a mandatory Vessel Reporting System to ensure the constant monitoring, safety and security of all vessels concerned within the region to the satisfaction of all authorities concerned.

The Danish Authorities announced in May 2006 an initiative to introduce a pilotage scheme for all vessels passing through Danish waters using the entrances to the Baltic Sea, which would include both the Öresund and the Storebaelt. This would require all commercial vessels using the straits to use a Danish pilot through these waterways. It is believed that the Swedish maritime authorities would take the same course of action concerning their side of the Öresund. This scheme would increase navigational safety through the straits, but would not overcome the issue of the nature of the vessel and the cargo being carried. There is still the need for the vessel to report not only its intentions but also its identity and cargo. It is accepted that the international law concerning the free passage of vessels exists, but where the strait is limited in width, where it contains an international border as a contiguous zone, or where it passes through national territory as in the case of the Storebaelt, then there is a need for the national maritime authority of the country concerned to identify the vessel and ascertain its complement, including its cargo.

Although the VTS system presently in use in the Storebaelt and intended for use in the Öresund may monitor vessels passing through both Straits, its use is limited in that it does not encompass a full Vessel Reporting regime such as that used in the Strait of Dover. The VTS regime simply allows the national authorities to monitor the passage of vessels through the Strait, but does not require such vessels to physically report in to the authorities stating details of not only their identification and course, but also their cargoes. Even the additional use of AIS transponders on board each vessel does not allow for such a reporting system, since the AIS system simply allows other vessels and land-based authorities to monitor a vessel's course while it is in motion, as long as the AIS system is active at the time. A fully integrative mandatory reporting system would account for all information pertaining to not only the vessel and its identification but also its origin, its destination and its cargo, and would thus enable the maritime authorities to have greater control over the passage of vessels through the Straits. Furthermore, the information provided as a result of such a reporting system would also be made available to all appropriate authorities involved with maritime activities in the Sound, from Coastguards and Royal Navies to other Maritime Authorities in both Denmark and Sweden. In this way, any incident recorded as a result of the Reporting System couple with any violation of maritime traffic regulations could then be conveyed to all such authorities and dealt with as appropriate.

The operation of such a scheme would naturally require the co-operation and collaboration of both the Danish and Swedish Maritime Authorities. The information collected by one national authority concerning shipping movements in one direction would have to be available and transmitted to the national authority on the other side of the Sound for action to be taken as appropriate. Equally, such information concerning the monitoring and recording of shipping movements could also be collated and analysed for the purposes of government statistics as well as ascertaining monthly and yearly levels of shipping in the region, showing levels of shipping sailing in each direction and divided into the following vessel and cargo categories:

- Car Ferries;
- Freight Ferries;
- Passenger Cruise Liners;
- Container Carriers;
- Bulk Carriers;
- Hazardous/Dangerous Cargo Carriers.

Cargoes could equally be classified as being General or Hazardous/Dangerous, and could be assessed as to their relative risk concerning shipping movements within the Sound. This information could then be analysed and maintained in much the same way as information gained from the reporting system used in the Strait of Dover. It would also show whether any vessels failed to report correct information about themselves or their cargoes, and whether remedial action would be required by any of the maritime authorities to investigate such vessels.

It is believed that a fully integrative and far more comprehensive and detailed reporting system would safeguard and enhance the process of maritime security within both the Storebaelt and the Öresund, but would also maintain the safety of the region as well as maintaining the efficient and smooth passage of vessels into, through and around both these Channels at all times. A more integrative and developed maritime reporting system would also ensure that more details could be kept pertaining to vessels transiting each Channel, and would enable more efficient databases of vessels to be kept, as well as providing an efficient statistical basis for the analysis of such maritime movements, especially where the security of vessels or the movement of hazardous cargo is concerned. Furthermore, for statistical purposes, it would also show the volume of maritime traffic passing through the straits, and could thus be used for commercial purposes to monitor and quantify maritime freight traffic within the region. Although some progress has been made, it is perceived that the system presently in existence is not sufficiently advanced to account for all safety and security needs within the region, and does not go far enough in ensuring a complete control over all shipping in the area. It would appear that only basic regimes have been implemented according to necessity, rather than examining the need for an all-embracing system which would be far more appropriate in such circumstances. The present regimes in operation are still lacking in their scope, and require considerable expansion to cover all aspects of the movements of vessels and their cargoes, especially where the movement of hazardous cargoes is concerned.

CASE STUDY 3 – UK WATERS: THE NORTH CHANNEL AND PENTLAND FIRTH

The North Channel is a sea area bounded by the coast of Northern Ireland to the west and Scotland to the north and east, and joined by a further sea area known as the Firth of Clyde to the north-east. It lies entirely within UK national territory, and is 75 miles long and 13 miles wide at its narrowest point, between the Mull of Kintyre and the Northern Irish coast to the east of Ballycastle. Elsewhere, it broadens to approximately 19 miles between Portpatrick, on the Scottish Galloway coast, and Donaghadee, on the Irish coast of County Down. Shipping passing between the north and the south of the Channel enters UK national waters at a point between the Scottish island of Islay and the northern Antrim coast on the Irish side, and exits the Channel at a point between Donaghadee and the Mull of Galloway on the Scottish side, or vice versa.

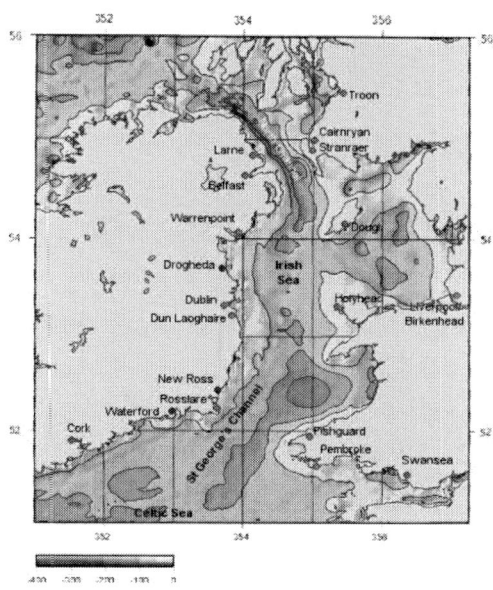

The Irish Sea and the North Channel

A following illustration of the Clyde and North Channel shows the extent to which the approaches of the sea area close to Islay and the Firth of Clyde to the north of the Channel narrow into the North Channel itself. Indeed, the channel between the Northern Irish Coast and the Mull of Kintyre (approx. 10 miles) is far narrower than the rest of the North Channel, to the south of the Firth of Clyde (approx. 19 miles). It can be seen how shipping moves through the Channel and either into the Clyde or into open water to the north-west, and out into the North Atlantic.

Furthermore, the extent to which the Channel narrows between the Irish Coast and the Mull of Kintyre can also be clearly seen.

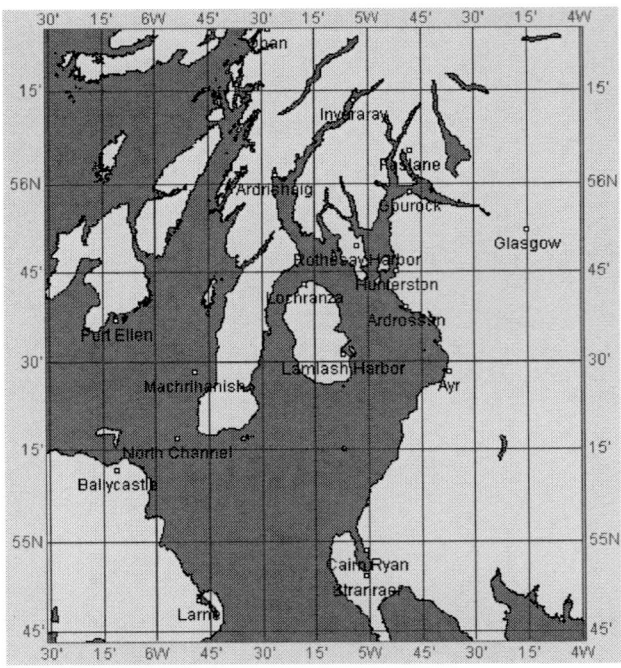

The Firth of Clyde and North Channel

All shipping leaving Liverpool and heading into the North Atlantic onto the Great Circle maritime route must therefore transit this Strait. This shipping is interspersed with cross-channel ferries from southern Scotland (Troon, on the Firth of Clyde, Cairnryan and Stranraer) to Northern Ireland (Belfast and Larne), other ferry services from north-west England (Heysham and the Mersey) to Northern Ireland, container feeder vessels out of the Port of Belfast and the Firth of Clyde, and naval vessels exiting the Firth of Clyde destined for operational services, especially the submarines of the Royal Navy based at HM Naval Base Faslane, on the Gare Loch. It should also be noted that the Firth of Clyde at its widest point, an imaginary line drawn across the Firth from Girvan, through the islands of Ailsa Craig and Sanda Island, to the tip of the Kintyre peninsula, is wider than the North Channel itself.

In reality, the Strait handles a significant volume of marine traffic, with a considerable volume of tonnage passing through the North Channel every year. This is represented by a variety of types of shipping, both commercial, military and leisure. As with all straits, there are essentially two main shipping lanes, a northbound lane to the east of the Channel, and a southbound lane to the west of the Channel. There is, however, much less maritime traffic density passing through the North Channel than there is through the Strait of Dover, where a Traffic Separation Scheme (TSS) is in force, detailed in a previous section of this study.

Although a nominal MCA (Maritime and Coastguard Agency) station is located at Portpatrick on the Scottish coast, it is used as a station for transmitting and receiving NAVTEX transmissions for the purpose of broadcasting and receiving maritime safety information. There is no significant vessel monitoring activity anywhere along the Channel for the purposes of Vessel Traffic Monitoring services, apart from two stations, Blackhead Lighthouse and Orlock Point, located to the north and south sides of the mouth of Belfast Lough, as well as the AIS facility at Liverpool, which gives access to marine traffic in the North Channel (www.aisliverpool.org.uk; www.shipais.com). The Irish stations are VTS manned, but deal primarily with traffic entering and exiting Belfast Lough itself. All other Coastguard activities for the Clyde, South and West Scotland area are controlled from the MCA centre at Fort Matilda, Gourock, close to the point where the Firth of Clyde changes direction from a general westward course to a southward course, some 100 miles away from the southern entrance to the Firth. The MCA centre at Gourock has confirmed that there is at present no VTS monitoring or control facility for the purposes of monitoring shipping in the North Channel, and the only activity carried out with relation to this area is the distance monitoring of the AIS signals broadcast by the vessels in the North Channel and the Clyde, with no direct control exercised by the MCA over the North Channel despite the volume of shipping transiting the Channel. Any incident would be reported to the MCA Clyde centre, with any major problem also reported to the nearest Air-Sea Rescue centre located at Prestwick. This implies that there is absolutely no direct control by Coastguards or any other national authority over the shipping in the North Channel, despite the fact that the Channel lies entirely within UK national territory, and is therefore classed as internal waters under the scope of the UNCLOS, in the same way that the Storebaelt is classed the same way given its status as Danish internal waters. This in turn creates a problem concerning the requirement by the UK national maritime authorities to implement a full VTS monitoring system in accordance with the EU VTMS Directive.

The problem faced combines a variety of considerations. Firstly, there are the various cross-channel ferry routes from Scotland to Northern Ireland. Then there are the short-sea and deep-sea container services through the Channel. Then there are the defence activities out of the Clyde interspersed with the movements of the Scottish Fishery Protection vessels and occasionally the Customs vessels on intelligence-based maritime activities. Add to this a considerable volume of both commercial shipping and leisure craft exiting and entering the Firth of Clyde, and the waterway becomes a well-used shipping area. This point of the Clyde / North Channel waterway is literally a marine crossroads, with Belfast Lough and the Clyde to the South-East and North-West, and the North Channel to the North and the South. But add to all this the location of a hazardous marine dumping ground in the middle of the Channel, and the scenario becomes more serious. At the southern end of the Channel lies the Beaufort Dyke, a deep submarine trench used for the dumping of munitions and hazardous waste of various kinds.

Should an accident occur, it will be dealt with by the MCA further up the Firth of Clyde. The nearest Search-and-Rescue base is located at Prestwick Airport, in the form of the Royal Navy's HMS Gannet, although the RNLI has lifeboat stations located closer to the Channel.

All the vessels transiting the North Channel use either VTS for the purposes of entry into and exit from Belfast Lough, or their AIS transponders for identification at sea. An interesting aside is that the AIS website used to display these movements also tracks the actual movement of vessels, so that the vessel's real-time course can be displayed over the period of several hours. This shows the exact course which would be directed by the vessel's master, and therefore tracks the exact position of the vessel at any specific time during the voyage.

Taking into account all the above information, it can be argued that a proper Vessel Traffic Monitoring and Reporting System is required for the Channel, which must also include the Firth of Clyde. It should also be pointed out at this stage that although some of the maritime traffic passing through or across the Channel is of a UK-owned or UK-managed nature, much is not. The vessels transiting the Channel en route from Liverpool to the North Atlantic are operated and owned by a variety of overseas concerns, and are carrying a vast range of cargoes, including hazardous goods. The purpose of a VTS regime is to control and monitor shipping through any restricted waterway, and considering its limitations, the North Channel and Firth of Clyde fall well within this category. Not only are they geographically-restricted waterways, but they are also waterways falling entirely into national territory. However, they do not handle just domestic shipping, as much of the traffic passing through it is of an international nature, some of which is involved in the North Atlantic run, and some is also of a military naval nature.

The submarine base is located on the Gareloch, and the submarines have to negotiate the upper reaches of the Firth prior to entering deeper water to the south, close to the Isle of Arran. These vessels are sharing the Clyde channels with commercial shipping, and close attention must be paid by all appropriate maritime authorities to ensure the incident-free passage of all these vessels. It is also well-known that naval exercises, especially using submarines, are carried out further down the Firth, and these must take place under absolute security conditions, while taking into account the commercial vessel movements.

The "port" extends from the City of Glasgow right down to the lower Firth of Clyde, with only the area south of Irvine not part of these controls. The ports of Troon and Stranraer lie outside the Clydport jurisdiction, whereas from Ardrossan to the North, the whole sea area falls within Clydeport controls. Within these areas, there is considerable cross-Firth activity, mainly as a result of the sailings by the vessels of Caledonian MacBrayne. The cross-Firth sailings intersperse with the movements of both commercial vessels and naval warships up and down the

Firth, and this requires some form of control from the Port Authority, which at present does not exist. Note on the maps how the Firth narrows considerably around the Hunterston area, where the Isle of Great Cumbrae is located more or less in the middle of the Firth, thus limiting access to and from the open sea. Given the expanse of the whole region covered by the Clydeport Authority, there is a great need to implement a control regime capable of controlling all such vessel movements and other maritime activities within the area, including leisure activities covered by the various marinas along the Firth. Once out of the scope of the Clydeport area and into the lower reaches of the Firth, there is less chance of incidents concerning vessel movements, as the Firth widens considerably and becomes open sea to the South, although it then becomes part of the North Channel, which remains equally uncontrolled by any form of VTS regime at present.

Movements of submarines, warships and even the Fishery Protection vessels clearly are less evident than the movements of commercial vessels in the Firth. The submarines leaving Faslane generally submerge off the Isle of Arran in the southern part of the Firth of Clyde, and are well beneath the waves by the time they fully exit the Firth. However, their presence remains unknown to other vessels transiting the North Channel for obvious strategic reasons. A further consideration is the existence of hazardous waste dumped onto the seabed in the region. At the southern end of the Channel, between the Galloway peninsula and County Down, lies the Beaufort Dyke, a deep submarine trench used for the dumping of munitions and hazardous waste of various kinds.

There are thus several main issues at stake. These are:

- The North Channel lies entirely within UK national territory and is thus subject to both domestic and international maritime rules;

- There is a wide variety of shipping passing through and crossing the Channel at any time;

- There are naval defence activities conducted within the region alongside commercial shipping;

- There is no evidence of a proper maritime reporting system in evidence at any point through the North Channel, other than the VTS stations at the mouth of Belfast Lough;

- There is a hazardous dumping ground on the seabed in the middle of the Channel.

Despite the status of the North Channel as a seemingly domestic waterway, allowance must be made for the passing through of international traffic. The International Law of the Sea requires that all vessels passing through a Strait have the right of innocent passage. However, each national authority reserves the right to monitor maritime traffic passing through a strait, and indeed is now required to implement a Vessel Traffic Monitoring System to ensure incident-free passage takes place through that Strait. However, in the case of the North Channel, there is no attempt made to monitor this traffic in the way that the CNIS monitors traffic through the Strait of Dover or even the VHF system is used to monitor traffic through either the Öresund or the Storebaelt.

The anomaly in this situation is that where the Strait of Dover and the Öresund are international waterways containing an international line dividing two countries, and which thus have the need of a maritime control system to ensure the safe passage of all maritime traffic through the Strait, the North Channel is entirely within UK national territory. In this respect, it is similar in its nature to the Storebaelt with relation to Danish national territory, where a vessel control system, however basic, already exists, and this therefore imposes an even greater need for a maritime traffic control system for the North Channel, given that it allows international traffic to pass through it without stopping. The very existence of the dumping ground for hazardous waste would suggest a breach of maritime law, other than the fact that the British government could use the excuse that the waters of the Channel were located within its own territory, and thus allowed it to carry out whatever action it deemed appropriate. The fact that such waste, should it break free from the seabed and contaminate the water, could pose a serious hazard to shipping in the area may have been conveniently overlooked. Some of the waste is extremely radioactive, while other waste is chemically-active.

And yet, shipping passes through the Channel without any apparent form of monitoring by the UK authorities other than some knowledge by the Port Agents and Port Authorities that a container vessel is perhaps inbound from the North Atlantic to the Port of Liverpool, as well as a VTS control over traffic movements into and out of Belfast Lough. The fact that vessels enter UK national territory of the southern Scottish islands and remain in national territory until they are well into the Irish Sea says much for the need to monitor a vessel's movement until it transits the Channel prior to crossing the Irish Sea and, for example, entering the Port of Liverpool. The Irish Sea is considered international territory, although the route of the vessels concerned skirts the Isle of Man before turning to port and entering the approaches to Liverpool Bay and thence the Port of Liverpool. This scenario is equally true for vessels entering the North Channel from the northern access point, and turning to port after the Mull of Kintyre into the Firth of Clyde bound for the Hunterston terminal, as well as other vessels entering the North channel from the south, then heading into the Firth of Clyde bound for the Greenock container terminal.

It is not suggested that there should be a reporting and monitoring system exactly identical to and as sophisticated as the CNIS system used through the Strait of Dover. The traffic through the North Channel is nowhere near as congested as that of the Strait of Dover. However, the need still exists for a full vessel monitoring system to monitor traffic movements through the North Channel, in order to ensure that no major incidents take place, especially as a Vessel Monitoring System is now a legal requirement as directed by the European Union. This system should bear some resemblance to other vessel monitoring systems in use, for example the system used in the Öresund and the Storebaelt, except with more details about the vessel's movement, its origin and destination, and its cargo. There are too many risks at stake not to employ such a system. Given the vigilance used for monitoring vessel movements through the Strait of Dover, it is some surprise that a similar system has not already been implemented for control and monitoring purposes over the North Channel.

One of the main issues concerning this control is how the MCA could monitor shipping movements if it does not have an active station overlooking the North Channel. It has already been shown that there is little control over shipping movements in the Firth of Clyde, as a VTS system has yet to be fully implemented. The NAVTEX system is both inadequate and inappropriate to control vessel movements, as it simply provides a means to report marine safety information as part of the GMDSS (Global Maritime Distress and Safety System), as directed by the SOLAS Convention. More needs to be done to create a full monitoring station facility if a proper vessel monitoring system were to be used not only in the Firth of Clyde but also in the North Channel. Both the Royal Navy and the Clyde Authorities have admitted the need for such a system, as at present there is no suitable VTS system in operation on the Firth of Clyde. Any attempts at control from a station based 100 miles away in the upper Firth would not be feasible, as there would need to be a point of visual contact based on the coast of the North Channel, perhaps on the Galloway coast, to monitor vessel movements through the Channel. The other alternative would be to create a station on the Northern Irish side, on the coast of County Down or County Antrim, alongside or as part of the existing VTS stations there, to monitor such maritime traffic movements. It is clear from the above graphics that there is substantial traffic movement through and across the Channel to justify having a VTS monitoring and reporting system overlooking the Channel, especially given the hazardous nature of many of the cargoes carried through the Channel.

The Firth of Clyde is not without marine accidents. In 2000, two vessels, the "Nordsee" and "Poole Scene" collided off Greenock Harbour in foggy conditions. In September 2004, the vessel "Jackie Moon" grounded off Dunoon because of crew negligence. The courses of all the vessels involved in both accidents could have been monitored prior to the collision had a full VTS regime been in force, and there is a possibility that both accidents could have been avoided, although with hindsight it is easy to state this.

The evidence points to the need to create a vessel traffic monitoring and reporting system in the North Channel as soon as possible, along the lines of the systems used both in the Strait of Dover and in the Danish and Swedish waters of the Öresund and the Storebaelt. This is reinforced by the existence of the VTMS Directive issued by the European Union, along with a further European Resolution, MSC 190(79) of December, adopting a mandatory tanker reporting system, the WETREP (West European Tanker Reporting System) for Sensitive Sea Areas along the coasts of Western Europe, including the Scottish and Irish Coasts and thus the North Channel.

THE PENTLAND FIRTH

A Vessel Monitoring and Reporting System exists in the North of Scotland, in the form of a VTS system operated by Orkney Harbours Authority, covering the Pentland Firth and Scapa Flow. The Pentland Firth is some 17 miles long and some 6-8 miles broad, separating the Scottish mainland from the Orkney Islands. The VTS system covers the stretch of water from a line in the west between Dunnet Head (Caithness) and Tor Ness (Orkney), to a line between Duncansby Head (Caithness) and Brough Ness (South Ronaldsay, Orkney). It also covers the ports within Scapa Flow, bounded by the islands of Mainland, Hoy, Flotta and South Ronaldsay.

Like the North Channel, the Pentland Firth is located within UK national territory, and handles large numbers of vessels through its waters every year, in reality some 6000 vessels per year. The vast majority of these vessel movements are for non-UK destinations, and include cargo vessels, Oil and Gas supply vessels, petroleum tankers and naval vessels. These movements are interspersed with several passenger/ro-ro vessel movements across the Firth, from the Scottish mainland to Stromness and Kirkwall in the Orkney Islands. Hence the need for a robust vessel reporting system. However, the VTS system is controlled by the Orkney Harbours Authority, and not the MCA. Other than the Control system in operation in the Strait of Dover, the other VTS systems in operation nationally are controlled by the local harbour authority, rather than the national authority, given that they are primarily used for the control of vessels into and out of the port, and along the waterways linking the port with the open sea, where specific channels must be used for access by all vessels.

The VTS system is used not only for the entrance to the port system in the Orkneys, but also for traffic passing through the narrow strait which constitutes the Pentland Firth. In a reply to a question from an MP in March 1994, recorded in the Hansard Government publication, the UK Secretary of State for Transport, Steven Norris, stated that there was an international requirement for laden vessels to report to the authorities their intention to transit the Pentland Firth.

A bulletin (**Press Notice 74/01, 27/02/2001**) from the MCA stated that calls for a mandatory ship reporting system or a dedicated radar surveillance operation located in the Pentland Firth could not be supported. The reason given was the anticipated phased introduction of the shipboard AIS systems from July 2000, further to the revision of Chapter V of the SOLAS Convention. It may be assumed that a similar argument has prevailed concerning the lack of a vessel monitoring system in the North Channel. The statement by the MCA appears to contradict the previously-mentioned statement by the former Secretary of State for Transport in 1994 that there was an international requirement for laden vessels to report into the authorities their intentions for passage through the Pentland Firth. What has been overlooked is that AIS is a non-contact system, relying on the broadcasting of electronic information from a vessel, rather than an active contact-based system such as that used by VTS systems. Admittedly, the VTS system is more for use by port and harbour authorities when controlling vessel movements into and out of port, but it can be used equally effectively in controlling vessel movements through international or domestic waterways linking open sea conditions, such as the Channel and the Strait of Dover, the Storebaelt, and, for that matter, the Pentland Firth.

The AIS regime, as shown earlier in the text, is limited in its scope as a security-based regime, and simply tracks a vessel's route by the positions shown on the AIS monitor. It does not give more detailed information about the vessel's intentions or even make contact with the vessel concerned where necessary. This stance by the MCA may be seen as being in direct contravention to the EU Commission's Directive of 2002 on Vessel Traffic Monitoring Systems, which required an active monitoring system to be installed in all locations where ports were located or where restricted shipping lanes were in force, such as in limited-width international or domestic shipping lanes. The Pentland Firth is a stretch of water linking two seas, and, like the North Channel, falls into the latter category. The difference concerning both stretches of water is that they both are located within national, not international, territory, and are both subject to the requirements laid down by the EU Commission Directive on Vessel Monitoring Systems.

Compare the The Pentland Firth's 6000 vessel movements per year with some 3500 vessel movements through the North Channel. Even this amount of vessel movements through the North Channel every year justifies the need for a vessel reporting system to be implemented in the North Channel region as per the requirements of the European Commission Vessel Monitoring Directive. It is not, therefore, that the legislation requiring such implementation of Vessel Traffic Systems does not exist, or even that the UK has failed to address vessel movements in Scottish waters. On the contrary, the legislation has been in place for some time, and VTS systems are used in this part of the UK. The issue at stake is the willingness of the maritime authorities to admit that their control over shipping is lacking in many areas, and that they must rectify this anomaly immediately. The risk of accidents in limited Channels such as the Pentland Firth and the North Channel is greater than that in wider waters, and this risk must be taken into account by the national authorities. The use of AIS does not reduce this risk in any way, given that AIS does not allow for any contact with the vessel. The VTS regime does allow for contact with any vessel in the vicinity, and thus can contribute to minimising the risk of collision between vessels. Hence the greater effectiveness of radar surveillance and VTS reporting regimes in both the Pentland Firth and the North Channel.

If such a reporting system is so vital for the Strait of Dover (which in reality includes all vessels passing through the Strait of Dover), then surely under the same rules a similar system is urgently required for the North Channel. The marine traffic may be less dense than through the Strait of Dover, but the reasons for such an operation remain the same. Without a reporting and monitoring system in place, there is a risk of incidents occurring over which there was no control, especially in bad weather or because of other circumstances relating to crew negligence. The increasing tonnage of shipping passing through the North Channel also increases this risk, and thus requires more vigilance in terms of the day-to-day monitoring of all traffic heading through or across the Channel. Besides which, unlike the Strait of Dover, all traffic passing through the North Channel comes under UK jurisdiction, and it would thus be the direct and ultimate responsibility of the UK maritime authorities should a serious accident occur, as in the case of traffic passing through the Danish Storebaelt. If the Danish authorities can implement a VTS reporting regime for the Storebaelt, then so too can the UK authorities for the North Channel and the Firth of Clyde. Safety must always be a higher priority than cost, especially given the hazards posed by the dumping of waster material deep in the North Channel some years ago. If vessels collide because of a lack of control over the area in which they were located, then the cost of recovery form any disaster becomes greater than the cost of implementing a control and monitoring system to prevent such accidents or disasters.

CASE STUDY 4 – CANADA: A BLUEPRINT FOR A MORE SECURE MARITIME FUTURE?

So far, the case studies addressed refer to European waters, and the anomalies connected with vessel control and monitoring in these areas. It has been shown that the AIS system is largely a passive system, whereas the VTS systems used in Europe are more pro-active, albeit with limitations. However, to ascertain how a more integrated and advanced system works, it is necessary to venture further afield and examine an overseas regime in place. The area chosen is that of Canada.

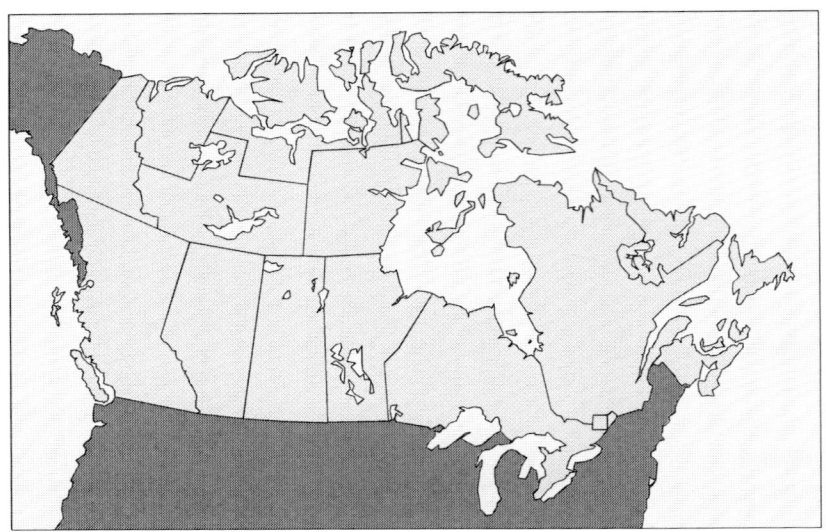

Map of Canada

The tragic events of 11 September 2001 in the city of New York showed the extent of vulnerability of any country, no matter how powerful it is on the world stage. Despite the military power of the United States, there was no defence system capable of detecting the power of the enemy within, and the use of clandestine means to inflict huge losses, in terms of both human and material resources, on such a nation. The aftermath was thus radical and far-reaching. The US Trade Act of 2002 imposed tight controls over incoming trade into the US, and also imposed a strict and disciplined regime over how any international consignments were imported by either aircraft of marine vessel into the US. One of the results was the CT-PAT (Customs and Trade Partnership against Terrorism) initiative, which requires all freight forwarders and agents to submit full details of any maritime or air cargo to the US Authorities, namely US Customs, 24 hours before the cargo is to be loaded aboard the aircraft or marine vessel. Details of these measures can be found on many websites on the Internet, as every freight forwarder arranging transport to the United States must comply with these regulations in full if consignments are not to be delayed. The presence of US Customs Officials in many EU ports reinforces this strategy, and ensures maximum security of shipments into the United States. Even US Coastguards may prevent a vessel from docking at a US port if they have reason to believe that incorrect or incomplete information concerning cargoes or passengers has been received.

The Canadian Government implemented similar measures in the wake of the 9/11 tragedy in order to ensure compatibility with US security measures, and thus reinforced existing maritime legislation already in place. A new regime concerning the 24-hour advance reporting of marine cargoes was implemented in April 2004, which required the same procedures for cargo arriving by sea into Canada as did the US regime. However, in terms of overall vessel reporting, a regime had existed in Canada covering control over Canadian waters long before the VTMS Directive of 2002 in the European Union. Long before the 9/11 events, a major maritime tragedy occurred in the Eastern Canadian Maritime Provinces which precipitated a need to address the whole issue of Vessel Reporting in Canadian waters. In 2004, further regulations were implemented in the form of **Notice 711**, applying to all commercial vessels entering Canadian waters. Marine Security (MARSEC) levels, based on the ISPS Code of the IMO, also apply, effective as at 1 July 2004.

The Notice also imposes a Pre-arrival Information requirement of a 96 Hour Notification prior to the vessel arriving at a Canadian port. This 96-Hour report must be submitted by the master of the vessel along with a true copy of their International Ship Security Certificate to a Canadian MCTS Centre when:

- En route to or transiting through Canadian territorial waters; or

- En route to or transiting through Canadian territorial waters and bound for a Canadian or US port; or

- 96 hours from entry to Canadian territorial waters;

- If the duration of the segment of the voyage before entering Canadian waters is less than 96 hours, vessels are required to send a pre-arrival report as soon as practicable before entering Canadian waters but no later than the time of departure from their last port of call.

Much of the reason for the implementation of a detailed vessel reporting system in Canadian territorial waters stems from a tragic accident in early December 1917, just outside the Port of Halifax, Nova Scotia. A Belgian Relief Vessel, the IMO, collided with the French munitions vessel MONT BLANC in the narrowest part of Halifax Harbour, resulting in the largest man-made non-nuclear explosion ever. The city of Halifax was utterly devastated, with some 2000 fatalities and several thousands injured. There had been no reporting systems in operation, and the harbour authorities were unaware of the proximity of both vessels to each other.

In the years that followed, many changes to the controls over vessel movements were implemented, eventually resulting in the creation and implementation of a vessel reporting regime designed to ensure that such an accident would never happen again in Canadian waters.

The **Canada Shipping Act** of 1989 required the implementation of a series of Vessel Traffic Services Zones in Canadian territorial waters, to be controlled by the Canadian Coast Guard (CCG), which is part of the Canadian Government Fisheries and Oceans Agency. This Act established the Vessel Traffic Services Zones Regulations, namely **SOR 89-98** and **SOR 89-99**, which established a robust and detailed vessel reporting regime. A series of Vessel Traffic Services Zones were established around Canadian territorial waters, in particular:

1. Placentia;
2. St John's;
3. Port aux Basques;
4. Halifax;
5. Strait of Canso and Eastern Approaches;
6. Northumberland Strait;
7. Bay of Fundy;
8. St Lawrence Waterway;
9. Vancouver;
10. Tofino;
11. Prince Rupert.

Of the above, the first 8 Zones cover Eastern Canadian areas bordering on the Atlantic Ocean, and the last 3 Zones cover the Western Canadian maritime areas bordering the Pacific Ocean. In the case of Western Canadian waters, the control system applies especially to the contiguous zone of the Juan de Fuca Strait to the west of Vancouver, separating the Canadian territory of Vancouver Island and the US coast of the State of Washington.

A further result of the regulations was the creation and implementation of a series of Marine Communications and Traffic Services (MCTS) Centres. These centres are the result of the integration of the Vessel Traffic Services (VTS) group and the Coast Guard Radio Station (CGRS) group. The purpose of the MCTS group is as follows:

- Safety of life at sea in response to international agreements;

- Protection of the environment through traffic management;

- Efficient movement of shipping;

- Information for business and the national interest.

(Source: www.ccg-gcc.gc.ca/mcts-sctm)

Within this framework, the activities carried out by the group are:

- Continuous monitoring of international distress and calling frequencies to detect distress situations and ensure speedy resolution of search and Rescue (SAR) incidents;

- Broadcasting marine safety information such as weather bulletins, ice information and notices to shipping concerning dangers to navigation by means of NAVTEX, Continuous Marine Broadcast and other electronic systems;

Vessel screening to prevent the entry of unsafe vessels into Canadian waters:

- Ensuring that vessels intending to enter Canadian waters must request clearance to do so and provide pertinent information concerning their status and compliance with applicable Canadian Acts and Regulations;

- Implementing compensatory measures for identified ship defects and/or deficiencies in order to minimise the possibility of marine pollution

Regulating Vessel Traffic Movements for marine risk reduction:

- Providing traffic and waterway information via VHF radio;

- Providing recommendations and directions, including the delivery of clearances, and under certain conditions, restricting traffic movement;

- Implementing actions necessary to ensure safe and orderly flow of marine traffic;

- Providing specialised surveillance for conservation and environmental protection in support of government agencies such as Environment Canada, RCMP, and Agriculture Canada.

Managing an Integrated Marine Information System in support of economic benefits and national interests:

- Collecting, analysing and disseminating marine traffic information in support of the activities of other government departments and agencies as well as the marine industry;

- Initiate, monitor and coordinate the communication network for Coast Guard's responses to emergencies, primarily in the area of search and rescue and pollution prevention;

- Relaying communications relevant to the efficient administration of other government operations.

The MCTS centres are operated by the Canadian Coast Guard (CCG) service, which monitors vessel movements into and out of Canadian waters. The Canadian Coast Guard has somewhat less powers than its US counterpart, but is still empowered with the control over vessels entering Canadian waters, including the ability to board and search vessels where required, and if necessary, escort them into the local Canadian port for arrest or seizure. However, the main function of the MCTS is to uphold and maintain the Vessel Traffic Services Regulations controlling the movements of shipping into and out of Canadian waters.

The main points of the Vessel Traffic Services Regulations established by the 1989 Shipping Act were:

- The master of the vessel must ensure that the vessel has adequate operating and functioning communications equipment on board;

- The communications equipment must be capable of transmitting and receiving radio communications on channels stipulated by the Vessel traffic Services Zones Regulatory Specifications;

- The master of the vessel must ensure that a report is submitted to a marine traffic regulator at least 15 minutes before the vessel enters a Vessel Traffic Services Zone;

- For vessels of 500grt or more, the master must ensure that a report is made to a marine traffic regulator at least 24 hours prior to the vessel entering a Vessel Traffic Services Zone from seaward, especially if the vessel is carrying pollutants of other dangerous or hazardous cargoes.

The vessel report must contain the following details:

- The name of the vessel;

- The radio call sign of the vessel;

- The name of the master of the vessel;

- The position of the vessel;

- The time of arrival of the vessel at the position;

- The course of the vessel;

- The speed of the vessel;
- The prevailing weather conditions;
- The estimated time that the vessel will enter the Vessel Traffic Services Zone;
- The name of the Vessel Traffic Services Zone the vessel intends to enter;
- The destination of the vessel;
- The estimated time of arrival of the vessel at the destination;
- The intended route of the vessel;
- The name of the last port of call of the vessel;
- The draught of the vessel;
- Any dangerous or hazardous goods or pollutants aboard vessel;
- Any defect in the vessel, including hull, propulsion or steering systems or navigational equipment.

THE ST LAWRENCE SEAWAY AND THE GULF OF ST LAWRENCE

The specific area chosen to analyse the regulations and how they function is Vessel Traffic Services Zone 8, the St Lawrence Seaway and the Gulf of St Lawrence, in Eastern Canada, governed by the **ECAREG** (Eastern Canada Vessel Traffic Services Zone Regulations) and the vessel traffic system operating as part of these regulations. In itself, the St Lawrence Seaway is a massive waterway extending from the Great Lakes, past the Port of Montréal, and out to the Gulf of St Lawrence. In the inner section of the seaway, the size of vessels using the waterway is restricted, owing the channels of the seaway and the Welland Canal between Lake Ontario and Lake Erie. However, the outermost parts of the St Lawrence (Laurentian) region are broad enough not to warrant specific traffic controls other than normal vessel reporting requirements for vessels entering Canadian territorial waters (the Cabot Strait is some 70 miles wide), as the vessels using the outermost parts of the waterway are of an ocean-going nature.

The actual area controlled by the MCTS regime under the ECAREG regime covers an area from the Jacques Cartier Bridge, spanning the waterway at Montréal itself out to a longitudinal point between the Gaspé Peninsula to the south and the coast of Québec to the north, at 66° West. The areas of water through the Honguedo Passage and the Cabot Strait, between Newfoundland and Nova Scotia, are not controlled by the MCTS regime. The seaway handles a large volume of shipping heading not only into the Ports of Montréal and Québec, but also into the Great Lakes network. The seaway handles not only cargo vessels but also passenger vessels, especially cruise liners during the summer season. It is also well-known for the fact that during the winter months it is ice-bound, thus necessitating the use of ice-breakers to carve a channel through the ice to allow the safe passage of the cargo vessels into and out of the Port of Montréal. The Port of Montréal is the home to the vessels of Hapag-Lloyd Canada ships (formerly CAST and CP Ships), as well as handling other overseas shipping lines, especially those from Europe.

It should be remembered that much of the North American logistics structure relies on waterborne transport from the seaway into the heart of the continent, up to the areas of Chicago, on Lake Michigan, and Duluth, on Lake Superior, using the famous "Laker" bulk vessels, and these operate along with the "Saltie" vessels, the ocean-going vessels which can also navigate the Great Lakes owing to the their restricted size. Most international vessels discharge and load cargoes at the port of Montréal, and any further waterborne transport is undertaken using the "Laker" vessels from Montréal omwards, into the Great Lakes network.

The MCTS control system allows for the close monitoring of vessels along the St Lawrence river and into the seaway, and is capable of monitoring each vessel by the transmission of its individual identification information. This information is then monitored by the CCG MCTS regime, and enables the CCG to ensure the safe passage of the vessel while in the seaway.

THE CCG MCTS MONITORING SYSTEM

Once a vessel has entered the St Lawrence MCTS system, its movement can then be monitored all the way to its port of destination, for example the port of Montréal, as shown by the red ring on the display. The system allows for the complete coverage of every vessel movement within the scope of the MCTS system, and enables the Coast Guard authority to control all vessel movements in Canadian waters from the various MCTS centres located around the region.

The AIS display does not give sufficient information to the Canadian maritime authorities of vessel activities in the St Lawrence. In this respect, it is a passive form of identification, and allows no control whatsoever over vessel movements in the area. The previous display, derived from the Canadian Coast guard website, enables the authorities to maintain a more rigorous control over vessel movements given that they can contact the vessel where necessary in order to establish its intended movement and course and re-direct it as appropriate. In this respect, the AIS system is totally inadequate for the needs of the Canadian maritime authorities, although it can act as a backup support with regard to up-to-date information on a vessel's movements. In reality, however, AIS cannot act as a substitute to the MCTS system, as it offers no form of direct contact with any vessel in the area, and cannot be used to intercept a vessel where deemed necessary.

In this respect, the HORIZON system developed by ICanMarine provides far more detail in terms of vessel location, contact and navigation status. The Horizon system, as described in a previous section of the study, allows for a far greater control over vessels in the area, although it does not control the identification of the vessel's cargo. However, the complexity and detail of the

HORIZON system does allow for a greater degree of vessel monitoring and control than simply using an AIS system such as that shown above. The system is designed for use both onshore and on deck, and in this respect has a wider variety of uses than does a simple AIS system, which in most cases is a passive tool rather than an active one. Whereas an AIS system displays a vessel's position as well as its basic identification details, the HORIZON system enables all users to identify the exact position of a vessel with relation to navigational tools such as electronic charts, and thus ensure their ability to navigate a channel safely, while observing and identifying other vessels in the area. This facility enables close contact between ship and shore, and also means that shore operators will also have the same electronic view of the channel as the master of the vessel concerned.

The effectiveness of the Canadian-designed system is that the same screen display can be used both on board vessel and on shore. This means that the onshore operator will have exactly the same view of maritime movements as will the master of the vessel or the Officer in charge. This also means that whatever instruction is given by the onshore VTS operator, this instruction will be directly understood and acted upon by the Officer in commend of the vessel receiving the instruction.

Despite the technological advances enabling the effectiveness of such a system, the European and Canadian views on the effectiveness of the AIS system differ radically. Where the EU has put considerable faith in the AIS system as a vessel monitoring solution, the Canadian authorities have been more intent upon the adoption of a pro-active position in the control over vessel movements into and out of Canadian territorial waters, which may in part result from their keenness to follow the US initiatives in the pursuance of rigorous maritime security initiatives in the wake of the 2001 terrorist attacks on the USA. The Canadian legislation with relation to maritime security and vessel monitoring has placed considerable importance on physical controls over vessel movement, and has thus facilitated the development of electronic means capable of achieving this. However, the EU VTMS Directive of 2002 was nowhere near as radical as Canadian legislation with regard to vessel monitoring and control, and indeed made no attempt to determine how such legislation should be implemented by each national maritime authority within the scope of the EU. Only in the Strait of Dover was there any major initiative to actively control vessel movements through limited international waters. In Canada, this control is part of the whole national maritime policy, and indeed goes much further in that it also monitors and controls cargoes loaded aboard vessels sailing into Canadian ports, which the EU system does not.

The following display shows the extent of the monitoring control regime over several sectors of the St Lawrence area, and how the various MCTS centres can monitor vessel traffic within each of those sectors.

The Canadian Marine Reporting model thus allows for the following sequence of reporting requirements. An example of a typical route into Canada would be that of the CAST sailings out of Liverpool into Montréal.

- The Cargoes to be loaded aboard vessel in the overseas port (Port of Liverpool) are reported to the Canadian Customs Authority at least 24 hours in advance of loading;

- Once clearance has been approved, the vessel is loaded and sails from Liverpool;

- A 96-Hour Pre-arrival Information Notification Report is submitted to the Canadian Coast Guard Regional Marine Information Centre (RMIC) by electronic means;

- A 24-Hour advance report is submitted by the vessel prior to entering Canadian territorial waters off Newfoundland;

- The vessel sails into through the Cabot Strait and into the Gulf of St Lawrence;

- The vessel reports in to the Canadian CCG MCTS Centre upon entry into MCTS-controlled waters in the St Lawrence;

- The vessel is monitored by the CCG authority up the St Lawrence River until it enters port and docks at its berth at the Port of Montréal;

- The cargoes are declared electronically to Canadian Customs and are cleared through all controls.

The resulting control, vessel reporting and monitoring structure has enabled the Canadian maritime authorities to exercise a complete control over not only vessel movements, as exemplified in the above diagram showing the CP Ships (CanMar) routes across the North Atlantic, but also their identification, their motive for entering Canadian territorial waters, and their cargoes. The system is all-embracing and far-reaching, and has allowed for a complete control by the Canadian Coast Guard authority over all related maritime activities. It has taken a series of national and international calamities, as well as the recognition by the national authorities of an urgent need to address the issue of maritime security to achieve the existing levels of maritime control, but the end result has shown itself to be extremely effective. In some ways, the system could be seen by some observers to be somewhat overkill, but it is better to have a comprehensive all-embracing system capable of supplying a blanket of information to a variety of authorities than to have a fragmented, piecemeal and incompatible system which overlooks important aspects of maritime security and thus allows for a variety of anomalies. These anomalies and oversights could lead ultimately to disasters or breaches in national security. The Canadian maritime reporting system is proven to work well, and can thus be seen as providing a more satisfactory answer to the whole issue of marine reporting, and could also be seen as a blueprint for developments elsewhere in the world concerning how to establish a robust, secure and all-embracing system of marine reporting.

REFERENCES:

Books:

Modern Admiralty Law (A Mandaraka-Sheppard)

The Law of the Sea (Churchill and Lowe)

Carriage of Goods by Sea (Wilson)

IMDG Code (IMO)

ISPS Code (IMO)

IMO FAL Convention

IMO Compendium on Facilitation and Electronic Business

Websites:

International Maritime Organisation (IMO)	http://www.imo.org
Comité Maritime International (CMI)	http://www.comitemaritime.org
Maritime & Coastguard Agency (MCA)	http://www.mcga.gov.uk
HM Revenue & Customs (HMRC)	http://www.hmrc.gov.uk
AIS Live	http://www.aislive.com
Ship AIS	http://www.shipais.com
Swedish Maritime Authority	http://www.sjofartsverket.se
Danish Maritime Authority	http://www.dma.dk
Canadian Coast Guard Authority	http://www.ccg-gcc.gc.ca